E. N. TIGERSTEDT

Interpreting Plato

INTERPRETING PLATO

BY

E. N. TIGERSTEDT

ALMQVIST & WIKSELL INTERNATIONAL

Published with the support of
Statens Humanistiska Forskningsråd

184
P71xtì

ISBN 91-22-00090-9

Printed in Sweden by
Almqvist & Wiksell, Uppsala 1977

FOR HAROLD CHERNISS

Contents

Preface

The present study is a continuation and, in a way, a conclusion of two earlier studies, *Plato's Idea of Poetical Inspiration* and *The Decline and Fall of the Neoplatonic Interpretation of Plato*. It was ready for printing in 1973, but for reasons for which the author is not responsible it has only now been possible to publish it. In the meantime, several studies on Plato have appeared which are of importance to my subject, but I have only in a few cases been able to take them into account. I hope to deal with them in a paper.

I am very thankful to my former University for including this book in its publications and to the Magnus Bergvall Foundation for having given me a substantial grant. My friend and successor, Professor Inge Jonsson, has given me a most helpful assistance.

My study is dedicated to a great Platonic scholar as a modest token of gratitude for all that I have learnt from him, not least when I have ventured to differ from him, and especially for the kind encouragement he has given my studies on Plato during the last years.

Samos, in April 1976

E. N. Tigerstedt

Interpreting Plato[1]

"Shortly before he died, Plato dreamt that he had become a swan which flew from tree to tree, thereby causing the utmost trouble to the archers who wanted to shoot him down. Simmias the Socratic interpreted the dream as meaning that Plato would elude all the pains of his interpreters. For to archers the interpreters are similar who try to hunt out the hidden meanings of the ancients, but elusive is Plato because his writings, like those of Homer, must be understood in many senses, both physically, and ethically, and theologically, and literally."

Olympiodorus, *Vita Platonis.*[2]

"Quidquid recipitur, ad modum recipientis recipitur."

Old scholastic saying.

I. The Problem

Simmias the Theban must have been a very old man when he gave his interpretation of Plato's last dream.[1] More than fifty years earlier, he had been present at the death of Socrates, with whom he had discussed the immortality of the Soul, if we are to trust the *Phaedo*. What he now said about the Disciple, he could as well have said about the Master: both of them face us as an irritating and provoking riddle, to be solved or ignored at our own risk.

As to Socrates, the existence of the riddle is easy to explain: he left no writings, so we are dependent upon the contradictory statements of his disciples. But Plato produced a substantial written *oeuvre* which ought to prevent any uncertainty about the scope and meaning of his philosophy. As all of us know, this is not the case. Of course, that can to a certain extent be said of all great thinkers. The interpreters of, e.g., Aristotle, or Kant, or Hegel by no means always agree. But the controversies about Plato are far more radical and fundamental. What some scholars regard as a faithful picture of Plato the man and his philosophy, is to other scholars an outrageous caricature or a pure invention. The dispute between the various schools of Platonic interpreters is not confined to judgement and evaluation but concerns the very essence of Platonism.

Was Plato a dogmatist or a sceptic, an un-systematical questioner or a rigid system-builder, a fervid mystic or a cool dialectician, a noble extoller of the freedom of the human spirit or a sinister herald of the totalitarian state? Are his thoughts to be found in his writings, open to every fair-minded and careful reader, or are they hidden behind the written work, a secret doctrine, to be extracted painfully from hints in him and other authors?

Thus the battle between the interpreters goes on, and it shows no sign of abating. On the contrary, just for the present it rages more furiously than ever. No scholar who in any way, be it ever so limited, is dealing with Plato and Platonism can escape from making up his mind about the vexatious problem of interpreting Plato. He cannot simply leave it to the "experts", i.e., the philologists and philosophers, for they disagree deeply. Moreover, Plato's central position in European civilization makes it difficult for a historian to evade the problem. It is better to face it squarely and try to analyse it. Even if he feels unable to present any final solution—and the disagreement of so many eminent scholars for so long a period ought to inspire him with diffidence—he may gain a deeper insight into the true nature of the problem and gather the reasons for its possible insolubility.

The great difficulty of interpreting Plato lies not so much in comprehending what he says. There are, indeed, difficult passages in his works, and there is a whole dialogue, the *Parmenides*, which ever since classical antiquity has troubled the readers. But generally speaking, even to philosophic laymen Plato is far easier to understand than many other great thinkers, e.g., Aristotle, or Kant, or Hegel. It is seldom difficult to make out what Plato is saying. But it is often difficult to be sure of what he really means.

The difficulty is in the first place due to the awkward fact, that *proton skandalon* of Platonic interpretation, that—save in his Epistles which may, for the time being, be left out of account—Plato never speaks in his own name, but always through other persons, in dialogues. And these dialogues are no systematic treatments of special topics or parts of philosophy but true discussions between two or several persons, which are not addressed to any reader. On the contrary, the reader becomes as it were, a silent listener to debates in which he does not join.[2]

This character of the Dialogues appears from the fact that—with six exceptions—they are called after a participator in the debate in question.[3] Subsequently, some editor—or editors—provided the Dialogues with two subtitles, in order to indicate their subject and character.[4] Thus the *Gorgias* got the subtitles "On Rhetoric, refutative". The Dialogue undoubtedly deals with this matter, but it deals with many other things, too. And it is not more "refutative" than many other Dialogues.

As to the six exceptions, they prove the rule. The first, the *Apology*, holds a place of its own, for it is simply not a dialogue. Of the others, the *Symposium*, contains speeches on love, but it contains much more besides. The *Republic* and the *Laws* treat of the matters promised in their titles but also of much which cannot even in a wide sense be said to belong to politics. The *Sophist* and the *Statesman* seem to constitute a special category. For at the beginning of each dialogue, it is stated that its object is to find a definition of the Sophist respectively the Statesman, and at the end we finally arrive at such a definition. But before then, the discussion has dealt with many matters which have little or nothing to do with the main subject.

In fact, if we have not previously read a Platonic dialogue, or at least a detailed resumé of it, we can never tell what all it may contain. Surely, this is a strange way of making that difficult thing, philosophy, still more difficult.

How do we then proceed, if we wish to establish what Plato thought about any given question? Well, first we read carefully through Plato's works, noting down everything that Socrates or any other person whom we regard as a "mouthpiece" of Plato—the Athenian in the *Laws*, the Eleatic stranger in the *Sophist* and the *Statesman*, the Locrian Timaeus in the *Timaeus, et alii*—has to say about our topic.[5] We then try to combine these various utterances, filling gaps by extrapolations, elucidating obscurities, emendating ambiguities, and, most important of all, neutralizing contradictions until we get a logically coherent, systematic body of doctrine which, with a sigh of relief, we present to the world of learning as *Plato's Idea of . . .*

But if we are endowed with normal powers of observation and selfcriticism, we can hardly fail to notice that Plato shows himself oddly refractory to our endeavours. There are obscurities and ambiguities in him which seem quite deliberate, as if Plato had not wanted us to be certain about his real meaning. These are gaps which can be filled only by ascribing to Plato thoughts of which we do not know whether he entertained them or not. Worst of all, there are contradictions which cannot be resolved, if we keep to Plato's own words.

More than a hundred years ago a German scholar, Heinrich von Stein, gave a vivid and still valid description of the bewildering and contradictory impression that a first acquaintance with Plato is likely to make on an unprepared reader.[6] Such a reader cannot but feel disappointed and vexed when confronted with a philosopher he has heard so highly praised—or so strongly reviled, as we must add today. A disappointment which, however, cannot be allowed to rest content with itself but leaves the reader astonished and upset. For he feels that the ambiguities, obscurities, gaps, and contradictions that perplex him could easily have been avoided by Plato, if only he had chosen to do so. However, he seems to pay no attention to our legitimate claim for clarity and coherence but rather to derive a malicious pleasure from eluding it.

Even to fix Plato's thought in any individual work is difficult enough, for many of the Dialogues do not arrive at any obvious conclusion. But it becomes still more difficult to discover a common denominator to several, not to say all, of his works. If we try to combine the statements on a certain topic in one Dialogue with those on the same topic in other Dialogues, we are only too often confronted with what, at least at first sight, appears to be direct contradictions. Of course, contradictions in a philosopher are no uncommon phenomena. But in Plato they are so flagrant as to suggest that he did not care about contradicting himself on fundamental points[7]—unless we believe him unaware of his contradictions,[8] a proposition which for several reasons seems hard to accept. And if we actually attempt to form an overall view of Plato's philosophy as a whole, then the difficulties threaten to get beyond our control, and it may well happen to us what happened to the great Eduard Zeller.

Zeller's Dilemma

The name of Eduard Zeller must always be mentioned with respect and gratitude by everyone who studies Greek philosophy.[9] He was the last scholar capable of surveying personally the whole field of this philosophy—from Thales and Anaximander to Proclus and Olympiodorus. He seems to have read everything that is extant of these thinkers and most of what has been written about them in the course of ages. He summed up his learning in a monumental work which still remains indispensable, *Die Philosophie der Griechen in ihrer geschichtlichen Entwicklung*.[10] But Zeller was not only immensely learned, he had also a clear and critical mind, a sturdy commonsense, and—last but not least—a lucid style. It is an intellectual pleasure to read about those ancient thinkers in Zeller, where they appear so much clearer than in their own works.

Zeller was, however, not only a philologist and a historian but a philosopher, too. In his youth, he had been an adherent of Hegel's, though he subsequently changed his mind and joined the distinguished company of ex-Hegelians, the foremost member of which was a certain Phil. Doctor Karl Marx. But, as was the case with Marx, Hegel never entirely lost his grip on his former disciple. Thus Zeller retained the Hegelian conviction that philosophy must be systematic—or cease to be philosophy. Every philosopher, worthy of the name, has a system.

Therefore, Zeller regards it as a matter of course that Plato, too, had a system, though, with a sigh, he speaks of Plato's "mit seiner Darstellungsweise verknüpften Mangel an vollständiger systematischer Durchsichtigkeit".[11] Plato having thus neglected to expose his philosophy in a truly systematic way, Zeller must make up for this neglect. Nor does he find it impossible to do so, provided that we "uns in den innern Quellpunkt des platonischen Systems zu versetzen, und um diesen die Elemente desselben in dem inneren Verhältniss, dass sie im Geiste ihres Urhebers hatten, anschliessen zu lassen".[12] The exposition of this presumed system has a strongly Hegelian flavour. Starting with "the propaedeutic foundation" of Platonism, Zeller subsequently gives a systematic survey of Plato's dialectics, physics, and ethics.

Zeller was, however, too learned, too acute, and too conscientious to be able to conceal—whether to himself or to his readers—the difficulties of his task. The less so, because he did not believe in the existence of any secret, unwritten doctrine which constituted the unity hidden behind the variety of the Dialogues. Nor did Zeller regard the dialogue as such as a mere external form.[13] Although he persisted in his belief in the unity of Plato's thought, he conceded reluctantly that Plato often contradicts himself. In his exposition of Plato's "system", Zeller several times exasperatedly complains of its "gaps".[14] And the Platonic myths meet with his strong disapproval. For they are "mehr ein Zeichen der Schwäche als der Stärke: sie zeigen die Punkten an wo es sich herausstellt, dass er (Plato) noch nicht ganz Philosoph sein kann, weil noch zu viel von Dichter in ihm ist".[15] If philosophy is systematic, rational thinking, then Plato is no real philosopher: that seems to be the inevitable conclusion of one of the foremost Platonic scholars of the last century.

Grote's Solution

But does not the very conclusion prove that Zeller started with a wrong assumption? Is there really any problem of Platonic interpretation? Is it not simply an invention of ours? Evidently, this was the opinion of George Grote, when, in his great, still eminently readable book, *Plato and the other Companions of Socrates*,[16] he flatly refused to impose any sort of unity upon Plato's various utterances and confined himself to rendering them faithfully as they appear in each Dialogue.[17] He declared it "scarcely possible to resolve all the diverse manifestations of the Platonic mind into one higher unity .... Plato was sceptic, dogmatist, religious mystic and inquisitor, mathematician, philosopher, poet (erotic as well as satirical), rhetor, artist—all in one: or at least, all in succession throughout the fifty years of his philosophical life".[18] As to the inconsistencies in Plato, Grote recognized them squarely "as facts in his philosophical character", in contrast to those scholars who "either force them into harmony by a subtle exegesis, or discard one of them as spurious".[19] And he sarcastically confessed himself unable to divine any sort of hidden wisdom, any *arcana*—whether *coelestia* or *terrestria*—"beyond what the text reveals".[20]

In the often misty realm of Platonic scholarship, such sturdy common sense is, indeed, refreshing. If Grote is right, there is no problem at all to worry about, if we only refrain from wondering, how one human being could harbour so various and different opinions and attitudes. And it is difficult not to wonder. Even Grote admitted that in his old age, Plato abandoned "his love of dialectic and the taste for enunciating difficulties, even when he could not clear them up". As the *Laws* shows, Plato became "ultradogmatical" and developed "a strict and compulsory orthodoxy".[21] Thus, senility turned a philosophic chameleon into a dogmatist.

Quite apart from the question, whether Grote's characterization of the Plato of the *Laws* is pertinent, it seems obvious that his refusal to look under the surface, to search for any unity in Plato, has led him into an impasse.[22] His is a counsel of despair, which does not work and which is silently refuted by the very existence of his own book. One does not write three big volumes about a chameleon. And Plato's sudden transformation into a rigid dogmatist does not carry conviction. Grote's work will always remain a healthy and necessary antidote against the never-ending attempts at systematization and harmonizing which overlook or explain away obvious contradictions, ambiguities, or gaps in Plato. But it cannot convince us that the interpretation of Plato constitutes no problem, for that thesis is disproved by the very attempts to prove it, of which the most radical and, in a sense, most successful is the elimination of the obnoxious texts.

II. The Resort of the Scalpel

"If thy hand or thy foot offends thee, cut them off and cast them from thee", we read in the Bible,[1] and since classical antiquity Platonic scholars have been only too ready to follow this exhortation.[2] If a Platonic text seemed to be opposed to their interpretation, it was simply declared spurious. This method of solving the Platonic problem by athetizing the recalcitrant texts could adduce the obvious fact that the *Corpus Platonicum* contains works which even in classical antiquity were considered un-Platonic. But the modern athetizers went much further, and in the middle of the nineteenth century there were not many Platonic writings which escaped their scalpels, especially in Germany, where scholars have always showed themselves inclined to extremes, today no less than a hundred years ago.[3]

However, at the end of last century and at the beginning of the present, there was a strong reaction against the athetizers. The new, "stylometric" method of linguistic analysis of the Platonic writings seemed to yield unassailable results concerning both their authenticity and their chronology. Fifty years ago, one of the leaders of this reaction, no less a man than Wilamowitz, declared in his peremptory way that the main problems of authenticity and chronology were solved.[4] It looked as if that most difficult thing, the *consensus philologorum*, was at last obtained. Thirty years after Wilamowitz, another eminent German Platonist spoke of this unanimity, "die man einen Triumph der literarischen Methode nennen kann".[5]

Alas, this happy state does not exist any more. Indeed, Wilamowitz's vindication of some of the Platonic Epistles—especially the *Seventh*—had never been accepted by several scholars, particularly Americans.[6] But now the doubts assailed even works whose authenticity, had for long been regarded as proved beyond reasonable doubt. The *Laws*, which during last century was rejected by many scholars, even by Zeller in his youth,[7] was once again suspected.[8] Recently, a German scholar declared curtly that the *Laws* is un-Platonic—without adducing any proof. The same scholar regards the *Phaedrus* as Plato's last work—a hypothesis which would have shocked Wilamowitz.[9] The *consensus* has no longer any general validity.

The disintegration of the Corpus Platonicum has begun again.[10] Once more, we are tossed on the sea of doubts and speculations.

This return to viewpoints and methods of an earlier age which for many years seemed entirely superseded is not due to any new philological arguments.[11] And the progress of Platonic scholarship has made it impossible simply to repeat the old arguments against the authenticity of this or that work. Nor are the new *chorizontes* moved by philological motives. Their real incentive is the incompatibility of the one or the other Platonic work with their general notion of Plato and his philosophy. Thus for instance, a modern German scholar suspects, or rather rejects, the *Laws*, because it does not correspond to his conception of Plato as "ein Ideenschauer".[12] To put it concretely, the Plato of the *Laws* is not the Plato of the *Republic*, therefore the former work must be spurious.[13] Much in the same way, Zeller had argued, when, in his youth, as stated above, he rejected the *Laws*. Later on, he changed his mind, and in *Die Philosophie der Griechen* the *Laws* is duly recognized as authentic. But by then, he had constructed his system of Platonic philosophy, into which the *Laws* did not fit, so he was compelled to the curious expedient of adding a sort of appendix to his survey of Plato's philosophy, called "Die Spätere Form der platonischen Lehre".[14]

Zeller's procedure is very revealing. He was too critical a scholar to be able to persuade himself for good that a work so well authenticated as the *Laws* was spurious simply because it was contrary to the opinion he had formed about Plato's philosophy. But he was unable to liberate himself from this preconceived opinion. So he had recourse to a compromise which satisfied nobody—not even himself.[15]

Zeller's scruples have not been shared by most of the old and new athetizers, their firm belief in their own view of Plato excluding any doubts. Knowing in advance what Plato thought and said, they do not hesitate to stigmatize as un-Platonic any text that opposes their interpretation.[16] Pruned by the critic's shears from all posterior excrescences and restored to its pristine purity, Plato's philosophy emerges as a lucid, coherent whole. By a stroke of magic, the contradictions, gaps, ambiguities, and obscurities that obsess weaker minds disappear. The problem that vexed us so much is no more.

It is easy to understand why many scholars, in the past as well as in the present, have been tempted to adopt this seemingly easy way of getting rid of the difficulty of interpreting Plato's utterances as they stand. As we shall amply see, all such "radical" solutions of our problem tend to deny its very existence. It is not so much solved as abolished.

The main argument against such a "solution" is, of course, as has been pointed out innumerable times, its arbitrariness. It may well be that no interpreter can escape from what Schleiermacher called the "hermeneutic circle",[17] that every interpretation of a text or an author must start with some preconceived view of them. But during the act of interpretation the scholar should always be able and ready to adjust or even to change his initial view, as his knowledge of and insight into his subject deepen. To make up one's mind in advance is deliberately to close one's eyes to evidence. Like the ancient astronomers, the interpreter of Plato should not forget his foremost duty: "to save the phenomena".

This is the more necessary, as there is no agreement among scholars as to the real nature of Platonic philosophy. If a scholar starts with some preconceived opinion about it, he can be sure that he will be hotly contradicted by other scholars. They, too, will athetize, but in quite a different way. As the history of Platonic scholarship proves, the critic's scalpel can be wielded with very different results. The way of the athetesis is not one way but many which diverge widely. As so often, the outcome of individual dogmatism is a general scepticism.[18]

III. The Triumph of Progress

To solve a problem of interpretation by athetizing the texts to be interpreted is a typically philological procedure, and the athetizers are mostly, though not exclusively, to be found among the philologists. The philosophers—especially in these times—have preferred another way, no less drastic, of disposing of our problem.

The contradictions, gaps, obscurities, and ambiguities that worry the interpreters of Plato are, indeed, real. But they are simply due to his incapicity for reasoning logically and coherently. Poor man, he could not help it! Living, as he did, before the foundation of Logic by Aristotle and, above all, before the rise of modern Logic, he could not discern the fallacies to which he fell a prey, uncritically trusting his dialectics.

Robinson

Such is the view of an eminent modern English philosopher and Platonist, Richard Robinson of Oxford.[1] Now, it would certainly be unwise to deny the possibility of logical fallacies in Plato's argumentations, for that would mean ascribing to him a superhuman infallibility which he himself would have been the last man to claim. However, what complicates the matter and makes us hesitate to embrace Robinson's explanation is first, the indisputable fact—admitted even by him[2]—that there are logical fallacies, or rather sophisms, in Plato which are consciously and deliberately used by him, *argumentandi causa*.[3] If this is the case, how can we ever be quite sure that the difficulties which oppose any systematization of Plato are not intentional? Secondly, our doubts are not abated by Robinson's assertion that Plato's inability to discern his own logical fallacies appears from the fact that he lacks terms for these fallacies, e.g., for ambiguity,[4] for if we accept this kind of argument, we arrive at some very strange conclusions.[5]

But the main reason for rejecting Robinson's thesis is that it is based on two by no means self-evident assumptions. The first is the belief in the unilinear evolution of human thought in general and of logic in particular. As, with laudable frankness, Robinson says he assumes "that each element of our thought has come into existence at some period of our history, so that at previous periods none of our ancestors possessed it". This is, indeed, "evolutionism" (as Robinson calls it) with a vengeance! Robinson knows in advance what sort of ideas Plato never could have entertained. That such a statement implies a deliberate and conscious argumentation *a priori*, has not entirely escaped Robinson, for he admits that "the risk of these assumptions and this procedure is an ungenerous narrowness or blindness to the range of an author's idea".[7] One cannot say that Robinson has escaped this risk.

But Robinson is silent about his second, no less important assumption: the absolute validity of modern Logic, such as he understands it, by which criterion he constantly judges Plato. In another context—discussing Karl Popper's attack on Plato—Robinson declares it impossible for anyone to judge Plato except by his own actual standards.[8]

This radical refusal to interpret Plato on his own terms, instead of judging him from the outside, according to standards not his own, has made Robinson blind to essential aspects of Platonic philosophy. Thus, he naïvely explains the dialogue form of it as "due in general to the fondness of the ancient Athenians for discussion", and in particular to Socrates' method of discussing philosophic problems, from which his disciple could not free himself, never fully appreciating "the distinctness of Socrates' destructiveness" from his own "constructiveness".[9] Plato's use of the dialogue was, consequently, due to a complete misunderstanding of his Master and himself.

The Socratic irony fares no better. Like Aristotle,[10] and much for the same reason, Robinson detests irony as "hypocrisy", "slyness", and "insincerity".[11] He is evidently quite unaware of its religious background.[12]

Bocheński

Not all modern philosophers have been willing to adopt so anti-historical an attitude to a thinker from the past. In his comprehensive work on the history of Logic, I. M. Bocheński points out as one of the prejudices in earlier historians of that subject, "a strange belief in the linear development of every science, logic included. Hence was a permanent inclination to rank inferior 'modern' books higher than works of genius from older classical writers".[13] Against this belief Bocheński declares: "Logic shows no linear continuity of evolution."[14] As to the problem of progress, he finds one thing certain: "that this problem cannot be solved *a priori* by a blind belief in the continuous growth to perfection of human knowledge but only on the basis of a thoroughly empirical inquiry into detail".[15] And he cautions the historian of Logic: "Now it is hard for a logician trained in the contemporary variety of logic to think himself into another. In other words, it is hard for him to find a criterion of comparison. He is constantly tempted to consider valuable only what fits into his own logic. Impressed by our technique, which is not by itself properly logic, having only superficial knowledge of past forms, judging from a particular standpoint, we too often risk misunderstanding and under-rating other forms."[16]

Nothing could be more sensible. Alas, the same scholar who gives this sage advice judges Plato in a way not very different from that of Robinson, when, only a few pages further on in his book, he speaks of Plato's contribution to Logic. True, Plato "rendered the immortal service of being the first to grasp and formulate a clear idea of logic". For he was "the originator of another quite original idea, namely that of universally necessary laws".[17] Nonetheless, Plato "tried throughout his life to realize the ideal of logic .... without success". He found it difficult to solve "logical questions that seem elementary to us".[18] Thus, his main contribution to logic consists in making possible "the emergence of the science with Aristotle". Here, Bocheński seems to have forgotten his own warnings.

The general objection to the attempt at explaining the contradictions, ambiguities, gaps, and obscurities in Plato as simply due to his muddle-headedness or primitiveness is that it flies in the face of facts. It turns Plato into a naïve and gullible fumbler, unconscious of what he was really doing,[19] whereas the *prima visu* impression Plato makes upon a reader is not that of a fumbler but rather that of an only too nimble manipulator of words and ideas. And it leaves unexplained, why Plato is still a living, topical, and controversial thinker, hotly discussed even outside the narrow circle of specialists. Whether we like it or not, Plato remains our contemporary.

Furthermore, this method of interpretation presupposes a superiority on the part of the interpreter which is not self-evident—at least not to him that does not believe himself superior to Plato, simply because he lives two thousand years later.

IV. The Genetic Approach

Athetizers and Evolutionists have always been in the minority—though sometimes a very enterprising one—among Platonic scholars of the nineteenth and twentieth century. The most popular of all the methods of interpreting Plato, ever since it was propounded by Karl Friedrich Hermann in the first and only volume of his pioneer work, *Geschichte und System der Platonischen Philosophie*,[1] has been the genetic or biographic interpretation. This method was applied in most of the comprehensive monographs on Plato in the nineteenth century and during the first decades of the twentieth, as also in innumerable studies on Platonic matters. It is still the prevalent method, though it has more and more been called in question and even radically rejected.

The Geneticists—if I may call them so—start out from a fact hard to deny, viz. that Plato must have been active as a thinker and writer for a comparatively long period, about half a century. It would, so they assert, be contrary to common human experience, if he had remained unchanged for so long a time. In fact, he had not, as the analysis of his works proves. All those obscurities and ambiguities, gaps and contradictions that trouble us in the Dialogues are as many testimonies to this change or rather evolution of his mind. In this way, Plato's works become milestones on the road his thought travelled.

Thus Hermann had argued against Schleiermacher,[2] who, in the Introduction to his famous translation, had asserted that Plato was from the very beginning in full possession of his philosophy, though for pedagogical and dialectical reasons, he expounded it gradually in the Dialogues, starting with the *Phaedrus*.[3]

Hermann's argumentation convinced the great majority of scholars, the more so as subsequently the so-called "stylometric" analysis of the Dialogues[4] proved beyond reasonable doubt that Plato's language and style underwent a profound change, which can be expressed in statistical tables and which has not been seriously questioned even by those that, for other reasons, feel dubious about the genetic approach.[5] It seemed only too plausible that the content of the Dialogues changed as well as their form.

But to what was this change due? Could it be interpreted as a purely intellectual, "autonomous" development of Plato's thought, an "immanent" philosophic phenomenon, a "dialectical" process, in which one idea gave birth to another?

Susemihl

Some scholars did, indeed, reason thus, one of whom was Franz Susemihl in his comprehensive work, *Die genetische Entwickelung der platonischen Philosophie*.[6] Although Susemihl sided with Hermann against Schleiermacher, he critized the former for having paid more attention to the development of Plato than to that of his philosophy.[7] Susemihl tries to redress this neglect by analysing in detail the evolution of Plato's thought in its different phases. Like Hermann before him,[8] Susemihl divided the Dialogues into three, chronologically and ideologically different groups: the Socratic or ethico-propaedeutic, the dialectical or indirect, and the constructive Dialogues. However, the last do not express the final form of Plato's thought, which is to be found in the *Laws* and in Aristotle's account of Plato's philosophy.[9]

Thus, according to Susemihl, Plato's philosophic evolution did not come to a halt with the "constructive" Dialogues, above all the *Republic*, but went on to what must be called a desintegration of his thought.[10] This was inevitable, because the whole evolution of Plato's thought was due to its *proton pseudos*. Plato did always remain "ein Werdender", "weil es eben unmöglich ist, mit einem unrichtigen oder einseitigen Zwecke, wie es die von ihm beabsichtigte möglichste Beseitigung alles Werdens ist, jemals zum Abschluss zu kommen. Das von ihm verschmähte Werden hat sich an ihm gerächt".[11] Plato changed his thought ceaselessly, because it was wrong from the very beginning, and he ended in a tragical selfdestruction. In this way, the evolution of Plato's philosophy is seen as a just punishment for its inherent vice. If Plato had not in his folly tried to eliminate "Change" (Werden), he would not have been compelled to change himself.[12]

Ribbing

For obvious reasons, such a view of Plato's intellectual development did not become popular with scholars.[13] It was sharply criticized in a contemporary work, *Genetische Darstellung der platonischen Ideenlehre*,[14] by the Swedish philosopher Sigurd Ribbing,[15] whose own position implied a return to that of Schleiermacher, whom he defended against Hermann.[16] For to Ribbing, Plato's philosophic development was an unfolding of the

26

latent potentialities of the doctrine of Ideas, which did not undergo any essential change.[17] Plato had no need to change his philosophy, because it was fundamentally right. To Ribbing, the *Republic* was the culmination of Platonism, "Zusammenfassung und Übersicht der ganzen Platonischen Speculation",[18] to which the *Timaeus* constituted a sort of appendix.[19]

That Plato's philosophy was a complete, coherent system, Ribbing took for granted; indeed, he never discussed any other possibility.[20] As much as Hegel, he believed philosophy to be possible only as a system. Therefore, he did not shrink from athetizing such Dialogues as seemed to him incompatible with the Platonic system, as understood by him. The criterion of authenticity was whether the Dialogue in question had a "natural" or even a "necessary" place in "the scientific order of Plato's writings", as constructed by Ribbing.[21]

It is easy to discern the naïve dogmatism of Ribbing's argumentation which he shared with many contemporary scholars[22] and which enticed him—like them—into some radical atheteses, above all that of the *Laws*.[23] Just this athetesis reveals the difficulty inherent in a purely dialectical interpretation of Plato's intellectual evolution. The *Laws* being, according to a trustworthy tradition, Plato's last work, published only after his death, it should represent not only the last phase of his thought but, granted the dialectical interpretation, its very culmination. Or, as earlier and recent discussions about the *Laws* have shown, this is not easy to conceive. For it seems difficult to deny that the *Laws* occupies a place apart in Plato's work,[24] and from classical antiquity until the present day, there have always been scholars who precisely for that reason declared it spurious,[25] in spite of Aristotle's testimony. The difficulty becomes still greater if, as many scholars believe, we should regard Aristotle's account of Plato's philosophy as referring to a last phase of this philosophy, for that account is, to say the least, difficult to bring into agreement with the *Laws*.[26] Susemihl regarded the Platonism of the *Laws* and that of the Aristotelian account as two different aspects of Plato's philosophic degeneration; the former being worse than the latter: "ein noch weiteres Schritt an der abschüssigen Bahn".[27] Here, we are confronted with the problematic nature of all the genetic or evolutionistic interpretations of Plato, which must be considered in a later context.[28]

Hermann

Most, however, of the Geneticists, beginning with Hermann, did not regard Plato's philosophic evolution as an autonomous, "inner-philosophic", dialectical process, but on the contrary stressed its dependence on extrinsic, not least un-philosophic factors. In the Introduction to his book, Hermann himself made the following characteristic and revealing declaration:

"Denn wenn es schon im Allgemeinen feststeht, dass kein grosser Geist, und sei er auch der originellste Schriftsteller oder der selbstständigste Denker, anders als aus der Vergleichung des Geistes und aller Verhältnisse seiner Zeit, insbesondere aber der äussern Umstände seines eignen Lebens, seinem wahren Werthe und seiner vollen Eigentümlichkeit nach betrachtet und begriffen werden kann ... so gilt dies von Plato wohl in höherm Grade als von irgend einem andern Philosophen der ältern Zeit."[29]

Here we have the notion, dear to romantic and post-romantic scholars, that writers and their works are permeated by "the spirit of the age", that they are expressions, if not products, of their time and milieu. To Hermann, this general maxim holds especially true of Plato. Far more than Aristotle, he was a child of his age—to such a degree that later generations could not wholly appreciate or understand him[30]—and dependent on his forerunners, whose ideas he summed up and carried forwards.[31] That, from a philosophic point of view, this circumstance amounts to a certain inferiority or weakness, Hermann freely admits, for thereby Plato's doctrine appears only "als ein vorübergehendes Moment in der Entstehungsgeschichte des menschlichen Geistes".[32]

This view of Plato naturally implies a denial of any purely immanent interpretation of his philosophic evolution. It was not due to any "absolute Notwendigkeit ... die mit eiserner Consequenz die Annahme jedes einzelnen Gliedes an die gleichzeitige aller andern knüpfte", but to his personality, which was the fertile soil of his ideas, his age being the propitious climate.[33] It is Plato's personality in all its variety that gives his writings their inner unity, not any preconceived system.[34]

For that reason, the only way really to understand Plato's philosophy, is to reconstruct his intellectual evolution, such as it appears in his life and works, for both belong together. Consequently, Hermann devotes the First Book of his work to "Plato's Lebensentwickelung und Verhältniss zur Aussenwelt" and the Second Book to "Plato's Vorgänger und Zeitgenossen in ihrer Bedeutung für seine Lehre", whilst the third Book discusses the authenticity and chronology of the Dialogues. Here, Hermann's work stops. The next volume, which should have contained an account of the development of Plato's philosophic principles and of his doctrine,[35] was never written. What we now have, is partly a biography of Plato, partly a history of Greek philosophy down to Plato, partly a contribution to textual and historical criticism. The real account of Plato's philosophy is missing, and Hermann's view of it must be gathered from casual remarks, above all in the Second Book, where it appears that he regarded it as being inferior to that of Aristotle, as has been pointed out above.

However, even in its unfinished state, Hermann's work has been immensely influential. It marks a new chapter in Platonic interpretation. This was not so much due to his learning and acumen—great though they were—as to his having voiced "the spirit of the age". "Evolution" (Entwicklung) and "Personality" (Persönlichkeit) were great contemporary slogans. When Hermann declared that "das Ganze der platonischen Schriften das Bild einer lebendigen organischen Entwickelung gewähre" and that Plato's writings must be regarded "als den treuen Abdruck seines Geistes",[36] his declaration found a ready echo in the minds of his readers. Here, so they could believe, spoke the true spirit of German Romanticism.

But a closer scrutiny of Hermann reveals that he is far less romantic than he sounds. For the "evolution" of which he speaks is, indeed, an evolution of Plato's "personality". But this personality is to such a degree subjected to external impressions and experiences, as well as to influences of other philosophers, that it threatens to become a mere product of all those factors. Hermann nowhere faces this problem squarely, but when he says that Plato's whole philosophy essentially emanated from the "need" (Bedürfnis) of his age,[37] it is only one of the many passages in his work that points to a very unromantic conception of intellectual evolution, though, in other passages, he speaks very romantically of the "harmonious organism" of Plato's system,[38] or praises the "inseparable and spontaneous unity of content and form" in Plato.[39]

But such romantic phrases cannot conceal that Hermann is basically a positivist. To him, at heart, Plato's philosophy is a heteronomous phenomenon, a product of extrinsic factors—though he would probably have rejected such a conclusion. But when he says of Plato's philosophy that "its real interest" essentially lies "auf der anschaulichen Entwickelung aller innern und äussern, persönlichen und geschichtlichen Motiven, die solche unabwendbare Nothwendigkeit herbeiführten",[40] it is manifest that the "necessity" of which he speaks is extrinsic, not purely logical or philosophic.

Thus, to Hermann, the main events in Plato's life which determined his philosophy were, first, the anti-democratic political spirit of his family,[41] secondly, the death of Socrates—far more than the acquaintance with him[42]—and, last but not least, the long travels Plato undertook after this event, which brought him into direct contact with several philosophic movements, especially Pythagoreanism, and thereby changed his thinking.[43] Although Hermann does not say so, it seems obvious that he regards Plato's mind as being a rather passive subject of these extrinsic influences.

Nor does Hermann have any high opinion of Plato's capacity for digesting those influences, for he says that, until Plato's acquaintance with the Pythagoreans, the elements (Ingredienzen) of his thought carried the character of their origins and that only Pythagoreanism enabled Plato to complete and finish his system.[44] And the three main parts of that system—Ethics, Dialectics, Physics—all go back to earlier philosophies—Socratism, Eleatism, Pythegoreanism—Plato's philosophy being a harmonious mixture of those three components.[45] Even the dialogue form of his philosophy was not peculiar to him or to the other Socratics. Plato's use of it was due simply to reverence for his master Socrates and to conservatism, not to any inner necessity.[46]

What really interests Hermann is the making of Plato's philosophy, not this philosophy itself. He says revealingly: "je mehr wir uns in den folgenden Büchern werden beschränken müssen, aus der reichen Fälle platonischer Weisheit einen gedrängten Auszug ihres wesentlichen Inhalts zu geben, desto nöthiger scheint es, dem todten Gerippe des System /!/ einem Überblick der organischen Entwickelung und thatkräftigen Gestaltung vorauszuschicken, die sich in den Schriften seines Urhebers als ewiger Quelle desselben ausspricht".[47] Small wonder, that the systematic section of Hermann's work remained unwritten.[48]

Positivism and Reductionism

It is not to my present purpose to describe and analyse in detail the many various genetic interpretations of Plato and Platonism.[49] Greatly though they may differ, they all share the conviction that Plato's works mirror a development of his mind, which is usually conceived as implying an emancipation from Socrates. For most of the Geneticists assume the existence of a Socratic period in Plato's evolution to which they assign a greater or smaller part of the Dialogues. What is more important, Plato's philosophic development is regarded, at least partially, as due to non-philosophic factors.

On this fundamental point, Hermann's attitude has decisively influenced generations of scholars, with many of whom, however, he would have deeply disagreed. Although, as we have seen, there was in him a strong inclination to stress the importance of non-philosophic factors to Plato's philosophy, he never went so far as to make it wholly a product of these factors, whether intrinsic or extrinsic. On the contrary, he regarded it as being to a large extent a summary of earlier Greek philosophies. However, the occurrence of this summing up was in its turn due to two non-philosophic factors: Plato's own personality, on the one hand, and his time and milieu, on the other.

After Hermann, the stressing of these two factors became the stronger, the more the romantic belief in "Personality" and "Organic Development", which Hermann had never entirely abandoned, faded away, confronted with an ever more victorious Positivism which turned all intellectual phenomena into products of material or pre-intellectual factors. To this influence of Positivism was, from the beginning of the present century onwards, added the growing influence of Psychoanalysis and Marxism, both of which, though mutually incompatible, cooperated in accomplishing the positivistic destruction of philosophic autonomy. The logical conclusion was a "Reductionism", based on a "Causal Monism": Platonism is "nothing but" a product and an expression of *one* non-philosophic factor, whether sexual-psychological or economico-social.

Political and Psychological Interpretations

Of these two trends of interpretation, the second—which can also be called the political interpretation—has been the far more popular, thanks to the renewed interest in Plato's political thought during this century. Earlier scholars, especially in the nineteenth century, tended to ignore it or push it into the background, considering it unessential, obsolete, if not embarrassing.[50] The fact that for centuries Plato's political speculations had captivated and stimulated other speculators—More, Campanella, Rousseau, and others—did not make them more palatable to Plato's professional academical interpreters in the last century.[51] True, in the Eighteen-seventies, a young professor of Classics in the University of Basle told his students that Plato is a political agitator, "der die ganze Welt aus den Angeln heben will und *unter anderem* auch zu diesem Zwecke Schriftsteller ist".[52] The professor's name was, however, Friedrich Nietzsche, and he was soon to say good-bye to Basle and Classical Philology.[53] Such heresies could not influence his colleagues, whose negative attitude was strengthened by the current rejection of the Platonic *Epistles* and the doubts about the *Laws* —both in their turn influenced by this attitude.

But at the turn of the century, a change set in. The authenticity of the *Laws* was now considered definitely vindicated, and as eminent a scholar as Eduard Meyer dared to defend the *Epistles*.[54] He found supporters, especially in Germany where the rejection of them had hitherto been generally accepted, and the case was by many considered settled, when, in his monograph on Plato, Wilamowitz peremptorily asserted the genuineness of *Epistles* VI, VII, and VIII. The verdict of the *Summus Philologus* carried weight, even far outside the German frontiers, and was gladly accepted by, e.g., most English scholars who had always felt inclined to accept the *Epistles*.[55]

This was of the greatest importance to the view of Plato and his philosophy. For, as many scholars believed and still believe, the *Epistles*, above all the *Seventh*, prove that Plato's interest in politics was the real inspiration of his whole philosophy. As a thinker, he was in the first place a political thinker, a theorist, indeed, but one who had tried hard to realize his theories in practice and action. That he failed, is the great tragedy of his life and thought. He was forced to confine himself to expose his ideas in writing and teaching. The *Dialogues* and the Academy became a sort of substitute for the Callipolis he was not allowed to build.

Of course, such a view does not necessarily imply that Platonism can be reduced to a mere political ideology. Nor is that the case with the most controversial modern work on Plato's politics, Sir Karl Popper's *The Open Society and Its Enemies*.[56] For Popper explicitly warns his readers that he is confining his treatment of Plato to the latter's political and social ideas and that he does not aim at giving a full *exposé* of Platonism.[57] Nor should we expect that the strongly anti-Marxist Popper would consider Plato's philosophy an inevitable outcome of contemporary Greek economic and social conditions.[58]

It is, indeed, perfectly possible to stress the political aspects of Platonism without in any way accepting a Marxist viewpoint, as appears from the interpretations of Plato current in Germany, during the first decades of this century, especially in the so-called "George-Kreis", in whose numerous writings[59] Plato is extolled as a heroic Founder and Leader of an aristocratic *Reich*,[60] if not as a forerunner of a still greater Leader and his *Third Reich*.[61]

Most of the many works which during the last four or five decades have been published outside Germany—and since 1945 in Germany, too—are, however, inspired by quite a different and opposite tendency. In them, Plato is hotly reviled as the infamous ideologist of political reaction, as the first Fascist or Nazi, his political philosophy being, as one of his most bitter critics, the Austrian legal philosopher Hans Kelsen, has called the "Ideology of any Autocracy".[62] Having in an earlier work discussed in detail these attacks on Plato,[63] I shall here, as always in this study, confine myself to the methodological questions.[64]

As the example of Popper—and of Kelsen, too—proves, a critical or negative attitude to Plato's political ideas does not in itself presuppose a Marxist position in the critic. Actually, however, many, if not most, of Plato's modern enemies have been more or less influenced by Marxist ideas, a fact which, unfortunately, compels me to enter a field set with snares for the unwary. Having no wish to lose myself in the abyss of Marxist exegesis, to discuss the true sense of "Dialectical Materialism" and of the relationship between "Basis" and "Superstructure", I keep to the conception of Marxism, such as it reveals itself in such books as Werner Fite, *The Platonic Legend*,[65] or A. D. Winspear, *The Genesis of Plato's Thought*,[66] or Benjamin Farrington, *Science and Politics in the Ancient World*,[67] or George Thomson, *Studies in Ancient Greek Society*.[68] Much as these and other books of the same kith and kin may differ, as regards the characterization and evaluation of Plato, they all agree in considering him and his philosophy a product of the Greek society of his times and especially of his own social status. To them, Plato is a mouthpiece of the reactionary leanings of the land-owning Attic and Greek aristocracy, full of resentment at its loss of power to the victorious democracy. That is to say, that these scholars embrace what many modern interpreters of Marx would call the "vulgar Marxist" interpretation, viz. a belief in a rigidly deterministic and one-sided causal relation between the economic and social Basis and its intellectual Superstructure, the latter regarded as wholly dependent on the former, without any autonomy of its own.

In a similar way, a stressing of the influence of Plato's personality, respectively his sexuality, does not necessarily imply a reduction of his philosophy to a mere rationalization of his instincts.[69] Such a conclusion would have been vigorously opposed by the many Platonic scholars of the nineteenth and twentieth century who stressed the importance of Plato's personality for his philosophy. But, as in the case of the political interpretation of Platonism, the psychological interpretation, too, has a strong tendency to Reductionism.

Kelsen

We can study this phenomenon in Hans Kelsen's paper on Platonic Love.[70] As we have seen above, Kelsen is mainly interested in Plato's political thought which he finds determined by Plato's sexuality, i.e., his homosexuality. Being a homosexual, Plato was beset by feelings of guilt and inferiority, which he tried to compensate by political and pedagogical activity. Remaining throughout his life a never-grown-up, an "eternal youth", he rejected the world of the adults and strove to create a new world, which meant a reactionary return to his own guiltless childhood, when he lived protected by the authority of his father, which he tried to restore in his ideal state. As a representative of a sexual minority, Plato was necessarily anti-democratic, an enemy of democratic equality, who believed in the rule of a small minority. Thus, the main aspects of Plato's political doctrine, its anti-democratic, authoritarian, reactionary yet re-volutionary character, are all due to his homosexuality.[71]

A great advantage of considering Plato's philosophy, especially his politi-cal philosophy, as determined by irrational and subconscious factors, is that in this way we can ascribe to Plato the very reverse of those ideas and sentiments that he professes in his writings. Thus, for instance, Plato's vehement condamnation of the tyrant in the *Republic* is to Kelsen simply a proof of Plato's secret inclination for tyranny. Plato's fear of the tyrant is his fear of himself.[72] In the same way, Kelsen interprets Plato's portrait of Callicles, the ruthless preacher of the "will to power", in the *Gorgias* as a self-portrait.[73] This is, indeed, to read Plato as the Devil is said to read the Bible. Applied to Kelsen's own writings, this method would yield some curious results.

The main objection to this kind of interpretation is not its anachronism, gross as it is,[74] but the fact that it is based on a purely *a priori* argumenta-tion. When, e.g., Kelsen states that Plato loved his father and hated his mother,[75] he does not do so, because he can adduce any "source" in favour of this thesis, for on this point the sources are silent,[76] but because, according to Freud, a homosexual does behave in that way.

A similar kind of *a priori* argumentation occurs in the Marxist in-terpretators of Plato. When, e.g., George Thomson, one of the most orthodox of them, asserts that Plato's philosophy "expresses the reactio-nary outlook of a selfish oligarchy clinging blindly to its privileges at a time when their social and economic basis was crumbling away", it is not because this assertion could be proved by any *a posteriori* arguments, drawn from sources accessible to us, whether Plato's own writings or other contemporary or later informations, but because any idealistic philosophy, such as Platonism, *must* be a "metaphysical mystification of reality",[77] created in favour of the ruling class, according to Marx, Engels, Lenin, and not least Stalin—a great authority of Thomson's.[78]

Thus, both the Psychoanalytical and the Marxist interpretations of Plato reveal themselves as based on *a priori* argumentations which convince only those that are convinced in advance. Such interpreters remind us of the French saying about *prêcher les convertis*. On the unconverted their teach-ing makes no impression.

If, from the loftly heights of *a priori* deductions, we descend to the low plains of *a posteriori* inductions, an objection which presents itself im-mediately is that the greatest part of Plato's writings deals neither with sexuality nor with politics,[79] but with matters which, for want of a better word, may be called "philosophic" and which must be left out of account or played down by anybody who wishes to turn Platonism into a sexual or

34

political "Ideology", in the sense of a rationalization of sexual desires or of class interests. This has not entirely escaped the attention of Psychoanalysts and Marxists, who occasionally condescend to bestow some perfunctory praise on, e.g., Plato's "contribution to epistemology",[80] or his "spiritual greatness".[81] The critical reader will not fail to scent in such phrases an uneasy feeling that Plato's philosophy cannot be entirely explained by—and reduced to—sexual or political factors.

As to the political interpretation—like any interpretation of Plato—it has to cope with the awkward fact constituted by Plato's ambiguity and especially by his irony. In an earlier paper, I have stressed the central part played by Irony in Plato and the obstacle it offers to the interpreters.[82] This becomes very manifest, when, in the *Republic*, Plato makes Socrates comment upon the Ideal City which he had proposed. After having at length expounded the plan of "Callipolis", Socrates concludes by accepting his interlocutor's remark that this Ideal City exists only ἐν λόγοις: "perhaps there is a pattern of it laid up in heaven for him who wishes to contemplate it and so beholding it constitute himself its citizen. But it makes no difference whether it exists now or ever will come into being. The politics of this city only will be his and of none other".[83] Surely, this is a curious way of concluding a blue-print for a Utopia. Nor are we made surer of Plato's intentions by the circumstance that in the *Republic* he so often speaks with his tongue in his cheek,[84] as, for instance, in the famous passage on the "noble lie", which has provoked so many of his modern detractors to shrill outbursts of indignation.[85]

The *Laws* is often pictured as inspired by old Plato's gloomy pessimism and harsh severity.[86] However that may be, the Platonic irony is by no means absent.[87] Repeatedly, the Athenian stranger, who is Plato's mouthpiece, speaks of his and the two other old men's long and serious discussions about the city to be founded in Crete as being a "play" of old men,[88] played "with the playfulness that is the sister of seriousness", as the *Sixth Epistle* has it.[89] Confronted with such statements, an interpreter may well hesitate to commit himself to the modern conception of a dogmatic and intolerant Plato, greedy for power and regardless of the ways os acquiring it.[90] It is difficult to believe that such a man could have expressed himself in that way.[91]

It is only fair to add that the sceptical and ironical aspects of Plato's philosophy have never been popular with Platonists—ancient or modern. With the exception of the so-called New Academy in Hellenistic times, their followers in later times, and a few modern scholars,[92] the overwhelming majority of Plato's admirers and followers—past and present—have seen in him the great, inspired and inspiring, Master and Leader, quietly disregarding those passages in his works that do not tally with such a view of their author. On this point, too, Plato's modern detractors have simply accepted the *opinio communis*, never questioning its validity, only replacing the love and admiration for Plato the dogmatist with the hate and scorn for the same mythical being.[93]

The interpretations of Plato, discussed above, give cause for some general remarks. As we have seen, most of them are very unfavourable to Plato. That is partly due to special circumstances, the iniquities of Fascism and Nazism being put down to Plato's account.[94] But even apart from actual political reasons, the general attitude of these interpreters is bound to give them a negative character. Marx, Nietzsche, and Freud have made a system of a method, hitherto only unsystematically used in polemics, especially theological: the ascribing of hidden, unclean, or at least subrational motives to the author interpreted. Thus, interpretation becomes an unmasking and "debunking", often performed with the moral pathos and the ferocious glee of an inquisitor.

The drawback of this method is that it is a terribly double-edged weapon. It is only too easy to turn the tables upon the interpreters and ascribe to their criticism of Plato unclean motives, similar to those which they attribute to him. Whereupon the interpreters in their turn will retort that the anti-critics are evidently inspired by the most unclean motives ... And so the dreary debate goes on *ad infinitum*—an infinite which only too much resembles what Hegel called *die schlechte Unendlichkeit*. The logical conclusion seems to be that, all interpreters being in some way prejudiced and determined by irrational motives, no rational discussion and interpretation of Plato is possible. We end up in an impasse. As in all similar cases, we begin to suspect that there is something fundamentally wrong with an interpretation that leads to such a conclusion.

The Ancient Biographical Tradition

The general objection to all attempts to explain Plato's philosophy by reference to his life and personality is the circumstance that we know far too little about both—except for what we imagine ourselves capable of gathering from his works. It is a curious and revealing fact that there is no exhaustive modern analysis of the sources of Plato's biography,[95] though more than a hundred years ago, in a book, often quoted above, Heinrich von Stein strongly criticized what he called "the biographical myth".[96] On some points—e.g., in regard to Plato's voyages—Stein may have gone too far in his scepticism, but it does Platonic scholarship scant credit that it has in the main left his arguments unanswered,[97] though some scholars have been well aware of the unreliability of the ancient biographical tradition.[98] One would have expected a real analysis of the sources from Wilamowitz, whose big book on Plato aimed at being a biography, at portraying Plato the man. But the Chapter "Das Material zu einer Biographie Platons"[99] is very disappointing. After some short introductory remarks, Wilamowitz concludes: "Mit dem überlieferten biographischen Materiale, wie es ist, kommt man nicht weit."[100] Or, as he states in another passage: "Was wir ausser der Werken Verlässliches über Platons Leben erfahren, lässt sich auf ein Quartblatt schreiben."[101] That does not unduly trouble Wilamowitz, for he believes that the works themselves are a sufficient source.[102]

Thus Stein's survey still remains the best point of departure for an analysis of the sources of Plato's biography. Such an analysis cannot be given here; I shall confine myself to general remarks about the character and value of the biographical sources, excluding the Platonic writings.

The Hagiographers

According to their tendency, Stein divided the sources into three trends: the panegyric, the satiric, and the micrologic—all of them biassed.[103] The first trend was originated by Plato's nephew and successor in the Academy, Speusippus, in a commemorative oration (ἐγκώμιον), in which, if we are to believe Diogenes Laertius, he hailed his uncle as the son german of Apollo.[104] Another of Plato's personal disciples, his second successor, Xenocrates, wrote a book on Plato's life, which is quoted by Simplicius in his Commentaries upon Aristotle,[105] and a third disciple, Hermodorus of Syracuse, wrote a more comprehensive work on Plato, treating both of his life and of his philosophy.[106] Other personal disciples of Plato's, too, are mentioned as having written about him.[107] We know very little about these works, which seem to have been lost early, without leaving any deeper traces.[108] So much, however, seems certain that they were strongly encomiastic, not to say hagiographic, tending to turn Plato into a semi-divine being, whose life from his birth to his death was full of portents and miracles.[109] The final outcome of this panegyric trend is the Neoplatonic biography of Plato, such as it appears in the so-called *Vita Platonis* by Olympiodorus,[110] or in the anonymous *Prolegomena*.[111] In them, biography has wholly become hagiography.[112]

The Detractors

This strong glorification of Plato, the Man and the Philosopher, was, however, counterbalanced by an equally strong denigration, for the modern detractors of Plato have their ancestors and models in classical antiquity.[113] From the very beginning, a man like Plato must have provoked opposition, anger, and resentment, even hatred; nor are traces of such reactions from the side of his contemporaries missing.[114] He is likely to have inherited Socrates' many enemies, and to have made himself new enemies of his own, not only among the politicians whom he despised and rejected, but also among the rhetoricians whom he criticized so sharply and, not least, among the philosophers, too, whom he had not spared. That the eager democratic politician and historian Demochares, Demosthenes' nephew, attacked Plato as well as Socrates, needs not surprise us.[115] But Plato's relations with Isocrates seem also to have been strained, [116] and the latter's disciple, the historian Theopompus of Chios, wrote a special work against Plato und attacked him in his big *History*.[117] Nor did Plato lack antagonists among his fellow-Socratics. Xenophon, whom he never mentions and who himself mentions Plato but once, is portrayed as his rival,[118] and Socrates' oldest disciple, Antisthenes, was famous for his animosity to Plato,[119] against whom he wrote a scurrilous pamphlet (Σάθων).

But it was a philosopher of a younger generation who became Plato's mortal enemy, his "first great calumniator",[120] the worthy *archegetes* of all anti-Platonists, ancient and modern, Aristoxenus of Tarentum.[121] For reasons that are not entirely clear to us,[122] this curious personage who combined hereditary Pythagoreanism with modern Peripatetic philosophy—he had been a personal disciple of Aristotle's—pursued Plato and his master Socrates with a hatred, as relentless as inventive, and a knowledge how to put the worst construction on everything. In this way, his anti-Platonic writings, especially his *Life of Plato*, became the *fons et origo* of that disparagement of Plato which ever since then has constituted a sometimes hidden but always existing counterweight to the official glorification until, at the present moment, it in its turn threatens to become the orthodox doctrine, whose heterodox critics make themselves guilty of *crimen laesae democratiae*.[123] Therefore, it is only fitting that Aristoxenus' late-born descendants have publicly defended their ancestor.[124]

It is a lurid portrait which Aristoxenus and his many sympathizers and followers among later philosophers, historians, biographers, and gossip-writers paint of Plato.[125] Physically repulsive, fat with a weak voice, he was morally corrupt and intellectually dishonest. Despite his outwardly severe countenance, he was at heart a voluptuary, a glutton, and a debauchee, a paederast and a whore-monger. Avid of power and trying in vain to realize his ridiculous Ideal State, he was yet an abject cringer before tyrants, and his own disciples revealed by becoming tyrants themselves, whenever they could do so, the real aim of their Master's teaching. Sternly rejecting poetry, because of his envy of the poets, above all of Homer, he was in his own writings a vulgar and extravagant poet, who did not care for truth and accuracy in the mendacious stories he told about people, not least about his master Socrates who protested in vain against Plato's lies. Nor were his writings really his own. For their form, the dialogue, was simply borrowed from earlier writers—Epicharm, or Zeno of Elea, or Alexamenus of Teos. As to its content, Plato's philosophy was nothing but a concoction of the ideas of other philosophers—whether his fellow-Socratics, Antisthenes and Aristippus, as Theopompus asserted, or the Pythagoreans, the Heracliteans, and Protagoras, as Aristoxenus maintained, or Epicharm, as Alcimus the Sicilian claimed, or even Zoroaster, as the Epicurean Colotes declared à propos of the final myth of the *Republic*. In short, an altogether disgusting and worthless fellow, whose contemporary and posthumous fame and influence remain a mystery. For the modern explanation of them as due to Plato being the mouthpiece of the ruling class of a slave-owning society was not yet invented.

The Gossip-writers

That is not to say that all the unfavourable stories told about Plato in classical antiquity are inspired by a real animosity against his person and philosophy, even if sometimes philosophic sympathies and antipathies have influenced them. For here the third of von Stein's trends comes into play: the "micrologic" one, the desire to know as much as possible about a historic personality, the pleasure in witty sayings and sentimental or piquant stories. Much of what is told about Plato is simply gossip, often malicious, sometimes amusing. The Greek biographers of Hellenistic and Roman times—from Duris, Chamaeleon, Clearchus, Idomeneus, Neanthes, Hieronymus of Rhodes, Satyrus, Ariston of Ceos, Hermippus of Smyrna down to Pamphila and Favorinus—aimed not so much at being truthful as at being entertaining. To subject their material to a criticial scrutiny was none of their business. They reported the stories found in earlier writers, adding new ones, which they had themselves collected or even invented—a story about quite a different person often being applied *sans géne* to Plato.[126]

Diogenes Laertius

Book III of Diogenes Laertius' *Lives of Eminent Philosophers* (first half of the third century A.D.?) presents us with an uncritical, undigested, and confused collection of biographical material about Plato, very little of it quoted at first hand.[127] One cannot speak of a "tendency" in Diogenes, for he cites impartially favourable and unfavourable statements and stories, without any obvious predilection for the one viewpoint or the other. This cannot be said of an earlier work. The *Dipnosophistae* of Athenaeus of Naucratis (ca. A.D. 200), for he shows an evident predilection for attacks on Plato.[128]

Confronted with this kind of sources, a modern scholar who contemplates writing a life of Plato finds himself in a difficult situation. He cannot simply disregard the sources, yet he can still less trust them unreservedly. Even a statement that looks probable may simply be due to a plausible invention. Nor are the earliest sources necessarily the most reliable, as the example of Aristoxenus proves. On the other hand, the tendentious character of a source does not in itself make it absolutely unreliable. Much of what Aristoxenus told about Plato might have been true, though he interpreted it to Plato's disadvantage. Above all, a scholar should never forget that many, if not most, of those ancient writers had no interest in telling the truth, if ever they knew it. They would have been astonished and amused, had they but known that, more than two thousand years later, they would be solemnly quoted as authorities concerning Plato's life and character.[129] *Rebus sic stantibus*, it seems difficult to escape Heinrich von Stein's conclusion that what the ancient sources offer us is not so much a biography of Plato as a biographical myth.[130]

Wilamowitz

Nor was this conclusion rejected by the foremost representative of the biographical interpretation.[131] For as we have seen,[132] in his great monograph on Plato, Wilamowitz strongly stressed the poverty and inadequacy of the ancient biographical tradition. He even went as far as to state that Cicero is the first mortal whose biography can be written.[133] But as we also have seen, this did not at all deter him from writing a voluminous biography, which aimed at giving an account not only of the Platonic works but of the man behind them, too.[134] For it was Wilamowitz's unshaken conviction that we can and must interpret Plato's works as expressions of his life.[135] They are "die Dokumente seines Werdens, seines Wollens, seines Lebens".[136] It seems that we are back to K. Fr Hermann again, and Wilamowitz praised, indeed, explicitly Hermann for having chosen the right path, though he did not attain his goal, owing to his wrong notion of the chronological order of the *Dialogues*.[137]

Nor seems Wilamowitz's programme, as stated in the introduction to his book, to differ essentially from that of Hermann: "Es (the book) wird für die Jugendzeit, über die es persönliche Überlieferungen garnicht geben kann, das allgemeine einsetzen, das auf den Knaben Platon wie auf die andern heranwachsenden Knaben Athens einwirken musste, wird herausholen, was die Familienbeziehungen und der Kreis seiner Bekanntschaft ergibt, auch die Bildungsmomente abwägen, die Zeit und Umgebung darboten. Bald kommen dann die Werke heran, von denen jedes ein Bekenntnis wird, das dem liebevollen Betrachter etwas Persönliches enthüllt, mag Platon auch nur einmal als Greis von der eigenen Person geredet haben, die er sonst fast ängstlich in dem Schatten rückte. So geht der Biograph von Werk zu Werk, von Interpretation zu Interpretation, und immer sucht er hinter dem Buche den Verfasser. Wenn dabei ein Mensch hervortritt, den wir als solchen anerkennen dürften, wenn sich die Einzelzüge zu einem Bilde zusammenschliessen, das als Ganzes glaublich wird, so ist die Aufgabe des Philologen erfüllt." The last words, however, Hermann would hardly have signed, still less what follows: "Er (the philologist) wird dann willig dem Philosophen Platz machen, der die Gedanken Platons dadurch erläutert, dass er sie weiterdenkt und kritisiert, dass er es macht wie Platon und sagt, den Menschen und das Buch lassen wir beiseite, weil wir mit ihnen nicht disputieren können und halten uns an den Logos."[138]

For, as the mere title of his work indicates, Hermann pretended to treat of Plato's philosophy, thereby earning the contempt of the philosopher Ribbing.[139] After all, Hermann was an heir to German Romanticism and Idealism, whereas the more naïve and less intellectual Wilamowitz gladly abandoned what to Hermann—as well as to his great adversary Schleiermacher—had been the main object of any study of Plato, the Platonic philosophy, to the professional philosopher.

Wilamowitz declares solemnly that the philosopher's criticism of Plato is a criticism "von der höchsten Warte" and "etwas viel Vornehmeres, als der Philologe kann und will". What then is the philologist's business? "Für ihn sind zunächst die Werke da. Ein jegliches ist für ihn, so wie es ist, etwas Lebendiges. Das will er verstehen, verständlich machen; von dem Wortlaute, an dem ihm alles wertvoll ist, bis auf den Klang, will er bis in die Seele dringen. Denn was lebendig ist, hat Seele. Hinter den Werken steht der Mensch, der sie geschaffen hat. Zu dem will er dann auch vordringen, auch bis in seine Seele, und dann will er diesen Menschen zeigen in dem, was er war und was er wollte. Er war ein Philosoph; weil sie platonisch ist, gehört seine Philosophie dazu, nicht weil sie Philosophie ist; soweit sie für den Menschen und seine Seele bedeutsam ist, muss sie auch kritisiert werden."[140] Not without astonishment, do we discover that, after all, the treatment and the criticism of Plato's philosophy *does* belong to the philologist, in so far as this philosophy "matters" to Plato the Man.

A reading of Wilamowitz's book proves amply that he does not hesitate to analyse and criticize Plato's philosophy without any inhibitions. Actually, the seemingly humble obeissance to the philosopher ill conceals Wilamowitz's contempt for him, which breaks out in the characteristically temperamental words: "Platon war nicht bloss ein Professor der Philosophie, den nur Kollegen verstehen können. Er wollte mehr sein: ich will zeigen, was er wollte und war. Ich will den Menschen zeigen."[141] The antithesis of "Man" versus "Philosopher" is revealing.

Thus, the Man Plato, not the Philosopher, is the main subject of Wilamowitz's book. But then to him, Plato is on the whole less of a philosopher than he was to Hermann. Therefore, Wilamowitz succeeds in describing Plato as a son of his time and environment, without making him lose his individuality. It is undeniable that in Wilamowitz Plato is far more of a living personality than in Hermann, where he threatens to become a mere product of external factors. Wilamowitz's romantic hero worship—which he had in common with his bitter foes, the disciples of Stefan George—keeps him from letting Plato be dissolved into super-individual currents and powers. Whatever Plato experiences and learns, he remains himself. Indeed, Wilamowitz shows a strong predilection—often ridiculed by his critics—for explaining Plato's philosophic works by unphilosophic, personal experiences, as when he calls the Chapter on the *Phaedrus* "Ein glücklicher Sommertag", or that on the *Philebus* "Ein letzter Kampf um das Lebensglück". This is not simply due to the bad taste which caused Friedrich Gundolf to call the book "a Plato for servant-girls"[142] but to his conviction that Plato's philosophy was an expression of his personality.

Hermann had said much the same, but to his mind the philosophic, super-individual factors were of greater importance to the evolution of Plato's philosophy than the latter's personal experiences. To Wilamowitz the reverse holds true, just because to him Plato is not in the first place a philosopher. Or rather, he became so only against his will.

For what Plato wanted to be, was not a philosopher, a "Weisheitslehrer", something which in his youth he heartily despised,[143] but a statesman, a reformer of Athens and all Greece. *That* he hoped to learn from Socrates, and it took him nearly his whole life before he gave up his expectations. His earlier Dialogues—the first of them written when Socrates was still alive[144]—do not contain any real philosophy; they are at the utmost discussions which do not conclude.[145] For Socrates did not teach any philosophy but how to live and—not least—how to die a philosopher.

Socrates' death meant the first great caesura in Plato's life. The *Gorgias* and Book I of the *Republic*—written well before the rest of the book but not published separately—testify to his bitter resentment against Athens, against humanity.[146] He takes refuge in science, philosophy. To further and deepen his studies he makes his great voyage to Egypt, Italy, Sicily, from which he returns as a new man, as the founder of the Academy as a school not only for philosophers but for statesmen—to Plato's mind one and the same thing.[147] In the *Menexenus* and in the *Meno*, he tries to make his peace with his native city, though without success,[148] even when, in the *Republic*, he propounds his great reform programme,[149] and in the *Phaedrus*, in a moment of happiness and harmony, extends a friendly hand towards his old foe, Rhetoric.[150]

In vain. The Athenians do not listen to Plato; the only ones who do so are his disciples in the Academy.[151] Plato is forced to remain a philosopher, a pure theorist, as he appears in the works he writes for his school: the *Theaetetus*, the *Sophist*, the *Statesman*, the *Philebus*. His intervention in Syracusan and Sicilian politics was foredoomed to failure; it ends in a catastrophe. Plato's last work, that "curious chaos", the *Laws*, still testifies to his unbroken will to reform humanity, even if he despairs of realizing his plans.[152]

As we see, the conviction that Plato's original ambition was to become an active politician is essential to Wilamowitz's conception of Plato. He states his conviction *in amplissima forma*, saying, at the beginning of his book, that the circumstance that Plato "Lehrer und Schriftsteller werden und bleiben musste, ist nicht sein Wille gewesen, hat er als den bittersten Verzicht empfunden".[153] And at the end of his long book, Wilamowitz exclaims: "Der versteht den Platon überhaupt nicht, der ihn als philosophischen Theoretiker wie Anaxagoras oder Spinoza oder Kant fassen will."[154]

In accordance with this view, Wilamowitz tends to depreciate those Dialogues that offer resistance to a political interpretation, such as the *Theaetetus*, the *Sophist*, the *Statesman*—at least partially—and the *Philebus*. They are what he disparagingly calls "Schulschriften", and he reacts strongly against the attempts to base the conception of Platonism on these works.[155] The enigmatic and cryptic *Parmenides* fares even worse: it is with disgust rejected as a mere school exercise in logic, unworthy of closer attention.[156] Generally speaking, there is in Wilamowitz a strong tendency to "play down" the theoretical aspects of Plato's teaching. True, he stresses Plato's decisive importance to the rise of "die strenge Wissenschaft". "Er hat sie in die Welt gebracht, kein anderer als er".[157] Wilamowitz even goes so far as to say that, at least later in his life, Plato felt it as a sacrifice to devote himself to politics instead of science.[158]

In spite of such statements which seem to clash with his general view of Plato—but we should not look for consistency in a scholar whose genius to a large extent lay in his inconsistency—it must be said that Wilamowitz lent his great authority to the support of the political interpretation of Plato, even if many manifestations of such an interpretation would have been deeply distasteful to him.[159] It can scarcely be denied that when, forty years ago, a French scholar called Plato "un homme d'action manqué",[160] he was inspired by Wilamowitz, as was certainly the case with Paul Friedländer, a personal disciple of Wilamowitz's, when, in the Introduction to his own book on Plato, he declared: "Er suchte den Staat und auf dem Suche nach dem wahren Staat fand er das Ideenreich."[161]

The Seventh Epistle

The basis of Wilamowitz's view of Plato is the Seventh Epistle, whose authenticity, after initial doubts, he so sturdily defended. But even those that share this opinion may question his interpretation of the Epistle.[162] As we have seen above,[163] in the nineteenth century, the Epistle was generally rejected as spurious, especially by German scholars. When the opinion changed, not least thanks to Wilamowitz's intervention, there happened what usually happens in such cases: one extreme gave way to another. What had formerly been contemptuously rejected as a worthless forgery—at the utmost containing some real facts—was now hailed as a fundamental document, the indispensable key to our understanding of Plato the Man and the Philosopher. Friedländer began his monograph with a lengthy quotation from the Epistle,[164] and scholars spoke of "Plato's Autobiography".[165]

Actually, the *Seventh Epistle* is nothing of the sort. It is no autobiography, still less a confession. It is a pamphlet, an apology,[166] written in a special historical situation, and addressed to the whole of the Greek world, "not a letter but a manifest".[167] The events in Syracuse and Sicily had aroused astonishment, indignation, and malicious pleasure among friends and foes. Plato and his disciples and collaborators in the Academy were subjected to sharp criticism and strong accusations which he tries to pare off in the Epistle.[168]

Plato's critics had asked: Why did he, who in his own city had carefully abstained from every kind of political activity, in his old age suddenly intervene in Syracusan politics—with such disastrous results? The answer to this question Plato gives in the so-called autobiographical section of the Epistle, which has been the pivot of the political interpretation of Platonism.

Plato justifies this self-revelation, unique in his entire work, with the argument that it will not be "without value" (ἀπάξιον) to young and old

44

alike to hear how he himself had formed those political opinions that Dion had learned from him. "And as the present occasion seems appropriate, I will try to describe how they originated in my own case" (324 B). Plato continues: "When I was young, I had the same ambition as many others: I thought of entering public life as soon as I came of age."

At that time, after the loss of the war and the fall of the democratic government, Athens was ruled by the so-called Thirty, some of whom, being Plato's relatives and acquaintances, invited him to join them. Although, young as he was, he was tempted to do so, as he thought "that they were going to lead the City out of the unjust life she had been living" (324 D), he soon found the present state of things far worse than the former. As an example of the iniquity of the new rulers Plato tells us that they tried to make "Socrates, an older friend of mine whom I should not hesitate to call the wisest and justest man of that time" (324 D–E) their accomplice in crime—but in vain. "When I saw all this and other similar things of no little consequence, I was appalled and drew back from those evil men" (325 A).[169]

After the fall of the Thirty and the democratic restoration, Plato felt once more, "though this time less strongly", the desire to take part in politics. But now the trial and execution of Socrates taught him how difficult and dangerous any political activity was bound to be. Such was the corruption of the public life, that Plato "became quite dizzy" (325 E) and though he "did not cease to reflect how an improvement could be brought about", yet he "refrained from action, waiting for the proper time" (326 A).

"At last I came to the conclusion that all existing states are badly governed and the condition of their laws practically incurable, without some miraculous remedy and the assistance of fortune; and I was forced to say, in praise of true philosophy, that from her heights alone it was possible to discern what justice is, either in the state or in the individual, and that the ills of the human race would never end until either those who are sincerely and truly lovers of wisdom come into political power, or the rulers of our cities, by the grace of God, learn true philosophy" (326 A–B).

Having thus looked back upon his own political evolution, Plato justifies his intervention in Syracuse with his hope of realizing his political ideas, "since it was only necessary to win over a single man" (328 C), and "it is not an unusual thing that a young man of native intelligence [Dionysius II] who has overheard some talk of lofty matters should be seized by love for an ideal of life". (339 E). The more bitterly disappointed Plato became with Dionysius for having refused to bring about a real union of philosophy and power, so that "all mankind would have been convinced of the truth that no city nor any individual can be happy except by living in company with wisdom under the guidance of justice, either from personal achievement of these virtues or from a right training and education received under God-fearing rulers" (335 D).

For a long time, Plato had lost all hope of achieving such a miraculous change at Athens—for admonition had shown itself vain and compulsion should not be used upon one's native city.[170]

Sicily was his last hope, and it was for that reason that, despite all his misgivings, he had visited Dionysius II twice. The Epistle concludes with these words: "Why I undertook the second voyage to Sicily I thought I ought to explain, because of the strange and improbable nature of these events. If then they appear more plausible as I have described them, and if it has been made evident that there were sufficient motives for what happened, this account will have properly accomplished it" (352 A).

The main content of the Epistle—the detailed account of Plato's visits to Sicily, particularly the last one, the philosophic excursus, and the some-what perfunctory political advice[171]—may here be left at that. Even from the incomplete résumé given above, it should be evident that the object of the autobiographical retrospect is to justify Plato's political conduct—his inactivity at Athens as well as his activity at Syracuse. This does not necessarily imply that the retrospect is insincere and deliberately mislead-ing, as some of Plato's modern detractors assert[172]—it agrees with the testimony of the Dialogues[173]—but simply that, in writing it, Plato had no intention of giving a complete picture of his intellectual evolution. Such aspects as were not necessary to an understanding of his political ideas and actions are omitted. No mention is made of such fundamental events in Plato's life as his meeting with Socrates—who is mentioned only in so far as his fates are of importance to the main theme—or the foundation of the Academy.[174] The *Seventh Epistle* is undeniably an important and valuable document. But its self-imposed limitation makes it impossible to base an all-round interpretation of Plato upon it.[175] It omits too many things that matter—to Plato and to our understanding of him.[176]

Even so, the Epistle itself speaks against a purely political interpretation of Plato, for it contains a lengthy passage—to be discussed in a later context[177]—the so-called philosophic Excursus (342 A–344 A). An ex-cursus it certainly is, though an excursus by Plato, and it cannot be denied that it interrupts the discourse in an awkward way, which has caused some scholars to athetize it as an interpolation. If we accept it as authentic, we must explain it as being due to Plato's overwhelming interest in philo-sophic theory, which made him for a moment forget Sicily, Dionysius, and politics. The Excursus stands by itself and though it "developes ... out of

46

the defense of Plato's dealings with Dionysius",[178] it must be regarded as an *opus supererogatorium*. It is more than what contemporary readers of the *Epistle* can have asked for. It is not essential to the apology. But it was essential to Plato.

The other possibly authentic Epistles do not add anything to our knowledge of Plato the Philosopher and little to that of Plato the Man. Even after the rehabilitation of the Epistles, the Dialogues remain the main basis of our interpretation of Plato. And, as we have seen, they do not favour a purely political interpretation.

The Reaction against Wilamowitz

Nor did Wilamowitz, as has been pointed out above, personally embrace such an interpretation, despite his accentuation of Plato's interest in politics. His interpretation is in the first place biographical, only in the second place political, in so far as Plato the Politician is an aspect of Plato the Man.

It was this biographical character of Wilamowitz's interpretation of Plato that, at the publication of his book, provoked fierce opposition, not least among readers of a younger generation to whom such an interpretation of a great thinker seemed an anachronistic example of myopic learning and trivial psychologizing, blind to spiritual greatness.

On a more scholarly level lay an objection which to a certain extent had been admitted by Wilamowitz himself, viz. the circumstance that the sources at our disposal do not allow of writing a real biography of Plato. Actually Wilamowitz's book abounds in probabilities, possibilities, hypotheses, and downright guesses, not to say inventions, which make it an easy prey to Paul Shorey's sarcastic appreciation that Wilamowitz's *Platon*, "if we regard it as an historical novel is deserving of all praise. But a historical novel it remains".[180]

Shorey did not stop at this objection, but delivered a vigorous blow at the very basis of Wilamowitz's work: the genetic interpretation of Plato. To Wilamowitz, it was self-evident that every single work of Plato expressed a certain phase of his evolution, intellectual and sentimental, and could and should be interpreted only as such an expression. For that reason, he rejected all talk about "The unity of Plato's thought". A unity there is, but not the unity of the result but that of the search.[181]

Consequently, if we ask Wilamowitz to what final result Plato came, the answer is ambiguous—or in the negative. As a practical politician, Plato was unsuccessful. But, Wilamowitz assures us, in the realm of theory Plato emerged victorious. No earthly state called him its legislator, "aber ein König im Reiche der Wissenschaft war er geworden". Thus, the summing up is positive. "Platon ist doch geworden, was zu werden in ihm lag. Was ihm in der Zeitlichkeit versagt war, hatte er für die Ewigkeit erreicht",[182] even if he himself did not feel it so, even if his dominating state of mind during his last years was resignation.[183] But a resignation to the will of God. Thus he could depart in peace. "Die irdische Welt hatte er *niemals* als seine Heimat betrachtet; da weilte er nur als Gast."[184]

The Plato that appears in the sentence just quoted is not identical with the politician about whom Wilamowitz has so much to tell. We are here confronted with a new proof of his inconsistent view of Plato. If we confine ourselves to asking what, according to Wilamowitz, the outcome of Plato's lifelong quest for truth was, we are left in the dark. For his last work, the *Laws*, is a chaos, better to be avoided by anyone who "Platons Philosophie als Philosophie sucht",[185] and the shape that in his last lectures he gave his doctrine eludes us.[186] In both cases, Plato's "last word" remains enigmatic.

After all, this is not to be over-much regretted. For although Plato, at any rate in his last work, wanted to be a teacher and a prophet, his own works testify against him. Whatever Plato himself may have believed, they contain no system, and the one thing that constitutes this unity is his own personality.[187] To the question: what *is* Platonic philosophy, Wilamowitz boldly answers: Plato. A seemingly identical answer was given by the disciples of Stefan George.[188] But to them, "Plato" was a time-less entity (Gestalt), though revealed in time, an incarnation of the Divine.[189] To Wilamowitz, "Plato" was a historical individual, an Athenian of the fourth century B.C., to be investigated and interpreted according to the rules of philology, history, and common-sense—not to say common-place—psychology, whose works mirror his varying thoughts, sentiments, and experiences. We are back at the starting-point. Asking for Plato's philosophy, we are offered his biography.

Shorey refused to take that for an answer. He questioned whether everyone of Plato's works was a complete expression of what at that moment happened to be in his mind, whether his "development in his extant writings was a hand-to-mouth evolution from dialogue to dialogue", whether in fact, there was no underlying unity of thought.[190] Shorey had no difficulty in proving that Wilamowitz himself often argued as if such a unity did in fact exist, as if Plato quite often kept some of his opinions *in petto*.[191] If only for that reason, the inquiry about Plato's philosophy cannot be evaded by a reference to his biography. Left to itself, the biographical interpretation turned out to be an impasse from which Wilamowitz's own disciples sought to escape.

The endeavour to liberate the study of Plato and Platonism from the fetters of a purely biographical and genetic interpretation characterizes a work which has often been quoted above, Paul Friedländer's *Platon*.[192] Not that Friedländer openly revolts against his old Master. On the contrary, the original edition of the book was inscribed to Wilamowitz, and in the subsequent editions we read "Udalrico de Wilamowitz-Moellendorff ΤΩΙ ΔΑΙΜΟΝΙΩΙ hoc opus manet inscriptum". But what sounds like a profession is in reality more of a concession.[193]

For, despite all his respect for Wilamowitz and the scholarly tradition which he represented, Friedländer does not accept the distinction Wilamowitz made between philology and philosophy. In the Preface to the third edition, he tells how, when first writing his book he found himself between two fronts: the philologists, headed by Wilamowitz, who left "das eigentlich philosophische den Philosophen", and the philosophers —Neokantians and others—who did not care for "das litterarische, dichterische Element in Plato". "Diesen Gegensatz zu überbrücken war damals und ist noch heute die Aufgabe", Friedländer declares.

This historical retrospect is, however, not complete. Strange to tell, Friedländer omits a third "front", that of Stefan George and his adepts, whose influence pervades his work, especially in its first edition,[194] though Friedländer was never really accepted by the School.[195] To this influence we must ascribe the way in which Friedländer tries to solve the problem of giving a full-length portrait of Plato, the Man as well as the Philosopher.

Friedländer's solution is to divide his book into two different parts. The first consists of several parallel and partly overlapping analyses of central aspects of Plato and Platonism, the second in a series of detailed analyses of all the works in a chronological order. In this way, Friedländer tries to escape from his philosophic-philological dilemma. He does not, like Wilamowitz follow Plato from the cradle to the grave, using his works as biographical documents. But neither does Friedländer give any comprehensive account of Plato's philosophy. What he says about it in the first part is wholly inadequate. True, many interesting, clever, even profound things are said about several important Platonic topics, such as the Irony, the Irrationalism, Socrates, the Academy, the Dialogue, the Myth. But no coherent view of Plato and Platonism emerges from these observations. Nor does Friedländer seem to have any clear notion of Plato's philosophy. In fact, like Wilamowitz, he cares more for Plato the Man than for Plato the Philosopher. Only, to Friedländer, Plato the Man is not, as to Wilamowitz, a historical individual but, as to the "Georgeans", a "Gestalt". Or rather, he tries to have it both ways, to combine Wilamowitz with George, to turn Plato the Athenian into a timeless hero.[196]

Nor are the analyses of the individual works substitute for the missing treatment of Plato's philosophy as a whole, the less so as these analyses are unsatisfactory from a strictly philosophic point of view. Friedländer has a better appreciation of Plato the writer than of Plato the thinker. Only too often the analyses become mere paraphrases or summaries, interspersed with eulogies of Plato. Generally speaking, the whole book suffers from a "Georgean" rhetoric, which sometimes, especially in the first part, becomes rather insufferable. But this is a superficial flaw, compared with the book's main fault: the absence of a logical, clearcut plan. There is no real intellectual penetration of the subject.

Friedländer tries to combine biography with philosophy, without succeeding.[197] Neither the reader who asks for Plato's life nor he who asks for Plato's philosophy gets his due. If any systematic account of the latter is impossible—as many scholars have thought and still think[198]—then we have more use for a sober account of the content of each Platonic work, such as A. E. Taylor's *Plato*.[199] This is not to deny that Friedländer's big book is very useful. The author's mastery of all matters platonic and of Platonic scholarship, which the copious bibliographies and the conscientious references to earlier scholars evince, makes the book an indispensable work of reference. But from a methodological point of view, Friedländer's *Platon* must be called a mistake. It falls between two stools; it does not achieve its aim.

Jaeger

More radical was the break not only with the biographical but with the whole genetic method in Wilamowitz's greatest disciple, Werner Jaeger. But to him, the interpretation of Plato was only one aspect—though a central one—of his general endeavour to renew the study of classical antiquity, to inaugurate a "Third Humanism".[200] While accepting the achievement of the modern historical and philological study of the Ancients, Jaeger yet claims for them a privileged position as the Creators and models of Western civilization, which always remains "Hellenocentric".[201] The history of this foundation of our civilization is what Jaeger tries to tell in his great work, *Paideia*,[202] whose German subtitle "Die Formung des griechischen Menschen" gives a better idea of the content than the English "The Ideals of Greek Culture".[203]

It is Jaeger's conviction that Plato had a decisive, even definitive influence on the "formation of the Greeks" and thereby on the whole of our civilization. For Platonism is "Paideia", formation of Man, at one and the same time Education and Science, Education through Science, and Science as Education. Plato is the Great Educator of Greece and the Western civilization,[204] he sums up and completes the work of his predecessors.[205]

In thus emphasizing the practical, educational object of Plato's philosophy, Jaeger was obviously influenced by the political interpretation of Platonism which, indeed, he embraced,[206] going as far as to say that "from the very start, Plato's thinking is aimed at solving the problem of the state".[207] It sounds like Wilamowitz. Actually, although Jaeger took his point of departure from Wilamowitz's and other German scholars' stressing of Plato's political interest, he differs from them—especially from Wilamowitz—in stressing equally "the *organic unity* of all his [Plato's] books and all his philosophical thought".[208] He openly reverted to Schleiermacher's view of the Dialogues as being deliberate expressions of an underlying unity. "The nineteenth-century development theory", Jaeger declares, "did not pay enough attention to the numerous connecting lines which Plato drew between his books, and which he meant to show us that they are all steps towards the revelation of a great and comprehensive system wherein everyone, from the first step to the last, becomes fully intelligible."[209]

These are strong words. They are, however, somewhat neutralized by Jaeger's insistence that Plato "chose to give unity to all his thinking on social and ethical problems, not within an abstract logical system, but within the vivid and tangible form of the state".[210] True, Jaeger here confines himself to Plato's political thought. But in the same context, he says that in the *Timaeus* Plato expounds his ideas on physics "not as a logical system of natural principles, but as a clear and palpable picture of the origin of the universe".[211]

Therefore, it seems that to Jaeger the unity of Plato's thought does not imply, but even excludes, a systematic unity. The difficulty in grasping Jaeger's position on this essential point is increased by the circumstance that his account of Plato's philosophy necessarily confines itself to what is of importance to the "Paideia". The dialectician, logician, and metaphysician Plato is neglected. So many essential aspects of Platonism are missing in Jaeger's account of it, that we are compelled to question whether Platonism really can be understood as "Paideia", even in the very large and loose sense in which Jaeger uses this term. No wonder that while some of his critics rejected his return to Schleiermacher,[212] others attacked his denial of the existence of a Platonic system.[213] Jaeger, too, fell between two stools. He contented neither the Geneticists nor the Unitarians.

V. The Search for Unity

Shorey

When Werner Jaeger openly sided with Schleiermacher, he did not omit to mention with approval an American scholar who for a long time had valiantly defended *The Unity of Plato's Thought*[1]—as Paul Shorey called the most important of his many writings on Plato. Published as early as in 1904, it had for many years been overlooked outside America, where Shorey exerted a great influence. Now at last, it appeared of topical interest to European scholars.

Writing at a time when the Genetic interpretation was predominant in Platonic scholarship, Shorey had the courage to question its premises and submit its conclusions to a critical scrutiny. He readily granted that "any author whose literary activity, like that of Plato, extends over half a century undergoes many minor changes of opinion, and reflects many varying moods of himself and his contemporaries. But—he added—it is not true of all, or of a majority, of the world's great thinkers that their first tentative gropings toward a philosophy and a criticism of life are depicted as in a votive tablet in their earliest published writings, or that the works of their riper years present a succession of shifting and dissolving views".[2] At the end of his investigation, Shorey repeated his main thesis: "that Plato on the whole belongs to the type of thinkers whose philosophy is fixed in early maturity (Schopenhauer, Herbert Spencer), rather than to the class of those who receive a new revelation every decade (Schelling)".[3]

But the "unity" of a philosopher's thought can mean many things. It can simply mean the recurrence of certain fundamental problems whose solution, however, may vary greatly, even change radically. Or it can mean the profession of certain general ideas, a *Weltanschauung* which does not exclude even important variations, contradictions, inconsistencies. Finally, it can mean the existence of a real, close-knit system. In the case of Plato, Shorey explicitly rejects the third possibility: "a complete system of philosophy with principles subordinate, derivative, and interdependent, and a fixed technical terminology, cannot be extracted from the Platonic writings". He adds: "This will not greatly grieve those who are aware of the perfect futility of all such system-building."[4] This is the exact opposite of

Zeller's attitude. To the latter, a true philosopher *must* have a system, consequently Plato has one. To Shorey, a true philosopher *cannot* have a system, consequently Plato has none.

Obviously, Shorey prefers the second of the three possible senses of "unity" mentioned above. Plato has, indeed, a coherent and constant philosophic doctrine. But it is flexible and variable for many reasons. First, "Plato is not only a thinker, but also a dramatic artist and an impassioned moral and religious teacher". This means that his writings abound in a "peculiar mixture of rhetoric and logic, of edification and science".[5] Furthermore, "Plato's dramatic quality affects not only the artistic setting and the personages, but the ideas which he brings upon the stage".[6] Arguing for victory, he—or his Socrates—may use arguments whose logical fallacy was perfectly clear to Plato himself. But above all, Plato was well aware of the limits set to all philosophy. He did not care for a rigid consistency in questions of pure metaphysics, which he "with sound instinct evaded by poetry and myth".[7] "When the interests of the moral and religious life, as he conceives them, are at stake he resorts to myth to express his hopes and aspirations. Where the epistemological problem compromises the foundations of practical certainty and sound method, he arbitrarily postulates the solution that will best serve his chief purpose—the extrication of a practicable working logic from the hopeless dialectical muddle of his time."[8]

Thus, to Shorey, Plato is primarily a great moral teacher who subordinates logic and metaphysics to ethics. Shorey is perfectly willing to admit that Plato sometimes contradicts himself,[9] as, e.g., in his various attempts to prove the immortality of the soul.[10] But that does not really matter. For, so Shorey asserts: "Plato's belief in immortality was a conviction of the psychological and moral impossibility of sheer materialism and a broad faith in the unseen, the spiritual, the ideal. The logical obstacles to a positive demonstration of personal immortality were as obvious to him as they are to his critics."[11] In short, Plato was a most sensible person, and if he sometimes does not seem so to us, this is due to our misunderstanding him. Why such a person nevertheless persisted in trying to prove the immortality of the soul, remains mysterious.

Nor is Shorey interested in Plato the dialectician. In the Introduction to his study, he speaks disparagingly of "a certain quaint and curious subtlety in the use of abstraction and antithesis characteristic of all Greek writers, but carried to its farthest extreme in Plato".[12] Like Wilamowitz whom he was to criticize so sharply,[13] Shorey, has little use for the *Sophist*, the *Statesman*, and the *Parmenides*, whose significance to Plato's later thought is said to be "very slight".[14] Why Plato devoted three whole dialogues to such questions, Shorey does not tell.

This is in accordance with Shorey's general tendency to deny as far as possible, or at least to minimize, the contradictions between Plato's statements on the same topic in different Dialogues, partly by declaring that these contradictions were mere mis-interpretations, partly by regarding them as due to polemical or rhetorical exaggeration, partly by considering them inevitable outcomes of the fundamental ambiguity of certain problems.

Although Shorey stresses the influence which the dialogue form had on the expression of Plato's thought, he never squarely faces the main objection to his thesis. The fact that Plato chose to express his philosophic thought indirectly, through the mouth of other persons, in dialogues, most of which are self-centred wholes, without any reference to other dialogues, means that the burden of proof lies with him who asserts the unity of Plato's thought. The primary evidence does not speak in favour of it.

In the Introduction to *The Unity of Plato's Thought*, Shorey, indeed, dealt briefly with "the difficulty of confining the infinite variety and suggestiveness of Plato's thought in the framework of any system, either of philosophy or of exposition".[15] As we saw, the former difficulty did not trouble Shorey. But the latter did: "the expositor of Plato can hardly avoid attempting to recast his exposition into some systematic form, and the recalcitrance of his material is to him a serious problem". Shorey rejected the "atomism" of Grote and others "that treat each dialogue as an isolated unit" as being a renunciation of all method.[16] But neither could he accept the systematic exposition in Zeller. His own treatment is "a compromise between the systematic and the atomistic" exposition.[17] He first demonstrates the unity of Plato's ethics, theory of ideas, and psychology, and then discusses several individual Dialogues.

But when, thirty years later, Shorey composed—or rather compiled—his thick book, *What Plato Said*,[18] he embraced the exposition which he had condemned as "a renunciation of all method". For the book is nothing but "a résumé of the entire body of the Platonic writings",[19] including even those Dialogues that are unanimously considered spurious, though not the *Epistles*, rejected by Shorey. The authentic Dialogues are arranged in "what seemed the most convenient sequence", as Shorey quaintly says,[20] actually in a more or less chronological order, from the *Eutyphro* to the *Laws*. These résumés are preceded by two short introductory chapters on *Plato's Life* and *Plato's Writings in General*.

This is a strange way of exposing Plato's philosophy in a scholar who is such a firm believer in the unity of Plato's thought, which Shorey does not weary of stressing in this new work of his. For no amount of cross-references in the margins or in the notes can atone for the lack of a systematic treatment. What we are offered are mere résumés of the individual Dialogues—résumés much inferior to those in Taylor or Friedländer. Sometimes—as in the case of the *Meno*—the résumé is so short and superficial as to be virtually useless.[21] The exasperated reader is tempted to embrace the opinion of a severe French reviewer: "Il a tout Platon dans ce manuel, à l'exclusion de ce qui fait l'essence même et la vie du platonisme."[22]

Nevertheless, a homogeneous view of Plato and Platonism emerges from all the disparate facts and quotations in Shorey's book. It is a view already known to us. Like his Plato, Shorey has not changed. He simply reasserts the opinion expressed in his earlier book and in his many papers on Platonic matters. To him, Plato remains above all a great moral teacher, while the metaphysical, logical, and other aspects of his philosophy are played down as far as possible.[23]

This view of Plato appears more clearly in Shorey's lectures, *Platonism, Ancient and Modern*[24], published after his death. There we are told that there is only one true Platonic tradition, "liberal theology and natural theology", and that "the true and typical Platonists in this domain are such men as Cicero, Plutarch, Schleiermacher, Matthew Arnold, and Martineau, with perhaps in second line the writers who may be represented by the ideas of Pope's *Essay on Man* and Leibnitz' *Theodicy*, to whom we may add, if we please, the Cambridge Platonists, Dean Inge, and Dr. Fosdick".[25] This is an astonishing and revealing list, to which Emerson must be added, whose essay on Plato in *Representative Men* contains, according to Shorey, "more essential truth about Plato than any equal number of pages ... in the literature of either scholarship or criticism".[26]

In short, what Shorey looks for and finds in Plato is not so much theoretical thought as moral edification, as understood by a serious-minded American academic, with a transcendentalist heritage and a utilitarian outlook, who tends to regard philosophic speculation as a loss of time if not worse.[27] As interpreted by Shorey, Platonism becomes, indeed, easy to understand, but we may wonder whether it is worth understanding. A benevolent critic complained that Shorey "seems at times reluctant to admit that there is anything difficult to understand in Plato's writings at all".[28] To turn Plato into a Greek Matthew Arnold, or Martineau, or even Emerson means not only a gross anachronism but also a shallow trivializing of his mind and thought,[29] which is not made more palatable by the complacent dogmatism with which it is professed.[30]

Nor does Shorey's assertion of the unity of Plato's thought carry conviction, for it is based upon his belief that to Plato ethics mattered more than logic and metaphysics, and that by ethics Plato meant much the same as the "liberal theologians" Shorey considers his true disciples, viz., an undogmatic, not to say agnostic, idealism,[31] not too different from a very broadminded Christianity.[32] Even so, Shorey can arrive at his unity only by blunting the edges and blurring the lines of Plato's statements.[33] The unity of Plato's thought, as seen by Shorey, is a sort of lowest common denominator. Plato's philosophy constitutes a unity because it is not really a philosophy.

Hoffmann

Such an opinion about Plato is utterly opposite to that held by Ernst Hoffmann, though his assertion of the unity of Plato's thought against the Geneticists earned him a *mention honorable* by Shorey.[34] For, when in his appendix to a reprint of Zeller, "Der gegenwärtige Stand der Platonforschung",[35] Hoffmann made up the balancesheet of Platonic scholarship since Zeller, he concluded that the nature of the Dialogues makes it impossible to utilize them "als wörtliche Dokumente eines geistlichen Entwicklung ihres Schöpfers".[36] Plato's "Lehrvorträge" were such documents, but of them we have only a vague idea, thanks mainly to Aristotle, and his testimony concerns only the last phase of Plato's thought. Hoffmann quoted with approval Werner Jaeger's distinction in an early work of his, between Plato's oral teaching, his *Logoi*, and his writings, his *Dialogoi*—to be discussed in a later context[37]—but did not, as other scholars were to do, insist upon this distinction. On the contrary, he sharply rejected the view that the Dialogues were totally unphilosophic, which had been advanced by some scholars, and asserted that at least "the systematic Dialogues" were fragments of Plato's philosophic "confession". Nor did he entertain any doubt that Plato's philosophy constituted a system which stood behind the Dialogues and could be reconstructed, and that it was an "allerreinste Wissenschaft und Weltanschauungslehre", whose character he very briefly adumbrated.[38]

Although he never lost his interest in Platonism and treated of it in several longer or shorter papers,[39] it was only many years later that Hoffmann summed up his views on Plato and Platonism in a small but substantial monograph,[40] which still remains one of the important modern books on Plato, characterized by an imposing—though not always, perhaps not even essentially, convincing—consistency. To Hoffmann, Plato is a philosopher, in the sense of being a systematic thinker, with a determined conception of the world which underlies all his writings and can be clearly defined.

It turns out to be a dualistic and theistic idealism. Platonism means the

56

belief in the existence of two worlds. On the one hand, the superior world of changeless eternity, consisting of the one and absolute Good, God, who transcends everything, and the many Ideas, which are in some mysterious way subordinated to God, yet independent of Him, and as eternal as He. On the other hand, the lower world of change and decay, the world of the senses, which "is", as far as it can be said to "be", only by participating in the superior world, which alone is true Being.[41] "Dies Dreierlei von Gottes Supertranszendenz, von der bestimmten Vielheit der Seinsidéen und vom grenzenlosen Bereiche des Entstehens und Vergehens kann man das Grundgefüge des Platonismus nennen."[42]

Yet, there is a fourth potency, the human soul. Man is a citizen of both worlds. An exile and a prisoner in the world of illusion, of non-being, he yearns to return to his true origin and home, God and the Ideas, and this yearning Plato calls *Eros*. If the radical separation of the two worlds is expressed by the Platonic word *Chorismos* and the participation of non-being in Being by *Methexis*, the Soul as an intermediary between the two worlds can be called *Metaxy*. The essence of Platonism is precisely "diese Problemverschlingung von Sein und Seele".[43]

That the human endeavour to escape from the world of non-being is at all possible is due to God. God is that dynamic force which draws the Soul back to its home and enables it to bridge the gulf. For He is not the Aristotelian unmoved Mover or the Plotinian impersonal One but the Father and Creator of the universe, though not in a Christian sense, the Ideas being uncreated.[44] *How* the Soul attains God remains a mystery, still more what constitutes this "attainment", which is no "unio mystica". To Plato, the Soul does not merge in God, as it does to Plotinus.[45]

Hoffmann's construction of Plato's philosophy endows it with a high degree of unity and homogenity but only at the heavy cost of some drastic reductions and simplifications.[46] Thus, he makes a radical distinction between Plato himself and later Platonists, from the Early Academy onwards all of whom have been traitors to Plato, especially the Neoplatonists.[47] Only in Kant do we find once more a thinker who returns to the Platonic dualism.[48] This implies that Hoffmann's conception of Platonism is deeply influenced by the Neokantian interpretation of Plato as formulated by Cohen, Natorp, and Cassirer.[49]

But it implies also that Hoffmann now abstains from adducing the testimony of Aristotle and other disciples of Plato's concerning his oral teaching, in which Hoffmann was previously interested. In the monograph, the account of Plato's philosophy is based exclusively on the Dialogues. But not on all of them. Earlier, as we saw, Hoffmann had been inclined to embrace Jaeger's view of the Dialogues as being in the main works of literary art, though even then he made an exception for the "systematic" dialogues. Now, he declares that the Dialogues written before and up to the *Gorgias* are a kind of comedies in prose which contain no philosophy at all.[50] Only with the *Gorgias*, written when in 387 B.C. Plato had returned from his long voyages and founded the Academy, the Dialogues became expressions of a positive philosophy, which Plato hitherto had not possessed.[51] Thus, a long series of Dialogues are simply ignored as giving only portraits of Socrates, the Sophists, and the Athenian society at the time of Pericles: the *Ion*, the *Hippias Minor*, the *Protagoras*, the *Laches*, the *Lysis*, the *Charmides*, the *Apology*, the *Crito*, the *Eutyphro*.[52] This is, indeed, a radical reduction!

From the *Gorgias* onwards, Plato had a philosophy, whose development we can follow in the Dialogues. For, contrary to his earlier attitude, Hoffmann now believes this to be possible. But he stresses that this development implied no radical change in Plato's thought: "Das Ganze seiner Lehre is kein Nebeneinander, sondern ein Nacheinander, wobei das Spätere das Frühere nicht aufhebt, aber voraussetzt."[53] Although Schleiermacher was wrong in believing that from the very beginning Plato had a clear idea of his whole philosophy, yet Plato was not decisively determined by external influences, as Hermann thought. For Plato's evolution was the logical outcome of his own original ideas, as manifested in the four phases of his thought—introduced respectively by the *Gorgias*, the *Parmenides*, the *Phaedrus*, and the *Timaeus*.[54]

It is easy to point out, as his critics did not fail to do, that Hoffmann's treatment of the Dialogues is very arbitrary. He adduces no real arguments for considering a great number of them non-philosophic and therefore not to be taken into account. And his treatment of the other Dialogues is open to many objections. The *proton pseudos* is, of course, his "undue desire to produce a single Platonic doctrine".[55] A particularly flagrant example of the over-interpretation—or rather misinterpretation—of Plato's statements that this tendency leads to, is the way in which Hoffmann identifies the Idea of Good in the *Republic* with the One in the *Parmenides* and the Demiurg in the *Timaeus*—for only thus can he construct a Platonic theism. Yet, as he himself admits, this identification cannot be proved by any explicit statement of Plato.[56] The same must be said of other constructions by Hoffmann: they go much further than Plato's own words authorize us to go.

Although he insists upon liberating Platonism from later excrescences, Hoffmann's own reconstruction of Plato's philosophy is not free from them, for, as has been pointed out above, it is strongly influenced by Neokantianism. Hoffmann's Plato is, in fact, a Christian, German, and

Kantian Plato, though he was well aware of the problems associated with any history of philosophy.[57] If his construction of Plato's system is so much more coherent than that by Zeller, it is because it omits or neglects aspects of Plato's thought that Zeller's conscientiousness forced him to include, though they were difficult to fit into the system he had constructed for Plato—or into any system at all.[58] Hoffmann's attempt proves once more the difficulty of extracting a philosophic system from the Dialogues alone.

Robin

In his monograph, Hoffmann paid no attention to another monograph on Plato, published fifteen years earlier by an eminent French Platonic scholar, Léon Robin,[59] though this book, too, attempted to construct a system of Platonic philosophy, conceived, however, in quite a different spirit.

Like Hoffmann—and like Zeller—Robin is convinced that Plato had a system, because he was a philosopher. It seemed to him "inconcevable qu'un philosophe puisse avoir réfléchi sur le savoir et sur ce qui en est l'objet et la méthode, sur la conduite et sur ce qui en est la règle, sans avoir fait effort pour systématiser les résultats de sa reflexion, après les avoir précisés et clarifiés".[60] Robin does not deny that Plato is a very great artist, but he does not find art incompatible with philosophy. Nor does he deny that to Plato practice might have meant more than theory. In a later context, Robin even says that Plato's main interest was in politics and education.[61] But although he devotes a substantial section of his book to what he calls "L'organisation politique de la Vertu",[62] to Robin—as to Hoffmann—Plato is above all a great theorist, a metaphysician and a dialectician.

But here, the ways of the two scholars part. In his Appendix to Zeller, Hoffmann had shown himself interested in Plato's "Lehrvorträge", but in his monograph he confined himself to the Dialogues, or rather only to a part of them. On the contrary, Robin bases his reconstruction of Platonism on the lectures, i.e., the account of them in Aristotle and other disciples of Plato. For, as he declares in his preface, the Dialogues present us with the reflections and debates of Plato's thought, seldom or never with a dogmatic exposition of the positive results. But behind this debate in the Dialogues, there was Plato's oral teaching, which to the philosopher himself, as he solemnly tells us in the *Phaedrus*, was the main thing. Or, if this teaching is wrapped in mystery,"il n'est pas douteux du moins que ce devait être quelque chose de fortement défini et peut-être même d'un peu raide".[63] Thus, behind the elusive debater and dialectician of the Dialogues stands the dogmatic teacher and lecturer of the Academy.

In thus distinguishing between two Platos and giving a clear precedence to the latter, Robin was paving the way for the modern Esoterists, to whom, as we shall see, he nevertheless does not wholly belong. Many years earlier, in his massive doctoral dissertation, *La théorie platonicienne des idées et des nombres d'après Aristote*,[64] Robin had laid the foundation of his conception of Platonism. True, as the title indicates, and as he himself stressed, he confined his exposition to Aristotle's account, without asking whether it tallies with Plato's own statements or not.[65] In reality, as appears from the exposition itself,[66] and as was pointed out by his critics,[67] Robin accepted Aristotle's account as essentially correct, even if making some serious objections.[68] Otherwise, he would hardly have devoted 700 learned pages to it.

The problem of the Aristotelian and other accounts of Plato's oral teaching will be discussed in a later context.[69] Here, it suffices to say that in his monograph Robin in the main accepts Aristotle's testimony and, as has been stated above, makes it the basis of his construction of Plato's philosophy.[70] But for that reason he does not reject the testimony of the Dialogues. To be sure, what Aristotle tells us about Plato's thought differs, "au moins dans l'expression", from that thought as it appears, e.g., in the *Phaedo*, the *Symposium*, and the *Republic*. But in return, it agrees excellently with the philosophy we find in Plato's "great Dialogues", the *Parmenides*, the *Sophist*, the *Statesman*, the *Philebus*, which cannot be properly understood without the aid of Aristotle.[71] Formerly rejected as spurious, these Dialogues now appear as the expressions of Plato's mature thought.

For Plato's philosophy, though constituting a unity, is a living unity: "elle se conserve en se transformant et en revêtant de nouveaux aspects".[72] Thus, in his exposition of this philosophy—divided into Epistemology, Metaphysics, Cosmology, Ethics, and Politics—Robin indicates the changes it underwent, above all the great change from a more or less rigid dualism to a supple system of multiple levels and relations.[73] The outcome was a complicated metaphysics of ontological hierarchies—from the One—or the Good, or the Being which in conjunction with the Dyad or the Great-and-Small— or the Illimited—generates series of Ideal Numbers and Ideal Figures, which in their turn generate the world of Ideas in the proper sense, down to the world of the Senses.[74] To quote a critic: "Thus the last word of Platonism is hierarchy and harmony."[75]

As Robin himself points out, such a Platonism has a Neoplatonic character, for it teaches a "procession" of Being,[76] and the very conception of a hierarchy and generation of ontological principles must be called Neoplatonic. Whereas Hoffmann tried to isolate Plato as far as possible from his successors, Robin is one of those many modern scholars—especially numerous today—who are eager to stress the connection between Plato and later Platonists. On this point, too, Robin's book has a very modern flavour.

When it was published, an eminent French scholar asserted that the author had proved "qu'on peut tracer aujourd'hui du platonisme un image sur laquelle à peu près tous les platonisants s'entendent sans grande peine".[77] He was immediately contradicted by an equally eminent compatriot, who caustically remarked that Robin's picture of Platonism was undoubtedly true, *if* Plato had really taught a philosophy similar to that of modern philosophers, *if* he had really wished to express a doctrine in the Dialogues, *if* he was primarily a professor.[78] It is a big If. But less sceptical critics, too, demurred to the systematization and "neoplatonization" of Plato's thought.[79] Curiously enough, they could invoke the author himself.

For Robin is well aware of the dangers that beset him who dares to construct a Platonic system. To Robin, one essential aspect of Plato's thought is "cette inquiétude qui sans cesse le stimule".[80] Robin refuses to admit that this "inquiétude" must exclude an effort at systematization, but he stresses that such an effort does not imply the end of the free evolution of thought. There can be no ultimate fixation, only an even deeper penetration into truth, to be ended by death alone. So far, the probabilism of the New Academy was as legitimate an heir of Plato's as Neoplatonism, even if the Academy turned what in Plato is only provisional into a permanently negative attitude[81]. For, "tous les visages de Platon ont leur vérité sur chacun des miroirs de la tradition."[82] In this way, Robin's seemingly rigid systematization of Plato concludes on a surprisingly sceptical note.[83] The last pages of his book seem to cancel—or at least to counterbalance—the preceding ones.[84]

Gomperz

No such autocritical scepticism harassed the mind of Heinrich Gomperz, when, in a booklet on the *Seventh Epistle*, he declared that a passage in this Epistle, which will claim our attention below,[86] proves that Plato had a definite doctrine which, however, he withheld from his Dialogues and reserved for his oral teaching, but which can be reconstructed from the account of it in Aristotle and other Platonists.[87] Gomperz promised to give a substantial description of "Platons philosophisches System",[88] but he only published a short lecture on this subject.[89]

Like Robin, Gomperz based his own construction of Plato's system on Aristotle and tried to show that it agreed with the later Dialogues especially the *Timaeus*, the *Philebus*, and the *Parmenides*, but he found it as early as in the *Republic*, where the Good must be interpreted as the One—as Hoffmann later thought.[90] Thus, although Plato's philosophic system is not "explicitly expounded" in the Dialogues—to Gomperz the distance between them and the oral teaching was greater than to Robin—it is presupposed by them, at least since the *Republic*. But to Gomperz this system is not—as to Robin—a neoplatonic hierarchy of Being but "ein dualistisches Ableitungssystem", which deduces the world from "zwei wesenshaft verschiedene Urfaktoren": The One, which is Order, Harmony, Symmetry, Proportion, and the Many, which is Disorder, Formlessness, Limitlessness, or, to put it more concretely, Good and Evil. It is a conception of Platonism which resembles that of Hoffmann.

Gomperz never elaborated his interpretation which seems to have been mostly ignored by his contemporaries.[91] Only many years later, his views were to experience at least a partial resurrection in the Esoteric interpretation of Plato.[92]

VI. The Hidden System

In the Twenties and Thirties of the present century, the search for a coherent, unambiguous, systematic Platonism and the experience of the difficulty, if not impossibility, of finding it in the Dialogues had, as we saw above, induced some scholars to base their reconstructions of Plato's philosophy not on the Dialogues alone but, to a lesser or greater degree, also on the account of this philosophy in Aristotle and other ancient writers which, so those scholars believed, reflected Plato's oral teaching in the Academy.

Yet, these reconstructions, such as they appear in Ernst Hoffmann, León Robin, and Heinrich Gomperz, did not go very far. Gomperz's reconstruction remained a mere sketch, while Hoffmann soon lost his interest and trust in any account of Platonism outside the Dialogues. Robin gave, indeed, a comprehensive exposition of Plato's thought which to a high degree followed Aristotle and brought Plato closer to Neoplatonism, but he neutralized the effect of this reconstruction by his sceptical reservations. As we shall see,[1] other contemporary scholars expressed their sympathy with a similar view, without, however, drawing the logical conclusions of their attitude. Evidently, the time was not yet ripe for a radical reconsideration of the problem of Platonic interpretation.

The Esoterists

Although several years earlier, the close connection between Platonism and Neoplatonism had been strongly stressed by scholars such as Philip Merlan[2] and Cornelia de Vogel,[3] it is only during the last decades—from ca. 1960 onwards—that the notion of an esoteric Platonic philosophy, essentially identical with Neoplatonism, has become popular with scholars. Its main propounders are two younger German scholars, Konrad Gaiser, in *Protreptik und Paränese bei Platon*[4] and *Platons ungeschriebene Lehre*[5]—a programmatic title—and Hans Joachim Krämer, in *Arete bei Platon und Aristoteles*[6] and *Der Ursprung der Geistmetaphysik*.[7] Although, as we shall see, the Esoterists—if I may so call them—have encountered sharp criticism, they have also won eager approval.[8] Today, many scholars seem to accept as an unquestionable fact that Plato had such an esoteric philosophy. It is therefore necessary to scrutinize this hypothesis.

Being mainly concerned with methods, I shall not go into detail, e.g., by analysing and criticizing the complicated metaphysical system which the Esoterists have constructed for Plato, but confine myself to a critical survey of the very foundations of their interpretation of Plato.

Like all radical solutions of the problem of interpreting Plato, the Esoteric one ruthlessly disposes of the problem itself. There are, indeed, contradictions, gaps, obscurities, and ambiguities in Plato's works. But they do not matter. For Plato's written works do not contain his real doctrine which he taught to his disciples in the Academy and did not divulge. Fortunately, thanks to Aristotle and other ancient authors, earlier or later, this oral, esoteric doctrine can be reconstructed. It turns ot to be a rigidly systematic, hierarchical metaphysics of Being, an "Ontology", very similar to Neoplatonism, whose direct forerunner it was. For Plotinus was in fact what he claimed to be: Plato's true heir and successor.

The Ancient Forerunners

Aristotle. The Esoterists proudly claim that this view of Plato and Platonism is a very ancient one, going straight back to classical antiquity itself.[9] But this claim is not so wellfounded as perhaps it seems. Aristotle, who is the main authority of the Esoterists, indeed mentions once—but once only—Plato's "unwritten doctrines".[10] But for the rest, as Schleiermacher pointed out,[11] Aristotle refers to and quotes the Dialogues, without in any way suggesting that they may not contain Plato's real thoughts. True, the Aristotelian account of Plato's philosophy presents us with a special problem, for it seems not to tally with the Dialogues—a problem which will be treated in a later context.[12] For the present, we only note that Aristotle does not distinguish between an exoteric and an esoteric Platonic philosophy.

Albinus. Nor can we find any such distinction in the extant fragments of the works of the old Academics. In fact, we must descend to Imperial times, before finding anything that looks like an evidence of esoteric Platonism.[13] It occurs in Albinus (middle of the second century A.D.). In his summary of Platonic philosophy, the *Didascalicus*, he says, à propos of the Supreme Good, that Plato "communicated his lecture on the Good only to very few and selected friends".[14] Albinus refers to the famous lecture *On the Good*, which will be discussed below.[15] Here, it must be stressed that Albinus does not talk about an esoteric Platonic philosophy as such,[16] only about a special—though certainly essential—aspect of Plato's doctrine which the Master kept secret.

Numenius. The same notion occurs in the pythagorizing Platonist—or platonizing Pythagorean—Numenius of Apamaea (second half of the second century A.D.).[17] We are told that he wrote a whole book, *On the Unspeakable* (i.e., secret) *Things in Plato* (Περὶ τῶν παρὰ Πλάτωνα ἀποῤῥήτων).[18] This looks as if Numenius really was a believer in an esoteric Platonism in the sense of the modern Esoterists. But the only extant fragment says simply that in the *Eutyphro,* Plato concealed his criticism of the established religion, so that the Athenians should not kill him as they had killed Socrates.[19] In his big work, *On the Apostasy of the Academics from Plato,* where the evolution of the Academy is condemned as an apostasy, Numenius repeats his criticism of Plato. Out of prudence, he did not teach in the usual manner, as Socrates had done, nor did he make his teaching very clear, "but he treated each point just as he thought wise, leaving it in twilight, halfway between clarity and obscurity. He did, indeed, thus attain security in his writing, but he himself became the cause of the subsequent discord and difference of opinions about his teaching".[20] As the context shows, Numenius is talking about Plato's theology,[21] the only aspect of Platonism that interests him.

The Neoplatonists

Numenius is usually regarded as a "forerunner" of Neoplatonism.[22] However, the Neoplatonists properly speaking—Plotinus, Porphyry, Iamblichus, and their disciples—do not distinguish between an exoteric and esoteric Platonism. To them, there is only an esoteric one. Plato's philosophy is by them regarded as a mystery religion, revealed by the gods to Plato —and, indeed, before him to the "Ancient Theologians" (Παλαιοὶ Θεόλογοι)—and through Plato to the elected few, as Proclus says in the First Book of his *Platonic Theology.*[23] Nor do the Neoplatonists oppose Plato's oral teaching to his written work. True, they occasionally refer to his lecture *On the Good,* i.e., those accounts that several of his disciples gave of it, but they do not in any way disparage the Dialogues.[24] On the contrary, Plato's "Theology", i.e., his metaphysics—which is what really matters to the Neoplatonists—is to be found in them. Proclus even goes so far as to assert that this teaching penetrates virtually all the Dialogues, though to a varying degree.[25] It is only a question of reading them in the right way.[26]

This attitude of the Neoplatonists should not astonish us. A great part of their extant works consisting of commentaries on the Platonic Dialogues, they could hardly be expected to declare that the writings they were interpreting did not contain Plato's innermost thought. Nor did the Neo-platonists say so, but, thanks to an ingenious method of interpretation, which has wrung an unwilling admiration from modern scholars,[27] they succeeded in finding their own opinions in Plato.[28] In desperate cases, there was always the last resource of allegorism. For the Neoplatonists did not read Plato as the Alexandrian philologists had read Homer, but as the contemporary Christian theologians read the Bible.[29] The Dialogues were to the Neoplatonists Sacred Books, full of divine revelation, intelligible only to the initiated.

Thus, the interpretation of Plato ceases to be a problem. There is one and only one way of understanding him, and that is to study the Dialogues as interpreted by the Neoplatonists. Neoplatonism being a metaphysical system, founded by Plotinus and brought to its perfection by Proclus, the difficulty of combining Plato's various often divergent statements into a unity disappears.[30] Only when the Neoplatonic interpretation becomes questionable or is openly rejected, the problem of Platonic interpretation emerges again.

However, that did not happen for a very long time. The Neoplatonic interpretation remained unchallenged for well over a thousand years. If any interpretation of Plato can lay claim to be "classical" and traditional, it is certainly the Neoplatonic one.[31] Or, as we saw, that interpretation does not know of any difference between an esoteric and an exoteric, a written and an oral Platonism.

The Dissolution of the Neoplatonic Interpretation

Brucker. How at last the Neoplatonic interpretation was first doubted, then criticed, and finally rejected, is a subject which I have investigated in another paper to which I must refer the reader.[32] There I have shown that the definite rejection occurred in the middle of the eighteenth century when it was authoritatively exposed in Jacob Brucker's comprehensive work, *Historia critica philosophiae* (1742), the first real history of philoso-phy.[33]

But as soon as the Neoplatonic interpretation was rejected, and the interpreters were reduced to using Plato's *ipsissima verba*, the problem of interpreting Plato became again urgent. This was the case with Brucker, who devoted many pages to the question of Plato's "obscurity", before giving a systematic exposition of his philosophy, based on the Dialogues.

Tennemann. What Brucker did, not without misgivings and hesitation, that, half a century later, Wilhelm Gottfried Tennemann did, with the

66

utmost selfconfidence, in his *System der Platonischen Philosophie* (1792–95), the first modern monograph on Plato.[34] Tennemann, not any classical author, is the real father of the modern Esoterists. He shares with them a positive and a negative assumption: the belief that any philosopher worthy of that name has a system, and the rejection—whether articulate or under-stood—of the attempt of the Neoplatonists to find their own system in Plato's writings. It is the combination of these two assumptions that has given birth to the modern Esoteric interpretation of Plato.

Hermann. To most scholars in the nineteenth century, Schleiermacher's refutation of Tennemann and other Esoterists[35] carried conviction, the more so as it was endorsed even by his great antagonist Karl Friedrich Hermann in his *Geschichte und System der platonischen Philosophie*, though with a certain hesitation. Talking about Aristotle's account of Plato's philosophy, Hermann declared—as subsequently Zeller[36] and Susemihl[37] were to do—that this account compels us to add a "last phase" to Plato's philosophic evolution, a phase which cannot be regarded as a culmination but rather as a decline, in which, however, Plato "nicht blos auf das Verhältnis der Ideen zur Welt, sondern auch auf die in den Ideen ver-einigten Elemente selbst tiefer einging, als er es mit dem Character schrift-licher Darstellung für vereinbar halten mochte".[38]

As if afraid of the logical conclusion of this statement, Hermann hastens to dissociate himself from the Esoterists, by firmly denying the existence of an esoteric Platonism, different from an exoteric one and reserved for Plato's disciples, so that he "durch seine Schriften nicht sowohl belehrend als vielmehr blos anregend zu wirken beabsichtigt habe". In Plato, there was not even that difference between an esoteric and an exoteric doctrine which existed in Aristotle whose "acroamatic" works alone contain his real system, missing in his popular works, "während Plato nur nicht dazu gelangte, alle Theile seines Systems gleichmässig in Schrift zu veröffentli-chen". Hermann ends the last section of the First—and only—Volume of his work with the solemn promise that the Second Volume—the account of Plato's system—would prove beyond reasonable doubt, "dass auch seine vollendeten Werke selbst alles dasjenige enthalten, was dem philoso-phischen Bedürfniss der Zeit entsprach, so dass die Annahme eines spezifischen Unterschieds zwischen ihnen und den mündlichen Vorträgen letztere gerade ausserhalb der weltgeschichlichen Notwendigkeit stellen würde, von der Plato ein so wesentliches Moment bildet".[39]

We may wonder whether Schleiermacher, who did not live to read Hermann's book, would have felt content with this final, ambiguous and contradictory retraction, in which, moreover, he would have sniffed a disgusting smell of Hegelianism. Any misgivings he might have felt would have been amply proved by a lecture which Hermann gave in 1839—the same year in which his book was published—but which was printed only ten years later, "Über Plato's schriftstellerische Motive".[40] For in this lecture, Hermann more or less joins the Esoterists, as their modern representatives have gratefully noted.[41]

True, even now Hermann refuses to call the Dialogues exoteric "in dem Sinne ... dass sie um der künstlerischen oder dialektischen Form willen, geschweige denn aus niedrigen Beweggründen, die wissenschaftliche Auffassung des Gegenstands verläugnet oder aufgegeben hätten,"[42] and he dissociates himself explicitly from Tennemann.[43] But on the other hand, he now wholeheartedly embraces an opinion which, in his book, he only hesitatingly proposed. It seems to him evident, partly from what Plato himself says in the *Phaedrus* and from what his disciples make him say in the *Epistles*,[44] partly from what Aristotle says about his philosophy, that the Dialogues do not contain the whole of it. In them, the principles of Plato's philosophy, the doctrine of Ideas, is only hinted at, the real treatment of it being reserved for his oral teaching, which was certainly as systematic as that of Aristotle.[45] In an earlier phase of his philosophic evolution, Plato had, indeed, tried to treat of the principles themselves—and failed, as the *Parmenides*, the *Sophist*, and the *Statesman* reveal. The Dialogue which was to crown and conclude them, the *Philosopher*, was never written, for by then Plato had realized that the highest principles could not be stated in writing.[46] For that reason, the later Dialogues are "psychagogic" aimed at the great public, while Plato reserved his deepest thought for the Academy.

Hermann is, however, anxious to stress the agreement between Plato's written work and his oral teaching. They are not parallel, but "die akroamatischen Lehren" must be regarded "als Fortsetzung und Schlussstein der schriftlichen ... die dort erst zur vollen Klarheit prinzipieller Auffassung erhoben werden, ohne jedoch über den nämlichen Gegenstand, so weit die Rede auf denselben kommen musste, etwas wesentliches Verschiedenes zu lehren".[47] In the final words of his lecture, Hermann makes a still greater concession, when he says that we should not expect to find Plato's highest principles in his works, "wenigstens nicht so ... dass man sie nur mit Händen zu greifen brauchte; solche Aufschlusse waren seinen mündlichen Vorträgen vorbehalten; darum aber liegen sie doch so ausgeprägt in denselben, dass wer Augen hat zu sehen, schwerlich ein wesentliches Stück vermissen wird, um sich daraus den ganzen Organismus platonischer Weltansicht zu reconstruiren, und insofern können sie auch als echte Quelle nicht allein seiner Methode sondern auch seines philosophischen Systems selbst gebraucht werden".[48]

Thus it seems that, after all, to Hermann the Dialogues in themselves give a sufficiently clear notion of Plato's philosophy. The relations between them and the oral teaching remain obscure. Hermann never says unambiguously whether we can understand the Dialogues without any knowledge of the oral teaching or not.[49] We are left wondering whether he knew it himself, for the Second Volume of his books where he would have been compelled to take his stand, was never written.[50] Even more than his false chronology of the Dialogues, this contradictory and ambiguous attitude made Hermann's defence of the existence and priority of an oral Platonic system fall on deaf ears. Only a hundred years later, when the genetic approach to Plato, whose originator he had been, seemed to have ended up in an impasse, the moment was ripe for a new and this time more successful attempt to ascribe an esoteric doctrine to Plato.

Plato's Testimony: the Phaedrus and the Epistles

Like Hermann, the modern Esoterists invoke Plato himself as the principal evidence of their thesis. Has he not opposed his written works to his oral teaching? Has he not in the *Phaedrus* extolled the spoken word at the expense of the written one, which is not the bastard brother of the true *Logos*, the one "that goes together with knowledge, and is written in the soul of the learner: that can defend itself, and knows to whom it should speak and to whom it should say nothing"?[51] Has not Plato in the *Seventh Epistle* solemnly declared that there is not nor will ever be any book (σύγγραμμα) of his upon the highest principles, "for this matter cannot be expressed like other sciences, but after community of life with much discussion of the matter itself, it suddenly appears in the soul like light kindled from leaping fire and thence forward substains itself"?[52] Has he not in the *Second Epistle* expressly stated that those first principles must be withheld from the multitude and revealed only to "gifted persons (ἐυφυεῖς)"? "The best precaution is not to write them down, but to commit them to memory; for it is impossible that things written should not become known to others. This is why I have never written on these subjects. There is no writing of Plato's nor will there ever be; those that are now so called come from an idealized and youthful Socrates."[53]

At first sight, these Platonic statements seem irrefutably to vindicate the Esoterists who have not failed to adduce them.[54] For that reason, it would be necessary to analyse these texts closely. Having, however, in an earlier study, discussed the passages in the *Phaedrus* and the *Seventh Letter*[55], I shall here confine myself to some general observations.[56]

As I pointed out in that study, modern scholars seem often to forget that

69

to Plato, as to any contemporary Greek, "reading" meant listening, whether to one' own voice or to that of somebody else.[57] That is just what was happening to Socrates in the *Phaedrus:* he has been listening to Phaedrus' recitation of a speech on Love by the famous rhetorician Lysias, but this truly "spoken" word is nevertheless mute, unable to explain or defend itself, or to choose whom it should address—the declamations of the Sophists being aimed indiscriminately at the general public. To such a word, Socrates opposes the true *Logos*, "living and animate", planted by a "dialectician" in the soul of the learner. It should be obvious that Plato here opposes passive reception to active collaboration, not the written word as such to the spoken one—in the modern sense. Even the spoken word can be dead and mute. The *Logos* is alive only as *Dialogos*.[58]

But that is precisely what Plato says in the *Seventh Epistle*, speaking about "the community of life" (συνουσία) and "the joint pursuit of the subject" (τὸ συζῆν)[59] which alone lead to a knowledge of the highest principles. Such a knowledge can only be acquired in the *Dialogos* between two minds.[60] It cannot be learnt by reading a book, nor—may we add—by listening to a lecture, as the younger Dionysius did. Hence, there is no contradiction between the *Phaedrus* and the *Epistle*—contrary to what many scholars have asserted.[61]

The case of the *Second Epistle* is different. Here, we find a Plato who has tried to gain the favour of the multitude in Syracuse but failed (312 A), who asks Dionysius to honour him so that the prince himself could be honoured by Plato (312 B), a Plato who has sent a pupil with this letter, written in enigmas, so that, if it falls in the hand of outsiders, it could not be understood (312 D), who begs Dionysius to take care that their correspondence should not be divulged (314 A) and not to write down Plato's doctrines but commit them to memory (314 B), who finally asks Dionysius to burn the very letter we are reading (314 C).

As scholars have not failed to point out, the picture that the *Second Epistle* gives of Plato's attitude to philosophy and of his relations with Dionysius does not tally with that given in the *Seventh Epistle*.[62] If the latter Epistle is by Plato, as most scholars today believe, then the former cannot be so. Both may be spurious. Both cannot be authentic.[63] Even the modern Esoterists hesitate to accept the *Second Epistle*,[64] which seems to imitate the *Seventh*, perhaps under Pythagorean influence.[65]

On the Good

But does not the famous lecture—or lectures—*On the Good* (Περὶ τἀγαθοῦ) prove that Plato reserved the essence of his philosophy for the members of the Academy? We have accounts of this lecture (ἀκρόασις) in Aristoxenus, Themistius, and Proclus. As most scholars nowadays agree in regarding the two last-mentioned accounts as mere elaborations of that in Aristoxenus,[66] I shall confine myself to what he tells us. Aristoxenus' relation occurs in the introduction to the Second Book of his *Harmonics*.[67] There he gives a preliminary view of his subject, so that his readers should not harbour a false conception of it:

"Such was the condition, as Aristotle always (ἀεί) related, of most of the audience that attended Plato's lecture (ἀκρόασις) on the Good. They came, every one of them, in the conviction that they would get from the lecture some or other of the things that the world calls good: riches, or health, or strength, in fine, some extraordinary gift of fortune. But when they found that Plato's reasoning was of sciences (μαθήματα)—numbers, geometry, and astronomy—and, to crown all (τὸ πέρας) that the Good is the One, methinks their disenchantment was complete. The result was that some of them sneered at the thing, while others vilified it. Now, to what was all this trouble due? To the fact that they had not waited to inform themselves of the nature of the subject, but after the manner of the sect of word-catchers (ἐριστικοί) had flocked around open-mouthed, attracted by the mere title. But if a general exposition of the subject had been given in advance, the intending pupil would either have abandoned his intention or, if he was pleased with the exposition, would have remained in the said conviction to the end. It was for that very reason that Aristotle himself used to give his intending pupils a preparatory statement of the subject and method of his course of study (πραγματεία)."[68]

The first question to be asked à propos of this famous and only too much discussed text is: who was Aristoxenus and what is the general validity of his statements about Plato? This is a matter upon which, for good reasons, the modern Esoterists do not like to dwell. For, as has been amply demonstrated above, Aristoxenus of Tarentum was a bitter foe of Plato's and lost no opportunity to slander and vilify him.[69] Any information about Plato which can be traced back to Aristoxenus should therefore *eo ipso* be suspect. The facts in themselves may be right but the malignant tendency is always present.

That is the case with our text. It is with a malicious glee that Aristoxenus tells how, through lack of commonsense and prudence, the great philosopher sorely disappoints his expectant listeners.[70] It seems pretty obvious that the story refers to some special occasion, a public lecture given to a numerous and mixed audience which had no idea of what Plato could possibly mean by "the Good". And so, until recently, the story has been generally interpreted.[71]

However, this interpretation is fiercely contested by the Esoterists. They assert that Aristoxenus meant not *one* lecture but a whole series of lectures, a real course, and that this course was regularly repeated in the Academy, constituting the very essence of Plato's teaching.[72] As in H. C. Andersen's fairytale one small feather becomes seven hens, so in the fertile imagination of the Esoterists this one public Platonic lecture—the only one known to us—changes "into something rich and strange", a whole systematic teaching of philosophic fundamentals.

As to Aristoxenus' account, the Esoterists have lately beaten the retreat. Obviously impressed by the criticism they have had to face,[73] they now admit that—as Gaiser puts it—"Aus der anekdotenhaften Darstellung geht nicht hervor, ob die ἀκρόασις nur einmal stattfand oder im Lauf der Zeit mehrfach wiederholt wurde".[74] But this admission is not sufficient. To say, as Krämer does, that "dieser knappe Text ... in diesen Fragen alle Möglichkeiten offen lässt" implies, indeed, a repudiation of his former way of regarding Aristoxenus' account as an irrefutable proof of Plato's regular lecturing in the Academy. But his new assertion that the text does not offer any certain information at all, is no improvement but only an attempt to fly in the face of Aristoxenus' clear words. What Krämer in the same context says about the possibility that the story was a stock "Kathederanekdote" and not a personal experience of Aristotle's and that the disappointment of the audience was repeated many times during Plato's lifetime can, indeed, as he points out, not be directly refuted,[75] but neither can it be proved. A possibility is not a probability, still less a fact. The burden of proof lies with him who, against the total silence of our sources, asserts that Plato regularly lectured on the Good in the Academy. On this point, too, the ancient scholastic rule should be applied: *quod gratis asseritur, gratis et negatur.*

But we can go a step further. The fact that this lecture—and only this one—was recorded by several of Plato's disciples—Aristotle, Speusippus, Xenocrates, Heraclides, Hestiaeus, *et alii*[76]—suggests that it was something unique. As Harold Cherniss has rightly said: "if in the school they regularly heard systematic expositions of Plato's ultimate philosophy, it is strange that they attached so much importance to this public lecture as to take it down and publish it alone of all the lectures which they heard".[77] When Krämer asserts that the statement in Simplicius' commentary upon Aristotle's *Physics* that these disciples "were present at the lecture On the Good" (παρεγένοντο ἐν τῇ περὶ τἀγαθοῦ ἀκροάσει) should be interpreted as meaning that they had several times and upon different occasions attended Plato's regular course of lectures on the Good, he asserts something which is not to be found in the text.[78] Nor should we, like Gaiser, from the circumstance that the catalogues of Aristotle's writings mention a work Περὶ τἀγαθοῦ in *three* Books,[79] infer that Plato must have given a course of lectures, for, as Gaiser himself points out, we do not know, whether Aristotle's work also contained a criticism.[80] Nor can the circumstance that later writers loosely speak of "lectures" in the plural (ἀκροάσεις, συνουσίαι) be taken as proving that there really were several.[81] And the fact that Aristotle gave regular courses does not prove that Plato did so too.[82]

Teaching in the Seventh Epistle

But does not Plato himself in the *Seventh Epistle* give a detailed account of his teaching in the Academy? So the Esoterists assert.[83] But what Plato relates is a unique experience in his life, his attempt to win Dionysius II for his philosophy. Of course, as clearly appears from the Epistle, Plato approached Dionysius as an experienced teacher and judge of men. But his way of treating Dionysius by putting him to a test (πεῖρα), "very appropriate for tyrants",[84] showing him the difficulties and pains attached to philosophy, should not indiscriminately be applied to his teaching in the Academy.[85] To assert that the disappointment felt by those that listened to the lecture on the Good was due to such a deliberate test on Plato's part[86] has no support in the sources.[87] When, in the Epistle Plato subsequently says that this test is "clear and infallible in the case of voluptuaries and idlers,"[88] we may well doubt whether such people ever joined the Academy. Plato seems rather to be thinking of the courtiers of Dionysius who, seeing their master interested in philosophy, tried to ape him.[89]

As has been pointed out above, the Epistle's famous rejection of the written word—like that in the *Phaedrus*—should be interpreted as stressing the fundamental importance to philosophy of the dialectical discussion.[90] If this interpretation is right, Plato's rejection of writing applies also to lectures, such as that on the Good. As a believer in the esoteric Plato, the late Philip Merlan, said: "Eine Schreibe bleibt eine Schreibe, auch wenn sie rezitiert wird."[91] Actually, in the *Epistle* Plato says explicitly that he is unable not only to write but also to speak about the highest matters.[92] "Speaking" must here mean "making speeches", "lecturing", for discussions are expressly mentioned as necessary to the search for truth.[93]

Commenting on the *Epistle* it is therefore with good reason that Krämer stresses that a knowledge of those highest matters of which Plato speaks can be acquired only orally "in einem allmählichen dialektischen Prozess geistiger Aneignung" and that this acquirement "sich ... stets nur in dialektischer Partnerschaft ereignet".[94] But, in the same breath, he speaks of Plato's lectures on the Good as constituting this "dialectic partnership" and tries to solve this contradiction by introducing the concept "Lehr-gespräch"—an invention which will be discussed below.[95] In the same way, Krämer rightly insists that the condemnation of the written word in the *Phaedrus* and the *Seventh Epistle* includes Plato's own dialogues,[96] but wrongly asserts—against the plain words of Plato[97]—that this condemnation does not include the disciples' accounts of Plato's "courses" on the Good, because such works circulated only inside the Academy and were not published books.[98] In this way, Krämer tries to escape from a dilemma of his own making. If, as he believes, the *public* lecture of which Aristoxenus speaks was in fact an often repeated course of lectures in the Academy, would not the accounts of the disciples conflict with the *Seventh Epistle's* severe condemnation of *all* attempts to write about the last and highest matters? Therefore, Krämer concludes, those accounts must have been "Schulschriften"—a new creation of his, which like the others lack support in the sources.[99] If we keep to what Aristoxenus really says, Krämer's hypothesis is unnecessary. In fact, it is Albinus rather than Aristoxenus who provides the foundation for the Esoterists' conception of the lecture on the Good,[100] though for obvious reasons they do not refer to him.[101]

Of course, the mere belief that Plato taught in the Academy and that in his teaching he may have advanced opinions not expressed in the Dialogues is no invention of the modern Esoterists', but a well-established view held by many authoritative scholars, such as K. Fr. Hermann,[102] Heinrich von Stein,[103] Eduard Zeller,[104] Wilamowitz,[105] and Paul Friedländer,[106] who only hesitated about the form of this teaching, whether lectures or discussions, concluding wisely that the one did not exclude the other. This, however, did not imply that these scholars were inclined to place Plato's oral teaching on a level with his written work, still less that they preferred the former to the latter. To them, Plato was essentially the Plato of the Dialogues.

The Depreciation of the Dialogues

Very different has been the attitude of the Esoterists and their modern forerunners. In 1912, the young Werner Jaeger declared peremptorily that Plato's true philosophy was not to be found in his Dialogues, which were conceived not as philosophic treatises but as works of art, but in his oral teaching, such as it can be reconstructed from the account of Aristotle and other disciples.[107] In the same way A. E. Taylor asserted that the Dialogues "were meant to appeal to the 'educated' at large and interest them in philosophy" but that "Plato's inmost ultimate conviction on the most

74

important questions" was exposed only orally,[108] and that to Plato his teaching was far more important than his writings[109]—a view shared by Taylor's Scotch fellow-Platonist John Burnet.[110] Although praised by the Esoterists,[111] Julius Stenzel was not nearly so radical but he, too, was convinced that the key at least to the later Dialogues was to be found in Plato's teaching in the Academy.[112] As we saw above,[113] at about the same time, Ernst Hoffmann, Léon Robin, and Heinrich Gomperz voiced similar opinions.

But the modern Esoterists go much further. To them, the only true philosophy of Plato was the systematic metaphysics expounded by him in regular lectures to his disciples in the Academy. Compared with these lectures, the Dialogues were only "paraenetic" and "protreptic", catering for the general public, whose interest in philosophy they sought to awake, in any case, subordinated to Plato's systematic oral teaching.[114] This thesis is in the first place justified by the misinterpretation of the *Phaedrus* and the *Seventh Epistle* criticized above.[115] Secondly, Krämer adduces as a proof also the many passages in the Dialogues, where Plato speaks depreciatingly of Man and human matters as being a mere play.[116] Krämer conveniently overlooks the deeply sceptical and pessimistic spirit of these utterances; he believes that they only apply to Plato's written works.[117] When, for instance, in the *Laws* Plato makes the Athenian speak of himself and his interlocutors as "playing a sage play about laws fit for old men",[118] or say that Man is created to be God's plaything and play His play,[119] is Plato then making an exception for himself and his teaching in the Academy?

To Krämer, a third proof—and one of the strongest—of an esoteric Platonism is the circumstance that in some of Plato's most important Dialogues—the *Protagoras*, the *Republic*, the *Phaedrus*, the *Sophist*, the *Statesman*, the *Timaeus*—the leader of the discussion—Socrates, the Eleatic, Timaeus—declares at the very climax of the discussion that he will not now indicate clearly the real nature of the matter they are discussing but may perhaps return to it another time.[120] This refusal to proceed further—so Krämer asserts—has no "protreptic function" nor does it express any real intention of dealing with the matter in a later work, but is due to Plato's aversion to discussing such matters publicly in writing. What Plato had to say about these central and important matters he reserved for his oral teaching.

Of the many examples of this "refusal" of Plato that Krämer adduces —some of them are not real refusals[121]—I shall confine myself to one, the most famous of them, Socrates' refusal in the *Republic* to tell his interlocutor Glaucon what the Good really is. As Socrates himself subsequently relates:

"It will right well content me, my dear fellow," I said, "but I fear that my powers may fail and that in my eagerness I may cut a sorry figure and become a laughing-stock. Nay, my beloved, let us dismiss for the time being the nature of the Good in itself; for to attain to my present surmise of that seems a pitch above the impulse that wings my flight to-day. But of what seems to be the offspring of the Good and most nearly made in its likeness I am willing to speak if you wish it, and otherwise to let the matter drop." "Well, speak on," he said, "for you will duly pay me the tale of the parent another time," "I could wish", I said, "that I were able to make and you to receive the payment and not merely as now the interest. But at any rate receive this interest and the offspring of the Good."[122]

It does not occur to Krämer—though it has occurred to other scholars[123]—that Socrates' smiling refusal could be due to Plato's earnest conviction that there were matters about which we could neither write nor speak directly but only deal with in the dialectical discussion in which our insight into them "emerges as a light" (ἐξέλαμψε φρόνησις).[124] Therefore, it cannot be expressed in any formula, whether in speech or in writing.[125] And when one of his critics suggested this interpretation,[126] Krämer strongly rejected it.[127] For to him a philosopher is a man who knows the answer to every question, though, for some reason, he may withhold his answer. So Plato did in the *Republic*, knowing perfectly well what the Good is and telling it to his disciples in the Academy, not only once but year by year.

If thus the Dialogues not only presuppose the Secret Doctrine but contain many hints of it,[128] then an uninitiated reader—i.e., any ancient reader who was not a member of the Academy or any modern reader who is not an Esoterist—is unable really to understand them.[129] But, so Krämer declares, Plato did not pay any attention to such readers, for what he wrote was in the first place intended for contemporary readers, "und als solches auf die geschichtliche Präsenz der Akademie und der Person Platons selbst unmittelbar bezogen".[130] A stiff saying, if we remember that Plato's *person* is singularly absent from the Dialogues! If Krämer is right, the overwhelming majority of Plato's contemporary readers must have been unable to understand him, and we are left with the riddle, why Plato bothered to write so many books instead of confining himself to his oral teaching.[131]

Actually, the Esoterists—especially Krämer—do not care much for the Dialogues, which to them are a nuisance they could well do without. If the Dialogues suddenly disappeared without a trace, this would not affect the Esoterists' conception of Platonism. For it is not based on an analysis of the Dialogues—though, as we have seen, the Esoterists have subsequently tried to find support for their opinions in them—but on an analysis of the

76

statements of *other* writers about Plato, above all those of Aristotle. To the Esoterists, these statements are of far greater value for our knowledge of Plato's real philosophy than his own writings in which, at the best, he only gives hints of it.[132]

The Secondary Tradition

A priori, such a position seems very paradoxical. And the paradox becomes even more glaring, when we consider that, whereas *all* of Plato's works are extant, the *Testimonia* of Plato's personal disciples concerning his teaching—with the partial exception of Aristotle—are known to us only at second or third hand.[133] They have to be collected from the works of later—in many cases very late—writers, and it is often extremely difficult to determine whether a certain statement refers to Plato or not, as the polemics between Platonic scholars have proved only too conspicuously.[134] We here deal with possibilities rather than probabilities, still less facts. To pretend, as the Esoterists do, that an interpretation of Plato which takes into account also such statements as may *possibly* refer to him is "historically better founded" than an interpretation which limits itself to statements which certainly do so, reveals a curious way of arguing.[135] If keeping to texts and facts is "philological Positivism", as the Esoterists contemptuously say, then we can never have enough of such Positivism.

The reason why the Esoterists prefer the secondary testimony of what they call "the Platonic tradition" to the direct testimony of the Dialogues is that only in this way can they reconstruct the philosophic system they believe that Plato had. Their argumentation is a silent admission of a fact, often stressed above, viz. the impossibility to extract a system from the Dialogues alone.

But is our knowledge of Plato's oral teaching only second-hand? If he lectured regularly in the Academy, did he not use notes? This question has been put and answered in the negative by A. E. Taylor, because otherwise Aristotle would not have "commonly" referred to the teaching given in the Academy as Plato's "unwritten doctrines".[136] Other scholars have been more positive. Thus, e.g., Julius Stenzel believed that the disciples' reports of the famous lecture on the Good were based not only on the Master's spoken words but on his own manuscript.[137] In this way, we are endowed with a written work by Plato, of the highest importance, lost, alas, for ever—whether destroyed by Plato or suppressed by the Academy, Stenzel fails to tell.

Our contemporary Esoterists have been somewhat more cautious. Krämer, indeed, believes that when he lectured Plato used notes, but adds that we can only presume the existence of a "Lehrschrift" on which the lectures on the Good were based, and leaves it open whether it was accessible to the disciples or not.[138] We are reduced to the secondary testimonies concerning Plato's oral teaching.

We must therefore ask, what precisely do these testimonies amount to and what is their reliability. It is a well-known fact, which has puzzled and worried generations of scholars, that there are in Aristotle—especially in the *Metaphysics*—several statements about Plato's philosophy, above all its essential aspect, the doctrine of Ideas, which only with difficulty or not at all can be brought to agree with Plato's own statements in the Dialogues. According to Aristotle, Plato professed "a 'vertical' dualism of supreme principles, the One and the Indefinite Dyad. The interaction of these principles 'produces' the Ideas (themselves in some way designated as numbers), and, as the Ideas are the causes of everything else, the two principles become universal causes. They are likened by Aristotle to the formal and material cause of his own system; and in some way they are also identified with the principles of good and evil".[139]

This summary of Aristotle's statements by the late Philip Merlan stresses their obscure and equivocal character. Similar—though not identical—statements can be found in later writers; they refer to other personal disciples of Plato's or to the lecture *On the Good*.[140]

The attitude of modern scholars to these statements in Aristotle and other Platonists follow five main trends.[141] First, there have been some few scholars who have had no difficulty in finding in the Dialogues the doctrines attributed to Plato by his disciples.[142] Secondly, there are those scholars—few but eminent, e.g., Paul Shorey and Harold Cherniss—who decisively reject the testimony of the disciples, especially that of Aristotle. Thirdly, there are the many scholars who with more or less reservation accept this testimony but regard it as referring to a last phase of Plato's thought which he did not find time to put down in writing. This was Zeller's position,[143] and thanks to his great authority it became the popular, one could almost say, the "orthodox" position.

The fourth position is that of the modern Esoterists. They accept wholeheartedly the testimony of Plato's disciples and later writers, in whom they see a never-broken chain of tradition from Plato down to Plotinus and the last Neoplatonists. They are not greatly worried about the discrepancy between this tradition and the Dialogues, for, as we have seen, they do not regard the Dialogues as expressing Plato's innermost thought which is only to be found in the tradition.

A fifth position has recently been taken up by an American scholar, Stanley Rosen.[144] "In order to 'save the phenomena' of dialogues, letters, and the tradition of esoterism" he maintains "that the dialogues themselves contain both an exoteric and an esoteric teaching"—a thesis he tries to prove by an analysis of the *Symposium*.[145] This position can therefore be considered as a combination of the first and the fourth position.

The first position differs from all the others in as far as the scholars who adopt it deny that there is any real difference between the opinions Plato expresses in the Dialogues and those attributed to him by other writers. As is the case with all such radical solutions of the problem of Platonic interpretation the problem itself disappears. This is, indeed, a convenient solution: the solution of the Neoplatonists.[146]

If, however, as far as I know, today no scholar adopts this attitude, it is, as I have said above, because no modern scholar—not even Hans Joachim Krämer—can read the Dialogues as Proclus read them.[147] Such a "systematization" of the Platonic texts is not palatable to modern readers, to most of whom it appears as an intolerable distortion. Nor is the last resort of the Neoplatonists, allegorism, open to us.

As to the fifth position, it shares the lot of all similar attempts to combine mutually exclusive views, viz., to fall between two stools. On the one hand, Rosen asserts that "the dialogues provide effective directions for the reconstruction of Plato's oral teachings", and goes as far as rejecting the attempt to reconstruct an oral teaching on the basis of documentary testimony by Plato's students as being "contradictory to the very passages from the letters and dialogues themselves concerning the nature of philosophy as unteachable or unsuited for writing".[148] On the other hand, he declares that "Plato, or for that matter any philosopher, was too sensible to publish openly all of his thoughts,"[149] adducing the examples of Leibniz, Hume, and Rousseau. Such a reticence, Rosen believes, was common before the Enlightenment. In stating this, Rosen joins the company not so much of the modern Esoterists as that of Numenius and Tennemann who believed that out of prudence Plato kept some of his philosophy secret.[150] Yet like them, Rosen does not doubt his own ability to unravel Plato's secret. But unlike them, he fails to demonstrate *why* Plato acted in this way.

Cherniss

The foremost living representative of the second position is Harold Cherniss. In his great, as yet unfinished work, *Aristotle's Criticism of Plato and the Academy*, and especially in his small but substantial book, *The Riddle of the Early Academy*,[151] he has with immense learning and great acumen denied the very existence of an Academic philosophic tradition, based on

Plato's oral teaching, which could supply, not to say correct, the teaching of the Dialogues. To Cherniss, there is only *one* Plato: the Plato of the Dialogues. Those statements in Aristotle and other writers that seem to contradict the Dialogues are simply due to a misunderstanding or a more or less deliberate distortion of them, as Cherniss tries to prove by detailed analyses of the principal texts. For neither Aristotle nor any other of Plato's disciples had sources of knowledge of his philosophy other than the Master's written works. Cherniss does not, indeed, deny that Plato delivered the famous lecture *On the Good*. But he thinks that this public lecture was a unique occasion, an exception which proved the rule and which was moreover so "enigmatic" that Plato's own disciples, who duly made their notes, could not make head or tail of it. The rule was that in the Academy Plato kept aloof, at least, did not teach any sort of philosophic system or try to force his personal opinions upon the members but granted them liberty to form their own opinions, also and not least about his Dialogues.

This short but, I hope, not incorrect summary does not do justice to the persuasive lucidity and polemical vigour with which Cherniss defends his thesis. As Aristotle's authority is invoked by those that believe in an oral teaching of Plato's, different from the Dialogues, Cherniss does his best to ruin that authority. In an earlier work, *Aristotle's Criticism of Presocratic Philosophy*,[152] Cherniss, with equal learning and acumen, had painted a most unfavourable picture of Aristotle as a historian of philosophy. Lacking understanding of philosophic ideas alien to him and interested in earlier philosophies mainly in so far as he could consider them more or less imperfect anticipations of his own philosophy, Aristotle was by nature unable to give a faithful and unbiassed account of other thinkers. This is especially true in regard to his master Plato of whose philosophy he was so highly critical. Therefore Cherniss subjects Aristotle's statements about Plato to a merciless scrutiny from which they seldom emerge unscathed. In the end, we are very much left with the strong impression that we can trust Aristotle only if we find his sayings supported by the Dialogues.

Cherniss's conclusions as well concerning Aristotle's general merit as a historian of philosophy as concerning the reliability of his statements about Plato have not remained unchallenged. Several scholars—some of them not too inferior to Cherniss in learning and sagacity—have tried to refute or at least to restrict them.[153] The Esoterists have in Cherniss seen a deadly foe and devoted much energy and space to polemizing against him. Even if I confined myself to the matter that interests me here, viz., Aristotle as a source of our knowledge of Plato, it is obvious that mere consideration of space would not allow me to discuss it in detail, provided I had the inclination and the competency to do so. Fortunately, it is not necessary to my purpose. For even without going into detail, it is possible to discern and discuss the methodological problems associated with this matter.

Plato in the Academy

In his endeavour to disparage any statement by Aristotle or any other else of Plato's disciples which does not seem to tally with the Dialogues, Cherniss has been induced to form an idea of Plato's rôle in the Academy which has not been accepted by other scholars. It is, indeed, difficult to believe that Plato rigidly abstained from discussing philosophic problems with the members of the Academy, for that would mean to turn "the riddle of the Early Academy" into an unsolvable mystery. If Plato behaved as Cherniss believes he did, why did he ever found the Academy? Why did he not remain a solitary thinker like Heraclitus and confine himself to writing and publishing his Dialogues?

Even Cherniss admits that Plato once lectured in public. But if he never discussed philosophic matters with his friends in the Academy, why should he then suddenly expound his opinions to a mixed audience which mis-understood him? Above all, Plato's own writings testify to the importance he attached to oral discussions. I shall not adduce the *Seventh Epistle*, as Cherniss considers it spurious. But the *Phaedrus* expresses the same at-titude, and the fact that Plato chose the dialogue as a form for his writings cannot be due to the example of Socrates alone. "Can we imagine the master of the written dialogue keeping away from oral dialogues with his disciples?"[155]

It is unfortunately true, as Cherniss stresses, that we know far less about the Academy than we would like to know. But what little we know points in the same direction, viz., that Plato had discussions with the members. There is, in the first place, the famous fragment from a comedy of Epicrates which should not be so lightly disposed of as Cherniss tends to do.[156] He admits, however, that it may prove that in the Academy "young students were encouraged to practice framing precise definitions"—something that does not speak in favour of a total withdrawal by Plato. Admittedly, Epicrates could have found this zest for definition in the *Sophist* and the *Statesman*, or, as Cherniss suggests, in Xenocrates. But, surely, the easiest explanation is that the poet had heard about excercises in dihaëresis in the Academy and amused himself and his audience by parodying them, making the students under Plato's guidance define a gourd.

If therefore Plato did not isolate himself from the Academy, that circum-stance does not necessarily imply that he gave regular lectures in systematic metaphysics, as the Esoterists wish us to believe (sometimes; for, as we shall see, they have also voiced a very different opinion),[157] "pronouncing *ex cathedra* an orthodox interpretation".[158] Following the indication of the Dialogues, we may imagine that in the Academy Plato taught more by listening than by speaking, more by questioning than by answering, more by doubting than by asserting, as becomes a true Socratic midwife of Souls.[159] Nor should we exclude the possibility that, in these discussions, Plato dealt with problems not treated of in the Dialogue and expressed opinions different from, even opposite to the Dialogues.[160] This possibility is the more probable as Plato does not hesitate to contradict himself in the Dialogues, as any sincere interpretation is forced to admit.[161] Bearing the *Phaedrus* in mind—also the *Seventh Epistle*, if we accept it as authentic—we cannot even exclude the possibility that Plato may have regarded his 'midwifery' in the Academy as more important than his written work.[162] I am well aware that this interpretation of the scanty evidence we have of Plato's teaching amounts only to a probability. But in such matters we cannot ask for more.

Aristotle on Plato

Even if we accept this probability, the question of Aristotle's authority is not settled. As I said above, I cannot discuss it in detail but must confine myself to some general observations. Aristotle's treatment of Plato is, of course, a very ancient controversial issue, and from classical antiquity onwards, there have always been those that have charged him "with lack of understanding or worse".[163] During the Renaissance, there was the famous controversy which culminated in Bessarion's apology, *In Calumniatores Platonis* (1469) and, in the next century, in Franesco Patrizzi's onslaught on Aristotle.

Nowadays, even those scholars who accept Aristotle's authority agree that he was not an impartial judge whether of Plato or of any other philosopher. Heinrich von Stein, who denied that there were any discrepances between the Aristotelian statements about Plato and the Dialogues, stressed that Aristotle judged Plato—as he judged all philosophers—from the viewpoint of his own philosophy.[164] A. E. Taylor, who believed in an oral teaching of Plato's differing from the Dialogues, declared that Aristotle was "a controversialist who is not unduly anxious to be 'sympathetic'".[165] And Taylor's friend, Burnet, even went so far as to state that Aristotle "never fully understood the head of the Academy".[166] True, they both hastened to add that, though Aristotle may not have understood what Plato said, yet, he faithfully reported it,[167] as if, in this convenient way, we could criticize Aristotle without impairing his authority.[168]

82

Still more revealing is the fact that the critics of Cherniss more or less openly admit Aristotle's shortcomings. Even Krämer condescendingly calls Cherniss' criticism of Aristotle "insoweit berechtigt und nützlich, als sie die schiefen Klassifizierungen und terminologische Umformulierungen der aristotelischen Berichterstattung aufdecken und ausscheiden konnte",[169] and Gaiser says that we must take into account a certain "Einseitigkeit der aristotelischen Berichterstattung".[170] Other scholars are more outspoken. Miss de Vogel concedes that "there are contradictions and misunderstandings in Aristotle's account, though perhaps not in the measure Cherniss thinks there are",[171] and Sir David Ross, while asserting that "Aristotle was not the pure blunderer that Prof. Cherniss makes him out to have been", admits that "he was too ready to adopt interpretation of Plato either because they fitted in with his own preconceptions, or because they gave him an opportunity of criticism".[172]

What these scholars do not seem to realize is how detrimental to their belief in Aristotle's credibility those admissions are. Granted—*argumentandi causa*—that Cherniss's general picture of Aristotle as an historian of philosophy is one-sided and that his criticism of Aristotle's statements is exaggerated, enough of it remains valid to make us hesitate before accepting Aristotle's account in cases where we cannot check it.[173] That Aristotle's account and criticism of Plato is often biassed and misleading is no invention of Cherniss's, but a fact, proved by earlier scholars and, as we saw, admitted by the very critics of Cherniss.[174] Nor does it help to invoke the testimonies of other Platonists, a Speusippus, or a Xenocrates, or a Hermodorus. For, as even the Esoterists concede,[175] they differ from each other—as much, we may add as the modern reconstructions of Plato's Unwritten Doctrine—besides being very scanty.

Direct and Indirect Tradition

Should we then argue, as a modern German scholar has done, that, although Cherniss undoubtedly is right on many points, nevertheless, for want of other sources, we must follow Aristotle.[176] But this was said à propos of Pythagoras. In the case of Plato, we have other sources, viz., his own Dialogues. It seems an odd perversity to reject or to depreciate a philosopher's *ipsissima verba* in favour of obscure and contradictory second or third hand reports of what he possibly might have said.[177] As a critic pertinently asked: what would we know about Kant, if we only knew him from the critical interpretations of later philosophers?[178] It is vain to adduce Plato's condemnation of writing, for, as we have seen, it affects *all* kinds of writing. It is a mere sophistry to invent a special kind, the "Lehrschrift", which might escape the condemnation.[179]

Nevertheless, it remains a legitimate and interesting task to collect and shift out critically whatever in later expositions of Platonism might possibly have originated in some oral teaching of Plato in the Academy. This possibility should not be rejected *a priori*, as Cherniss does. If he was right in pointing out how easily such teaching could be misunderstood and distorted,[180] Philip Merlan was equally right, when he stressed that "any interpretation of Plato resulting in the assertion that he was misunderstood by Aristotle and 'betrayed' by Speusippus, Xenocrates, etc., will forever have to remain on the defensive".[181] It is only fair to add that, although trying to bridge the gap between Platonism and Neoplatonism, Merlan refused to commit himself to any final conclusion, whether the disciples' interpretation of Plato's philosophy—an interpretation which Merlan regarded as being essentially akin to the Neoplatonic one—was legitimate or illegitimate.[182] Such a restraint was certainly wise, for it lies in the nature of our sources that the margin of error is so broad as to exclude any certainty.[183] If by a lucky chance the Egyptian desert sand presented us with copies of all the different accounts of *On the Good*, it is to be feared that we would be more, not less, at a loss as to the real sense of this lecture. For in that case, even more than now, we would be confronted with several diverging interpretations: *Quidquid recipitur, recipitur ad modum recipientis*.[184]

The Final Wisdom

It is tempting to evade these difficulties, by assuming, with Zeller and the majority of modern Platonic scholars, that everything in the accounts of Plato's philosophy in Aristotle and other disciples of Plato's that cannot be made to tally with the Dialogues refers to Plato's oral teaching as constituting a final phase of his thought, which he did not manage to express in writing.[185] However, this convenient explanation meets with the obstacle that Plato was writing until the very end of his life—the *Laws* was published posthumously and bears obvious traces of being unfinished —and that it is extremely difficult, to say the least, to discover in the *Laws* or in any other work which can be assigned to his last years any unambiguous expression of the essence of the Unwritten Doctrine, viz., the dualism of first principles and the system of derivation.[186] If this doctrine was a final phase, we would still have to explain *why* Plato did not choose to write it down.

Another difficulty is that Aristotle, who is our main authority for the

Unwritten Doctrine, joined the Academy in 367 B.C., twenty years before Plato's death,[187] and it is not easy to prove that his account of Plato's philosophy refers only to the last years of Plato. Other disciples, like Speusippus and Xenocrates, whose accounts of the Master's thought are similar, even if not identical, with that by Aristotle, must have joined the Academy much earlier, probably from its beginning.[188] Here, as in other cases, a purely 'genetic' explanation reveals itself as inadequate.

This explanation is naturally rejected by all those modern scholars who react against the very notion of an 'evolution' of Plato or any other thinker or writer.[189] The modern Esoterists subscribe wholly to this reaction, thus returning to the position of Schleiermacher. As we have seen, the latter believed that from the very beginning Plato was in possession of his philosophy, though, for pedagogical and philosophic reasons, he only gradually unfolded it in his Dialogues, for Schleiermacher strongly denied the existence of any esoteric doctrine.[190] Later scholars generally accepted this denial however without accepting the view that Plato's philosophy did not undergo any essential change.

The System versus the Dialogues

On the contrary, it is precisely the second thesis of Schleiermacher that the Esoterists embrace.[191] To them, too, Plato's philosophy was the same from beginning to end, but it was the esoteric doctrine of his oral teaching which thus remained unchanged while the Dialogues seemingly present an image of change and variation. But this is a mere illusion which only deceives him who does not know of the Secret Doctrine which stands behind the Dialogues and to which they all point.[192] "Von ihrem esoterischen Kern her betrachtet stellt sich die platonische Philosophie als ein im wesentlichen streng gefügtes System dar, dessen Aussenseiten in den Dialogen durchschlägt", Krämer says.[193] Only the scholar who knows his esoteric core of Platonism is able not only to interpret the hints of the Secret Doctrine in the Dialogues but also to assign to each Dialogue its place in the totality of Platonic philosophy: *"die besondere Erscheinungsweise, die jeder einzelne Dialog den esoterischen Gehalten gibt, von seiner spezifischen inneren Form und Psychagogie zu erhalten".*[194]

As we have seen, this implies that to the Esoterists the Dialogues are purely "protreptic" and "paraenetic", to use their favourite catch-words, "Werbe- und Mahnschriften" in German.[195] The task of the Dialogues was to interest and prepare their readers for that insight into philosophic problems which could only be acquired through the oral teaching in the Academy. Therefore, the real function of the Dialogues is "psychagogischer, nicht dialektischer Art".[196] Their teaching remains provisional; they are but a "prelude".[197] Thus, they constitute "gleichsam den äussersten Kreis und die unterste Stufe in der erzieherischen Arbeit der Akademie".[198] Without knowledge of the Secret Doctrine we cannot really understand the Dialogues. But a knowledge of the Dialogues is not necessary to him who is initiated in the Doctrine, as the history of the Platonic tradition proves, whose two "Stränge", the Dialogues and the Esoteric Doctrine, run parallell to each other, without the former ever being able to take the place of the latter.[199] On the contrary, it is the Esoteric Doctrine which orally—"subterraneously"—transmitted through the centuries has constituted Plato's real influence on posterity.[200]

Thus Platonism becomes identical with the Secret Doctrine or rather System. In that case, however, it seems difficult not to draw the conclusion that, as Schleiermacher believed, Plato's philosophy was complete from the onset, i.e., that the System the Esoterists attribute to him was present behind the very earliest Dialogues.[201] This conclusion the Esoterists, indeed, draw, though with some hesitation, for they find it difficult to discover even traces of the System in the early Dialogues.[202] If nevertheless they are in favour of an early date, it is because they—especially Krämer—do not regard Plato as the true originator of the Esoteric Doctrine. This honour belongs to Xenophanes who was the real founder of Plato's metaphysics of Being, the doctrine of the One from which everything derives, though Plato radically changed Xenophanes' teaching by putting the Many at the side of the One.[203] In *Der Ursprung der Geistmetaphysik*, Krämer has expounded this thesis further and developed it into a general view of the evolution of Greek philosophy from Xenophanes to Plotinus, with the "Geistmetaphysik" as the highway.

It is a conception which does not lack a certain grandeur but which invites criticism.[204] I shall confine myself to one aspect: the practically total absence of Socrates. In *Der Ursprung der Geistmetaphysik*, he is mentioned once, casually. In *Arete*, he plays, indeed, a greater part, but only as an immature dialectician.[205] For the Socratic ignorance and the Socratic irony Krämer—like the Neoplatonists—has no use.[206] That holds generally true of the Esoterists.[207] Their Platonism is a Platonism without Socrates—a Hamlet without the Prince of Denmark. It is impossible not to feel that this amounts to a disastrous mutilation of Plato's thought.[208]

The same must be said of the Esoterists' treatment of the Dialogues. I have earlier given some samples of this,[209] and shall now only point out, how misleading their general and undiscriminating characterization of the Dialogues as "protreptic" and "paraenetic" is, at least if we keep to the proper sense of these words. Can we really call Dialogues like the

Theaetetus, the *Parmenides*, the *Philebus*, the *Sophist*, the *Statesman* "protreptic" and "paraenetic"? Are they not difficult and highly technical philosophic discussions which presuppose a very select public? And when Krämer calls the *Laws* "ein Lesebuch für den Jugendunterricht und ein Muster für die Auswahl anderer Lektüre",[210] his statement is so misleading as to be ludicrous. The reading matter of the young is, indeed, discussed in the *Laws*, but that giant dialogue deals with many other subjects, some of them deeply philosophic and religious.

By thus denying or minimizing the philosophic content and importance of the Dialogues, the Esoterists widen the gap between the author of the Dialogues and the teacher of the Academy. On the one hand, we have a thinker who at an early age constructed a metaphysical system which, during many years, he expounded in regular lectures to his students. On the other hand, we have a writer who to his dying day wrote dialogues which, at least to the uninitiated multitude for which they were intended, did not reveal any such system. Dialogues, we may add, which are masterpieces of profundity, wit, irony, charm—something nobody would gather from what the Esoterists say about them. This Janus-headed Plato is such a psychological improbability that we must ask for very strong proofs, if we are to believe in him. And the proofs are not forthcoming.

This difficulty did not escape the keen attention of Philip Merlan. Being himself a believer in the Esoteric Plato and having many years worked to bridge the gap between Platonism and Neoplatonism, as he himself stated,[211] he was nevertheless not able to accept the Esoterists' image of Plato. To Merlan, there were, first the aporetic Plato of the Dialogues, secondly the systematic Plato of the Academy, but thirdly yet another Plato, lurking behind the first and the second. And this Plato did not reveal his innermost secret, indeed, as the *Seventh Epistle* clearly states, he could not do so. Plato's last wisdom is hidden from us.[212]

Merlan's opinion carries weight, as coming from an eminent scholar who devoted a good deal of his life to a study of Plato and Platonism. Nevertheless, it seems even more difficult to believe in this Πλάτων τρικάρανος than in the Janus-Plato of the Esoterists. Nor is our willingness to believe strengthened by Merlan's acute criticism of the Esoterists, in spite of his qualified acceptance of their creed,[213] for this criticism affects Merlan himself, too.[214]

The Systematical Fallacy

As Merlan rightly pointed out, the *proton pseudos* of the Esoterists is their conviction that a philosopher must have a system—the conviction of Tennemann, Hegel, and Zeller. One of the Esoterists, Klaus Oehler, has expressed this conviction with such a revealing naïveté that his confession must be quoted *in extenso:*

"Man sollte sich lediglich daran erinnern, was man selber empfand, als man zum erstenmal Platonische Dialoge las, oder was man empfindet, wenn man nach der Lektüre Aristotelischer Texte wieder in Platons Dialogen liest. Es ist das Gefühl des Genarrten, das Gefühl, dass man von jemand, der das Ganze weiss, mit Absicht in dem Zustand dessen gehalten wird, der nur ein bisschen mehr als gar nichts weiss, dass man es gewissermassen mit einem Eisberg zu tun hat, dessen sehr viel grösserer Teil unsichtbar ist, mit anderen Worten, dass hinter den Dialogen eine grosse Konzeption steht, die alles in den Dialogen Gesagte umklammert und umgreifend zusammenhält. Diese Vermutung, von der sich wohl kaum ein Leser Platons ganz wird freisprechen können, ist durch die neueste Forschung im Rahmen der uns zur Verfügung stehenden Mittel der historischen Erkenntnis zur Gewissheit geworden, und ich behaupte, dass es heute möglich ist, klar zu sehen, wie die exoterische Lehre Platons in einer esoterischen Lehre verankert ist."[215]

Habemus confitentem reum. There *must* be a Plato akin to Aristotle who gives positive answers to all our questions.[216] As this Plato is not to be found in the Dialogues—on this point Oehler silently accepts the anti-systematical interpretation of them as opposed to the Neoplatonic one[217]—he *must* be constructed from what the 'tradition' tells us about him, regardless of the validity of this 'tradition'. It is strange to hear a modern scholar invoke the 'tradition', as if we ought to be fettered by it in our interpretation of Plato. Krämer asks his critics pathetically whether they fancy themselves capable of understanding Plato better than Aristotle or Plotinus.[218] Indeed, they do—precisely because they are not Aristotle or Plotinus, not great philosophers defending their doctrines against Plato or attributing them to him. They have no philosophic axe to grind.

The Self-Contradictions of the Esoterists

The strangest thing about that strange phenomenon, the modern Esoteric interpretation of Plato, is that its supporters are by no means insensible to the objections that can be made against it. On the contrary, several of the arguments their critics have put forward can be found in the writings of the Esoterists themselves, not least in those of the seemingly most dogmatic of them all, Hans Joachim Krämer.

Thus we read in Krämer's *Arete* that, in contrast to Aristotle, Plato's lectures were, in fact, no real lectures *ex cathedra,* but "Lehrvorträge" or rather "Gespräche", i.e., that Plato's teaching consisted in discussions, not unlike the written Dialogues.[219] But then, according to Krämer, the Dialogues are not "echte Zwiegespräche gleichberechtigter Partner" but "überwiegend ... Lehrgespräche mit einem Hauptreder, dem Gesprächsführer, und einem ausgesprochenen Lehrer–Schüler-Verhältnis".[220] Subsequently, Krämer goes so far as to say that in those "Lehrgespräche" Plato probably proceeded "sokratisch indirekt".[221] As we saw above, Krämer believes that Plato used notes but does not wish to decide whether they were accessible to the disciples or not. However, there were the notes of the latter which circulated inside the Academy as "Schulschriften" but were not published, at least not until long after Plato's death.[222]

In this way, the gap between the "lectures" and the Dialogues lessens, especially in the case of the later Dialogues which became more and more similar to these "lectures", showing "dass sich hier in Wahrheit die Grenze zwischen Schule und Schriftwerk verschoben hat".[223] This concession by Krämer was anticipated by Gaiser, who in *Protreptic und Paränese* had stressed the special character of the later Dialogues,[224] and in *Platons ungeschriebene Lehre* asserted that the distinction between Plato's exoteric-public activity and his esoteric-Academic teaching was not identical with the distinction between his written work and his spoken word. Gaiser even added that in many ways the Dialogues belong to the activity of the 'School', while, on the other hand, the lectures (Lehrvorträge) were accessible to the general public—a view which Krämer does not share. But Krämer, too, has, in a later paper on the problems of the indirect Platonic tradition, declared, "dass die immanente Interpretation der Dialogen neben der indirekten Überlieferung ihr gutes und selbständiges Recht behält und durch die Beschäftigung mit der ungeschriebenen Lehre nicht etwa ersetzt werden kann". The indirect tradition cannot invalidate the Dialogues; it can only supplement and enlarge them and Krämer insists: "Für einen Absolutheitsanspruch zugunsten des Ungeschriebenen fehlt jede Grundlage und von irgendeiner Abwertung des platonischen Schriftwerks kann nicht in Ernst die Rede sein."[226] These statements may well astonish a reader of *Arete*. But now Krämer also asserts—contrary to his former opinion—that, in writing the Dialogues, Plato was thinking of his influence on posterity, too.[227]

The Unsystematic System

The conviction that, in his oral teaching, Plato expounded a systematic metaphysics is the fundamental tenet of the Esoterists. But even this tenet is not inflexible. Actually, in his programmatic book, *Platons ungeschriebene Lehre*, Gaiser declared that, although Plato had a system, yet this system was "hypothetical and open"[228] and this in a book that tries to reconstruct the system! Krämer, too, insists on the 'elasticity' and 'flexibility' of Plato's thought. "Die These ist durchaus vertretbar, dass Platons Prinzipien- und Ableitungssystem in einzelnen lediglich Entwurfscharakter gehabt habe. Die erstaunliche Freiheit, mit der die Schüler in der Akademie neben Platon abweichende Entwürfe vorlegen konnten, spricht dafür, dergleichen Platons dynamischer Philosophiebegriff." In the same way, Klaus Oehler declares that to Plato the System was "nur das dialektisch verständliche Abbild der einen, absoluten Wahrheit und war deshalb für ihn immer etwas Hypothetisches, nichts Fertiges, Endgültiges, Abgeschlossenes, es war ein flexibler System, dessen literarische Fixierung für Platon ein Widerspruch in sich gewesen wäre".[230]

It is certainly strange that neither Gaiser nor Krämer nor Oehler seems to realize how such statements sap the very foundation of their tenet. For an "open and flexible" system is no real system at all, at least in the sense of Hegel, whom Oehler invokes in the very paper from which the above quotation is taken.[231] If Plato had a fixed system which he expounded in regular lectures *ex cathedra* to his disciples in the Academy, *then* we could hope to reconstruct it from their accounts, though even in that case we would be compelled to make due allowance for subjective misunderstandings and distortions. But if Plato had no such system at all, but expressed his general principles in different ways at different times to different disciples, how could we ever make out his teaching? If, as Oehler says, Plato himself found it impossible to fix his 'flexible' system in writing, how could *we* achieve it?[232] Thus, there remains a residuum of Platonism, inaccessible to anyone that has not been a member of the Academy and participated in Plato's "Lehrgespräche". To this must be added that even the highest human wisdom is ignorance, compared to God's wisdom.[233] For that reason, there remains "bei den höchsten Gegenständen dieser Philosophie stets ein letzter Vorbehalt", as Krämer says.[234]

The Self-Destruction of the Esoteric Interpretation

Before our eyes, the mighty palace of Plato's systematic philosophy, such as the Esoterists have constructed it, threatens to dissolve and disappear. It is obvious that the Esoterists cannot make up their mind about Plato's teaching. Therefore, they have invented those pseudo-notions behind whose ambiguity they hide their confusion: The *System*, which is and is not a real system, a logically coherent whole, the *Lehrgespräch*, which is and is not a real discussion, a dialogue, the *Lehrschrift*, which is and is not a real, published book.

After all, the Esoterists are the inheritors of many generations of Platonic scholars. Hard as they try, they cannot undo the critical work of those scholars. They lack the calm self-confidence of the Neoplatonists, certain of finding in the Platonic Dialogues whatever they wanted to find there. Instead, the modern Esoterists waver between depreciating the Dialogues and trying to interpret them in the Neoplatonic way—both half-heartedly. They dare not wholly to disregard the Dialogues nor wholly to force them into their system. When Krämer recently solemnly recognized the legitimacy of an 'immanent interpretation' of the Dialogues, he signed the death-warrant of the Esoteric interpretation, for a long experience has proved that an immanent interpretation of the Dialogues is fatal to any attempt to systematize Plato's thought. Thus, it can be said of the Esoterists that they have refuted themselves and continue to do so.

VII. The Fair Risk

The Unsolvable Problem

Our critical survey of the various attempts to solve the problem of Platonic interpretation seems to have come to a dead end. As we have seen, most of the solutions deny the very existence of such a problem, whether by athetizing the obnoxious texts, or by finding Plato a fool, or by ascribing to him an unwritten doctrine which deprives his written works of any real significance, or, most radically, by denying the independent existence of any Platonic philosophy at all.

The still most popular solution to our Problem, the Genetic interpretation, differs from the other solutions by loyally accepting the existence of a problem. Yet its way of solving it by explaining the obscurities, ambiguities, gaps, and contradictions in Plato's works as simply due to changes in his philosophic opinions has proved a failure.

For, if these changes are to be understood as constituting a continuous evolution of Plato's mind, then we have to be absolutely certain about the chronological place of each Dialogue, if we are to reconstruct this evolution. Or, such a certainty does not exist. Even if we accept the *opinio communis* of scholars as to the chronological order of the Dialogues, this agreement does only apply to the groups into which they are divided, not to the relative position of the single Dialogues within the groups. And it does not appear as if on this point an agreement could ever be reached.

But even if it were, that would not necessarily imply that our Problem was solved. For, as a study of the various Genetic interpretations proves, the interpreter is finally forced to choose between two forbidding alternatives. Either he abandons all attempts to discover a unity in Plato and acquiesces in registering the changes as they occur in one Dialogue after the other. This was the choice of Grote. Or, the interpreter tries to find a unity by arbitrarily rejecting or depreciating some Dialogues—e.g., the *Laws*—and giving prominence to other Dialogues, as most of the Geneticists have done. But in acting thus, they have in both cases joined the ranks of the scholars, just mentioned, who solve the problem of Platonic interpretation by abolishing it.

All these attempts have been criticized in detail above. The one decisive argument against them is that all of them have conspicuously failed. The Problem is still with us, as the most superficial knowledge of recent discussions about Plato proves. To day Plato still remains an unsolved riddle.

A Modest Proposal

Yet, it seems that some conclusions could be drawn from this very failure. After all has been said, it seems reasonably sure, that there is something, whatever it may be, which must be called Platonic philosophy and which cannot be reduced to nonphilosophic factors, that this philosophy is to be found in Plato's written works and nowhere else, and that the author of these works was a very intelligent man. Modest though these propositions are, none of them is self-evident, and each of them has been rejected by several learned and ingenious persons. But in the opinion of the present writer, they constitute the *conditio sine qua non* of Platonic interpretation.

The Initial Shock

Bearing this in mind, we may go back to the point from which we started; the ignorant—and therefore presumably to a certain degree unprejudiced—reader's first direct acquaintance with Plato.[1] He finds himself confronted with some thirty, longer or shorter pieces of prose, "Dialogues", with two or three exceptions pretending to give an account of discussions between two or several persons and mostly carrying the name of one of these persons. The author himself is not so much as mentioned.

Platonic Anonymity

This is odd and must have appeared so to Plato's contemporary readers. For the authors of the great Greek prose writings of the fifth and fourth centuries B.C. proudly introduce themselves at the very beginning of their works: "Hecataeus of Miletus ... Herodotus of Thurii ... Thucydides of Athens ... says thus and thus".[2] Not so Plato. The greatest masterpieces of Greek prose are anonymous. Naturally, every reader knew that the author was Plato of Athens, and presumably his name was written on the papyrus. But in the Dialogues, Plato's name occurs only twice, mentioned quite casually. There is no preface, no appeal to the reader, no *captatio benevolentiae*, no *envoy*.

Nor does the author take part in the discussions which are related in the Dialogues. These discussions are either represented directly: the reader is without further ado put *in medias res*, much as if he were reading a play, to which the Platonic dialogues have so often been compared.[3] Or they are narrated, either to some anonymous listener—or listeners—or to some explicitly mentioned person—or persons. The narrator can be a participator in the Dialogues in question, or at least a witness to it. Or he can be a person who on his part refers to somebody else, who was present at the discussion or had been informed about it in some other way. These ways of introducing a Dialogue, sometimes rather complicated, seem all to aim at widening the gap between the author and the reader, so that a direct contact between them is excluded.[4] Plato is speaking to us at second or third hand.

The Prologue to the Parmenides

This curious dissociation of Plato from his own work can be still more emphasized by the way in which the narrator or his informant is portrayed in the Prologue.[5] Let us take the case of the *Parmenides*. The discussions which form the main body of the Dialogue are narrated to some anonymous listener—or listeners—somewhere—evidently not at Athens—by an otherwise unknown Cephalus of Clazomenae. Having heard of a famous discussion which many years ago had taken place at Athens between Parmenides, Zeno, and Socrates, Cephalus arriving in that city and meeting Adeimantus and Glaucon in the market place, asks them for their half-brother, Antiphon. For some of Cephalus' countrymen, who have come with him to Athens, have told him that Antiphon remembers this discussion, because in his youth he had a great deal to do with a friend of Zeno's, Pythodorus, who often had repeated it to him. Unfortunately, Antiphon has abandoned philosophy for horse-breeding, but after some resistance—"for he said it was a great deal of trouble"—he repeats what Pythodorus had told him. The tale which this lover of horseflesh tells turns out to be the most abstract, most enigmatic, most controversial of all the Platonic Dialogues. Surely this is a curious way of introducing a work of high metaphysics.

The reader can hardly escape an uneasy feeling that Plato is pulling his leg—a feeling which a naïve reader of Plato often experiences, in contrast to the immense majority of Platonic scholars whose serenity is not troubled by such misgivings. Being themselves very serious-minded persons, it does not occur to them that Plato could possibly enjoy a joke, even at their expense, although, at the beginning of his philosophic fight with Socrates, old Parmenides speaks of the "laborious pastime" in which he now must engage.[7]

In this case, scholars have not failed to point out the parallels between the *Parmenides* and the *Republic*. In both Dialogues, Adeimantus and Glaucon—Plato's elder brothers—meet a Cephalus, though that of the *Republic* is a Syracusan, whereas that of the *Parmenides* is from Clazomenae. But the latter city was the home of Anaxagoras, whose philosophy young Socrates—and in the *Parmenides* he is young—was pondering, if we are to believe the *Phaedo* (97 B). Nor is the portrait of Antiphon to be overlooked: he is found giving instructions for forging a bit to a smith, a circumstance which clearly indicates "an agressive personality, with a strong desire to compete and dominate", as an imaginative scholar says.[8] A still more imaginative scholar informs us that this mention of horses recalls to his mind "both the impressive figure of the chariot of the soul in Parmenides' poem and the soul-chariot of the *Phaedrus*".[9] This is the spirit in which the Neoplatonists read the *Parmenides*.[10]

Although such interpretations—or overinterpretations—cannot be strictly refuted, neither can they be proved. Or, at least in the case of the *Parmenides*, they do not seem to tally with Plato's simply matter-of-fact account. We are left with the picture of an ex-philosopher, turned horse-breeder, reluctantly reciting a series of dialectical tours-de-force, which, in some mysterious way, he has succeeded in remembering.[11] We cannot help wondering what this may mean—if it means anything.

Platonic Irony

Alas, it is not the first nor the last time that Plato in this way leaves his readers wondering, and his only answer to our entreaties seems to be that of Dr Johnson: "Sir, you *may* wonder". For here, that trouble-maker, the Socratic-Platonic Irony, comes into play. In an earlier study, I have dealt with this problem and demonstrated in detail how the irony impedes our understanding of the Dialogues.[12] I shall not repeat my observations but confine myself to pointing out the two functions of the Platonic Irony.

First, the Irony still more weakens the contact between the readers and Plato, who seems to keep us smilingly at a distance. Secondly, the Irony troubles and upsets us, by making us uncertain of the author's intentions. Nay, we are uncertain about the Irony itself. For it lies in the nature of Irony that its occurrence in a text can hardly be proved to a reader who denies it. We can seldom be absolutely sure that Plato is not speaking ironically.

But this insight into the fundamental role of irony in Plato should not entice us into attempting a "pan-ironical" interpretation of Platonism. Nothing can be more detrimental to a true understanding of Plato than this way of exaggerating a legitimate and faithful viewpoint by making it the exclusive one.[13] When an American scholar recently asserted that we must recognize Irony as *"the central problem in the interpretation of Plato"*,[14] he made himself guilty of such an exaggeration, being inspired less by Plato than by German Romanticism, as his mention of Friedrich Schlegel proves.[15]

A "pan-ironical" interpretation of Plato is not only anachronistic but selfdefeating—as the Romantic Irony turned out to be. By becoming absolute Irony destroys itself. It can exist only as the opposite to Seriousness. And there are some matters about which Socrates-Plato is deadly serious. The "pan-ironical" interpretations entirely overlooks the religious basis of the Platonic Irony and its inseparable companion, the Socratic Ignorance.[16] Human life in general and philosophy in particular are, indeed, but a play. But this play is God's own play, which we must play in all seriousness.[17] Therefore, the riddle with which the irony confronts us cannot be solved—or rather abolished—by proclaiming its universality. We cannot escape the trouble it causes us; we are not left in peace.

The Challenge of the Dialogues

If, in a sense, Plato keeps aloof from his readers as no other philosopher has done, in another sense, he approaches them more closely than any other philosopher. His appeal has a strength which can only be compared to that of the great religious teachers. Plato's own teaching is at one and the same time forbiddingly impersonal and compellingly personal. His Dialogues are discussions which are not addressed to any reader or which the reader is invited to join but to which he is admitted only as a silent listener.[18] Yet, in a strange way, the same Dialogues are *argumenta ad hominem*, more impressive than most sermons. As we read them, it seems to us as if Nathan's words to David were ringing in our ears: "Thou art the man."

This unique personal impersonality of the Platonic Dialogue and of Plato's whole teaching is, of course, due to the fact that Plato encountered philosophy not in a book or a theory, but in a living man, a fellow-Athenian, Socrates. That this was the great, decisive event of Plato's life cannot be doubted, though he himself never speaks openly about it.[19] The only time he speaks about Socrates without a mask, in the *Seventh Epistle*, he does so in curiously reticent words: "an older friend of mine whom I should not hesitate to call the wisest and justest man of that time".[20] Laudatory though these words are, we surely miss a personal accent, for which, however, there was no place in the Epistle, and—we may add—

which a forger would not have omitted.[21] "We cannot do more than sense a self-confession in the account given in the Dialogues of the Athenian youth to whom the encounter with Socrates means the beginning of a new life."[22]

Socrates never wrote, he talked. And his talks were not lectures, such as the Sophists glorified in giving, but discussions, questions—and—answers, dialogues. Whatever "the origin of the Dialogue" may have been[23]—if there is any need to look for a special origin of so natural a thing—the Platonic Dialogue springs directly from the person and teaching of Socrates—these two inseparable things. It belongs to the Σωκρατικοὶ λόγοι of which Aristotle speaks, as constituting a literary genre. And how much the various λόγοι may have differed, common to all of them seems to have been precisely this indissoluble unity of Socrates the Man and his message.

The Necessity of the Dialogue

In the case of Plato, this means that the Dialogue is essentially a talk, a discussion between real persons, not a treatise dressed up as a dialogue. This holds true even of the last Dialogues,[25] where Socrates more or less withdraws from the discussion or, once, in the *Laws*, is totally missing.[26] Even when the role of the interlocutor seems to be confined to concurring in what the leader of the debate—Socrates or some other person—is saying, he is not a *quantité négligeable*, whose rejoinders may conveniently be omitted in a translation.[27] To do so, is to falsify Plato. For, as we have learned, it was his deepest conviction that truth can be searched for and reached only in the free exchange of thought between two minds.[28]

Ever since Schleiermacher, and especially at the present moment, this fundamental importance of the Dialogue to Plato has been stressed so often that it may seem superfluous to expatiate once more upon such an obvious fact. Alas, it is not. Not only have some eminent scholars in the past—Hermann,[29] Wilamowitz[30]—considered the Dialogue a mere external form, not necessary to Plato's thought, if not downright detrimental to it, there are still several prominent Platonic scholars, who share this opinion.[31]

This is only too easy to understand. As we have seen, now as formerly most people read Plato in order to learn "what Plato said" on this or that point, to extract a fixed doctrine. To such readers, the dialogue is only a nuisance which they disregard or push aside irritatedly, because it prevents them from finding out the true content. As we also have seen, these readers sooner or later end up in an impasse, if they have not a systematic *a priori* interpretation of Plato, as the Neoplatonists had. In that case, however, the readers do not need to search for doctrines in Plato, because they know in advance what they will find.

But if we accept the Dialogue as an essential aspect of Platonism, we should not confine ourselves to regarding it merely as a pedagogic convenience, as, in a way, Schleiermacher did, and especially Zeller. With his usual lucidity, the latter formulated this view in his polemics against Hermann. Zeller defended the *raison d'être*, of the Platonic Dialogue as a way of treatment, "bei welcher der Leser angeregt würde, das Wissen nur als ein selbsterzeugtes zu besitzen, bei welcher die subjektive Bildung zum Wissen bedingt wäre".[32] Thus, to read a Platonic Dialogue is like going to school and listening to a master teacher who persuades us that what he has taught us we have found by ourselves. Small wonder, that Zeller immediately adds: "In der Folge hat allerdings die strengere Wissenschaft diese Form mit Recht verlassen."[33] The teacher who discusses with his pupil—Socrates-Plato—has given way to the professor who lectures ex cathedra to his students—Aristotle or Hegel.

This view of the Dialogue is clearly superficial and insufficient.[34] Despite his criticism of Hermann, Zeller could not bring himself to take the Dialogue seriously.[35] It remained to him an imperfect form of which Philosophy in its maturity has to rid itself. For, being systematic, Philosophy needs a systematic exposition.[36]

The Double Dialogue

To Plato, the Dialogue is the only natural way of treating of philosophic matters. Even when alone, the human mind converses with itself. In the *Theaetetus* (189 E) and in the *Sophist* (263 E) thought (λόγος, διάνοια) is called "a silent inner conversation of the soul (ψυχή) with itself". To question and to answer is to Plato the natural way of thinking. The written Dialogue is therefore the externalisation of this inner dialogue. But it is at the same time something more: the meeting of two minds. In the first place, the minds of Socrates and his interlocutor; in the second place, the minds of Plato and his reader.

These two dialogues are not identical.[37] What Socrates says, he says to a certain person in a certain situation, and we cannot simply apply it to ourselves.[38] But—and that is the paradox of the Platonic Dialogue—neither can we refrain from doing so. We follow the discussions, as if we took part in them. To read a Platonic Dialogue, means silently to participate in a discussion.

98

The Discontinuity of the Dialogues

But in order to do so loyally, we must abide by the rules of the game. In most cases, the discussion starts without any reference to earlier discussions. There are in the more than thirty Platonic Dialogues only two clear exceptions to this general rule: in the *Statesman* the preceding *Sophist* is explicitly quoted,[39] and the *Critias*, which remained a fragment refers to the *Timaeus*.[40] These are the exceptions that prove the rule. For the rest, the *Sophist* (216 A) refers to the *Theaetetus*—not however, to its content but to Socrates' promise at the end of this Dialogue to pursue his discussion with Theaetetus. But in the *Sophist*, it is not Socrates but an anonymous stranger from Elea who leads the new discussion. In the *Theaetetus* (183 E), and in the *Sophist* (217 C), there are furthermore allusions to a discussion between Socrates and Parmenides which evidently refers to the *Parmenides*. And the *Timaeus* opens with what seems to be a reference to the *Republic*, so curiously worded, however, that it has provoked all sorts of explanations. That is all. For the rest, each Dialogue stands by itself. Even the Dialogues just mentioned can be read and understood without a previous knowledge of the Dialogues to which they refer.

This is a curious fact. We have to accept that it has pleased Plato to express his thought in such a discontinuous way, always starting from the beginning, seemingly without bothering about whether the conclusion—or non-conclusion—of one Dialogue agrees with its counterpart in another Dialogue or not. We have no choice but to follow the discussion of each Dialogue; their possible agreements or contradictions must remain a *cura posterior*.

But if we thus naïvely confide in Plato, we are out for some rude disappointment. Even if we keep to one Dialogue, we meet with ambiguities, obscurities, gaps, and contradictions. Perhaps the Dialogue does not conclude at all, or the conclusion is expressed in such a way to arouse suspicion, as, for instance, when we are offered a myth which, though beautiful, does not yield an unambiguous answer. And if we move on to another Dialogue, we may discover that it contradicts or questions the result to which the former Dialogue seems to have arrived.

The Reader's Responsibility

In this way, we are all the time compelled to be on our guard. Nothing is a matter of course; everything can be called in question. To read Plato demands a far higher degree of vigilance and activity than any other philosopher asks for. Time after time, we are forced to make our choice, to decide how we should interpret what we are reading.

Yet, when reading a Platonic Dialogue, the reader is not wholly abandoned to himself. The participators in the Dialogue have a leader, a guide—Socrates or some other person—who patiently urges them forwards, unravels the knots and simplifies the problems. The reader, too, seems to feel himself under a similar guidance.

Only, this guidance does not deprive the reader of his liberty or lessen his responsibility. The great guide of the Dialogues, Socrates, is, as all of us know, a man whose wisdom consists in his ignorance: he knows that he does not know anything. Therefore, his guidance is negative, not positive. As he says in the *Theaetetus* (149 B-151 E), he is "sterile in point of wisdom", but a wonderful midwife in helping others to bring forth "real and genuine offsprings". "I am, then, not at all a wise person myself, nor have I any wise invention, the offspring born of my own soul; but those who associate with me, although at first some of them seem very ignorant, yet, as our acquaintance advances, all of them to whom the God is gracious make wonderful progress, not only in their own opinion, but in that of others as well. And it is clear that they do this, not because they have ever learned anything from me, but because they have found in themselves many fair things and have brought them forth. But the delivery is due to the God and me."[41]

This "midwifery" takes the curious form of benumbing and bewildering Socrates' interlocutors. Young Meno complains of Socrates' spells and incantations which have reduced him to utter perplexity (ἀπορία) and compares Socrates to the torpedo-fish which benumbs anyone who approaches and touches it. Socrates' retorts that he would be like this fish only if it benumbed itself. "For it is not from any sureness in myself that I cause others to doubt: it is from being in more doubt than anyone else that I cause doubt in others."[42]

Something similar to what happened to Meno is happening to us who read Plato. At first, we find him, as the Athenians found Socrates, "a most eccentric person" (ἀτοπώτατος) who drives us to being perplexed"[43] (ἀπορεῖν). *Aporia*—this is the feeling of bewilderment and perplexity which seizes us, when first confronted with Plato. It is the right reaction, for it reveals that his words have met with response in our minds. For that reason, a bewildered naïve reader is nearer to the spirit of Plato than the learned scholar who calmly and confidently constructs a system of Platonic philosophy.

Later on, we may feel that we are going from strength to strength, becoming evermore certain about Plato's intentions, and, at the end, bringing forth 'a fair offspring of thought'. Only, this offspring is ours, not Plato's. In some cunningly hidden way, Plato has managed to make us think for ourselves, though believing that we only reproduce his thoughts. In fact, our interpretation of Plato is not a reproduction but a creation. As an American scholar has excellently expressed it: "No interpretation of Plato's teaching can be proved fully by historical evidence. For the crucial part of his interpretation the interpreter has to fall back on his own resources: Plato does not relieve him of the responsibility for discovering the decisive part of the argument by himself."[44]

Platonism and Existentialism

Should we then say that—to use a modern jargon—Plato puts us into "an existential situation"? This would mean to turn Plato into a Kierkegaard, or a Jaspers, or a Heidegger—that is into something quite different.[45] There is in modern Existentialism a pathetic subjectivism and irrationalism which is wholly alien to Socrates and Plato. Socrates is never pathetic, not even on the threshold of death. When he seems so, as, for instance, when extolling Love in the *Phaedrus*, he makes a point of warning us not to take him in deadly earnest.[46] Therefore, to say, as a modern scholar does, that Plato's aims include, among other things, "forcing men ... to submit to the divine mania" and that an interpreter of Plato must bear in mind that "excessive sobriety and caution, in obedience to standards derived from another and later tradition, violate Platonic accuracy",[47] is to show oneself insensible to the Platonic irony.[48]

Nor is the Existentialist subjectivism Platonic. True, Plato's "aims include forcing men to think for themselves",[49] and the truth towards which Plato goads his readers is, indeed, a truth of their own, found by themselves for themselves. Nevertheless, this truth is not a purely subjective one. For it is not won in loneliness. Like the disciples of Socrates, the reader of Plato is not alone in a hostile universe, like Sartre's hero, or alone with a terrible, transcendent God, like Kierkegaard's "hin Enkelte". He has a friend and guide at his side. And there is a third in their company, the *Logos*.[50]

Plato's adamantine faith in the power and the right of the *Logos* separates him from all ancient and modern sceptics and irrationalists, though he sometimes seems to speak with their tongue. Plato would never have said with Kierkegaard that "Subjectivism is the Truth". To Plato, Truth and Right Reason which leads to it are superior to and independent of the individual. Truth and Right Reason are Man's Masters. Even Socrates is but the servant of the *Logos*, of *Aletheia*. When in the *Symposium* (101 C), Agathon says to Socrates that he cannot contradict him, Socrates retorts: it is Truth that you cannot contradict; Socrates you easily may. In the *Phaedo*

(91 C), Socrates beseeches Simmias and Cebes to give little thought to Socrates but far more to truth.[51]

Right Reason, *Logos*, is the only true leader of the discussion, and where it goes there we must follow,[52] for it constrains us.[53] No worse evil can happen to a man than to be stricken with "hatred of Reason" (μισολογία), so Socrates asserts in the *Phaedo* (89 B). "Therefore let us be on our guard against this and let us not admit into our Souls the notion that there is no soundness in arguments at all. Let us far rather assume that we ourselves are not yet in sound condition."[54]

Much as Socrates insists upon his and other men's ignorance, he refuses to take it for a final answer. Arguing about virtue with Meno, he concedes in his usual self-depreciating way that the points which he has made in support of his argument are not such as he can confidently assert. "But", he adds—and this time the *Eiron* is quite serious—"that the belief in the duty of inquiring after what we do not know will make us better and braver and less helpless than the notion that there is not even a possibility of discovering what we do not know, nor any duty of inquiring after it—this is a point for which I am determined to do battle, so far as I am able, both in word and deed."[55]

These and many similar statements express an unshaken conviction that there is an objective, immutable, eternal Truth, which it is Man's duty to search for, even if, owing either to his weakness or to the difficulty of the matter, he may be unable to attain it, and that it is likewise his duty to render in any case a well-reasoned account of his views (λόγον διδόναι). To Plato, Truth cannot be found by an irrational act of faith—Kierkegaard's "leap of 10 000 fathoms"—or by a mystic illumination, but only by the dialectical argumentation of the Dialogue. This must be emphasized, for in their laudable endeavour to liberate Plato from the dogmatic systematization of Platonists, some of his modern admirers tend to deprive his philosophy of any concrete content. It is easy to understand that the Existentialist Karl Jaspers says of Plato: "Der Sinn seiner Mitteilung ist, die Nothwendigkeit, den Weg zu finden, zum Bewusstsein zu bringen, und das Beschreiten des Weges aus der Kraft des Suchens zu veranlassen. Der Weg selbst wird nicht als eine in bestimmter Weise zu befolgende Anweisung ausgesprochen. Denn er kann nicht durch Zeigen eines angebbaren endlichen Zieles in der Welt gewiesen worden."[56] Here, the Socrates ignorance is turned into an Existentialist "putting into the situation".[57]

We notice the same transformation in another modern interpreter of Plato, Leo Strauss, quoted above, when he asserts: "Plato composed his writings in such a way as to prevent for all time their use as authoritative texts. His dialogues supply us not so much with an answer to the riddle of being as with a most articulate 'imitation' of that riddle. His teaching can never become the subject of indoctrination. In the last analysis his writings cannot be used for any other purpose than for philosophizing."[58] Here, truth and falsehood are mingled. But the tendency is the same as in Jaspers: to turn Platonism into an empty "philosophizing".

In this way, Plato's philosophy becomes identical with Philosophy as such, regardless of its character. Thus Jaspers declares: "Plato ist wie der Stellvertreter des Philosophierens überhaupt."[59] Surveying the many shapes the ages have given to Plato —transforming him by turns into a Neoplatonist, a Christian, a Kantian, a Hegelian, etc.—a modern English scholar complacently concludes: "All of this is to the good." No doubt, this has often led to anachronism, but "in the end, the good outweighs the evil". For Plato, "more than a philosophy, is philosophy itself".[60]

Such praise of Plato sounds magnificent, but is really hollow. What is a philosophy worth that can be turned into anything its interpreters want? It is more than questionable whether Plato would have felt flattered by this praise, and we can easily imagine his Socrates ironically declining the compliment of being identified with so many "wise and divine men".[61]

The naïve reader—and, as I have said in an earlier study,[62] compared with Plato everyone of his reader is naîve—feels instinctively that there is something fundamentally wrong with this way of understanding Plato. The 'pan-aporetic' interpretation of Plato is as one-sided as the 'pan-ironical'.

Platonism and Scepticism

For an unprejudiced study of Plato's work establishes beyond reasonable doubt that he believed firmly, even passionately in a great many things: God, the world of the Ideas, the eternity of the Soul, Reason, Virtue, etc.[63] Yet, as soon as we try to fix these beliefs in exact formulas, they tend to elude us. We are once more confronted with the problems of Platonic interpretation, so drearily well-known to us. It seems as if the interpreter who wants to remain true to Plato will have to steer his course between the Scylla of Scepticism and the Charybdis of Dogmatism. And, as in the myth, the latter monster is the more deadly of the two.

Any 'aporetic' interpretation of Plato—not to speak of the 'panaporetic' one—must take into account the impressive fact that, as has been pointed out above,[64] the overwhelming majority of Plato's readers, in the past as well as in the present, have in him seen a great, inspired Teacher and Leader. When a modern scholar in a statement just quoted,[65] says that Plato's teaching can never become the subject of indoctrination", the answer is that it *has* become such a subject. The Platonic Tradition is in the main not a tradition of Scepticism but of Dogmatism.

The New Academy

But not entirely so. There is the curious exception and episode of the so-called New Academy.[66] Not a short episode either, for it lasted nearly two hundred years, from Arcesilas (scholarch in 268/4 B.C.) up to and including Philo of Larissa (to ca. 80 B.C.). As the New Academy's foremost representatives, Arcesilas (or Arcesilaus) and Carneades, imitated Socrates also in confining themselves to oral teaching, and the writings of their disciples are lost, we are reduced to using the statements of other writers, contemporary or later, most of them inimical. The only exception is Cicero, who called himself "Academic", but being neither a profound nor a consistent thinker, he is a somewhat muddy source.[67]

Contemporary adversaries and later Platonists, beginning with Philo's rival and successor, Antiochus of Ascalon, accused the New Academy—the very name was coined as an insult[68]—of betraying Plato by stealthily propagating the teaching of Pyrrhon the Sceptic under the label of Platonism.[69] The role of Pyrrhon, who left no writings, in Greek philosophy and his possible influence on the New Academy are very controversial matters.[70] But it seems certain that both Arcesilas, and Carneades, and their disciples regarded themselves as true followers of Socrates and Plato,[71] and that they believed they had returned to their Master's free spirit of doubt and inquiry, from which Plato's immediate successors, Speusippus, Xenocrates, and others had deviated.[72] The statement that the New Academy possessed a secret doctrine of dogmatic Platonism is certainly a legend, concocted in order either to maintain unbroken the tradition of dogmatic Platonism or to accuse the New Academy of dissimulation.[73]

The state of our sources makes it difficult to judge the Platonism of the New Academy. But if we can trust what especially Cicero tells us, it seems as if in the New Academy the Socratic ignorance and the Platonic dialectics had so to speak run wild. The former had hardened into an un-Socratically dogmatic "withholding of judgment" (ἐποχή),[74] and the latter had deviated into a purely negative criticism of any positive position. It seems as if Socrates-Plato's unshaken confidence in the *Logos* were no more, as if the New Academy was its master, not, like Socrates, its servant.[75] What is told about the oratorical triumphs of Arcesilas and Carneades testifies also to an alien spirit, and these two Academics' fights with the Stoics remind us of the eristic battles of the Eleatics and Sophists.

Thus referring to Arcesilas Cicero could say of Plato that in his books "nothing is stated positively and there is much arguing both *pro* and *contra*, all things are inquired into and no certain statement is made".[76] The Reasonable (εὔλογον) of Arcesilas or the Probable (πιθανόν) of Carneades was but a poor substitute for Plato's Truth. We are a long way from the Platonic Socrates who in the *Phaedrus* (272 D–E) bitterly accuses the rhetoricians of caring only for the Probable not for Truth.[77] To be sure, the Probable of which the rhetoricians were speaking was not identical with that which Carneades had in view. But common to both was the assumption that Truth cannot be reached, if it exists at all.

But, even if one-sided and superficial, the New Academy's reaction against the dogmatism of the Early Academy testifies to the strength of the Socratic spirit in Platonism. And thanks to Cicero's enormous influence, this aspect of Plato has for centuries constituted a counterweight to the ruling dogmatism of the Platonic tradition.[78] It is not a negligible fact that during many generations Plato's Academy was a seat of doubt and inquiry.

The Awkward Dilemma

The history of Platonism seems to confirm the impression conveyed by a study of modern Platonic scholarship, viz., that the interpretation of Plato hovers between two extremes. Either it stresses the sceptic, aporetic element in him so strongly that the positive message of his philosophy tends to evaporate. Or it emphasizes the dogmative, assertive element so that Plato's philosophy becomes a closed system. In that case, however, experience proves that the interpretation cannot be founded on the Dialogues alone. The interpreter is forced to appeal either to a preconceived system of Platonism—as the ancient Neoplatonists did—or to an oral doctrine, reconstructed from the statements of other writers—as the modern Esoterists do. None of these three solutions to our Problem is attractive.

The Unceasing Inquiry

Is there not a way out of this impasse, an interpretation which "saves the phenomena"—the phenomena of Platonic doubt and Platonic assertion, Platonic question and Platonic answer? Such an interpretation has, indeed, been proposed by a modern Italian scholar, Luigi Stefanini. In the remarkable Introduction to his big monograph on Plato,[79] Stefanini tries to do justice to both aspects of Plato's thought, which he pertinently delineates:

"Una certezza assoluta e un dubbio radicale, un oggetto fisso e immutabile proposto alla conquista dello spirito, e un suggetto ansiosamente proteso incontro ad esso e sempre respinto dalla meta; un' intuizione che instantamente e prodigiosamente si eleva in alto, e una dialettica faticosa che non riesce mai a imprigionare la subitanea rivelazione e pur è necessario presupposto e conseguenza di questa: ecco l'atteggiamento essenziale del pensiero platonica".[80]

After having surveyed and rejected earlier attempts at solution to the problem of Platonic interpretation, Stefanini presents his own solution, by characterizing Plato's philosophy as a "constructive scepsis"—the word "scepsis" taken in its original Greek sense of "inquiry".[81] This inquiry never stands still; each partial solution reveals itself as a new problem. But the Platonic *Scepsis* should not be mistaken for a probabilism, whether that of the New Academy or that of modern philosophy. In Plato, reason is the master, not the servant, of life.[82] Therefore, the goal of Plato's thinking is not the Probable but the Verisimilitude (εἰχός) of which the Platonic Myth is an expression.[83] The Verisimilitude is not an appearance of Truth but an approximation to it, emanating from a continuous confrontation with Truth and therefore presupposing a certain knowledge of it.[84] To Plato, Truth is something objective, independent of the subject, the human mind. To turn him into a modern criticist is to distort him.[85]

Yet although Stefanini thus refuses to modernize Plato, he interprets him and judges him from a viewpoint alien to Platonism: Christianity. In Plato, as in other ancient philosophers, we can notice the profound discontent with certain doctrines in which they were imprisoned and follow their vivid strife for a higher truth, sometimes obscurely sensed, Stefanini declares.[86] What Plato had prepared but did not understand is fulfilled in the philosophy of the Fathers of the Church.[87]

Thus, Platonism is reduced to a *Praeparatio Evangelica*—to use the Latin title of Eusebius' famous work—an important, may be even necessary preparation, but still only a preparation for a higher state, which alone gives Platonism its true significance and perfection. Plato cannot be properly understood out of himself alone; ultimately, his thinking points beyond its own limits. Stefanini asserts that Plato—substantially though not formally—abandoned the Greek belief that Truth belongs to the object alone and that the only true knowledge is that of immutable Being, whereas we can only have a relative knowledge, opinion, of the world of Change.[88] Plato's whole philosophic evolution, was a logical consequence of the inner conflict which drove him restlessly from one position to another.[89] In the last works, e.g., the *Timaeus*, the Platonic philosophy still remains an open system.[90] Even the so-called unwritten doctrine does not constitute a radical innovation but only a further clarification and exploration in depth.[91] The Scepsis goes on, as long as life endures.[92]

Such an interpretation of Plato resembles that which, many years ago, Franz Susemihl had attempted.[93] Susemihl, too, regarded Plato's teaching as continually changing, owing to a basic flaw. True, Stefanini has a far higher opinion of Plato, and he does not, like Susemihl, make him end in self-destruction. But common to both scholars is that they judge Plato from without, according to a norm not his own—Aristotelianism or Christianity.

It is to be regretted that, in this way, the deep and just insight into the nature of Plato's philosophy which Stefanini expounded in his Introduction remained barren, not being really applied in the book itself, which is just another of the many genetic interpretations of Plato.[94] However, Stefanini's recognition of the Platonic Scepsis as the inseparable unity of inquiry *and* solution, doubt *and* assertion can be appreciated and accepted at its own valuation.[95] Only, we should not imagine that, by doing so, we have acquired an easy method of solving once and for all the problem of Platonic interpretation.

The Fair Risk

Such a method does not exist. To decide in each controversial case how Plato should be interpreted, is a matter of personal judgement and responsibility. If all reading implies an interpretation and all interpretation a transformation, this harsh fact—*durus est hic sermo*—holds especially true of Plato. But, as a modern scholar has excellently put it: "This does not mean that the interpretation of Plato is essentially arbitrary. It means, on the contrary, that the rules of exactness governing the interpretation of Plato's books are much stricter than those governing the interpretation of most books."[96]

We are in duty bound to do our best to ascertain in accordance with the rules of historical and philological criticism, what Plato's words mean—even and especially when meaning something contrary to our own beliefs and tastes. But Plato's works being what they are, there will always remain a margin of subjective interpretation, of error, far larger than in most other works. It is vain and dishonest to try to conceal this difficulty from ourselves and others. We have to accept it squarely. In that sense—and in that sense only—Kierkegaard's saying about the subjectivism of Truth holds true. But we have to make sure that we have exhausted the possibilites of objective interpretation, before abandoning ourselves to the lures of subjectivism. It is Plato's voice we should listen to, not our own, disguised as Plato's. That we can never be absolutely sure that we are not mistaken, is a risk which all of us who study Plato must take. At the utmost we can only say as, in the *Phaedo* (1 14 D), Socrates does, having just before his death told the lofty myth about the underworld:

"Now it would not be fitting for a man of sense to maintain that all this is just as I have described, but that this or something like it is true ... I think that he may properly and worthily venture to believe, for the risk is well worth taking."

List of Abbreviations

AGPh= Archiv für Geschichte der Philosophie.
AJPh = American Journal of Philology.

CPh = Classical Philology.
CR = Classical Review.
CW = Classical Weekly.

DLZ = Deutsche Literatur-Zeitung.

F Gr Hist= Die Fragmente der griechischen Historiker ed. Felix Jacoby.

GGA = Göttingische Gelehrte Anzeigen.
Gn = Gnomon.

H = Hermes.
HZ = Historische Zeitung.

JHI = The Journal of the History of Ideas.
JHS = The Journal of Hellenic Studies.

KP = Der Kleine Pauly.

LCL = Loeb Classical Library.

M = Mind.
MH = Museum Helveticum.
Mn = Mnemosyne.

OCD² = The Oxford Classical Dictionary. 2d ed. 1970.

Ph = Philologus.
PhW = Philologische Wochenschrift.

RE = Real-Encyclopädie der classischen Altertumswissenschaft. A after the number of the volume indicates the Second Series (R–Z). The First Series is cited by volume, the Second by half-volume.
RES = Real Encyclopädie. Supplement.
REA = Révue des Études Anciennes.
REG = Révue des Études Grecques.
RhM = Rheinisches Museum für Philologie.

WS = Wiener Studien.

Interpreting Plato

1. The present study is an outcome of an earlier one, *Plato's Idea of Poetical Inspiration* (Societas Scientiarum Fennica. Commentationes Humanarum Litterarum, 44:2, 1969). It is not a survey of Platonic scholarship and makes no claim to any bibliographical completeness. The scholars who are cited and discussed are chosen as representatives of attitudes and opinions, shared by many others.—A history of Platonic scholarship is, indeed, a *desideratum*. The only work which, to some extent, may be regarded as such, Heinrich von Stein, *Sieben Bücher zur Geschichte des Platonismus* (I–III, Göttingen, 1862–75; I quote from the reprint Frankfurt, 1965), though in many respects a remarkable work, well worth reading, is now quite out of date and very incomplete. As to earlier scholarship, J. A. Fabricius, *Bibliotheca Graeca*, must still be used, see the fourth edition, by Gottlieb Christoph Harles, III (Hamburg, 1794), pp. 141 ff. The nineteenth century scholarship is very completely recorded in Eduard Zeller, *Die Philosophie der Griechen in ihrer geschichtlichen Entwicklung*, II:1 (I use the sixth edition, Hildesheim, 1960, a reprint of the fifth edition, Leipzig, 1922; the text is that of the fourth edition, 1888). Later scholarship can be found in Karl Praechter's revision of Ueberweg's *Grundriss der Geschichte der Philosophie*, I, *Die Philosophie des Altertums*, 12th ed. (Leipzig, 1926), in Johannes Geffcken, *Geschichte der griechischen Literatur*, II:1–2 (Heidelberg, 1934), and in Hans Leisegang, *Platondeutung der Gegenwart* (Leipzig, 1929), cf. also his article on Plato, *RE*, XX:2 (1950). More recent literature is quoted in Albin Lesky, *Geschichte der griechischen Literatur* (3d ed. Bern, 1971), and especially in Paul Friedländer's comprehensive monograph, *Platon*, I–II (3d ed., Berlin, 1964), III (2d ed., Berlin 1960). There are two good surveys of modern scholarship, that by Harold Cherniss, "Plato 1950–1957" (Lustrum, 4–5, 1959–60) which is very complete, and that by E. M. Manasse, *Bücher über Plato*, I–III (Philosophischer Rundschau, Sonderheft, 1–2, 7, 1957–76), which confines itself to works in German, English and French. The *Année Philologique* (from 1914 onwards) is, of course, indispensable, but the reader must bear in mind that it is not always complete.

2 The so-called *Vita Platonis* by Olympiodorus actually constitutes the introduction to his commentary on the *Alcibiades Maior*, see L. G. Westerink's edition (Amsterdam, 1956), p. 6.

I. The Problem

1. We know next to nothing about Simmias, see Zeller, *op. cit.*, II:1⁶, pp. 241 ff. H. Hobein's lengthy article, *RE*, IIA:1 (1927), cols. 144–155, is full of loose guesses. All of Simmias' works are lost and many of them seem to have been regarded as spurious. It would be hazardous to vouch for the historicity of his appearance at the deathbed of both Socrates and Plato. See further Léon Robin's Introduction to his edition of the *Phaedo* in the Budé-Plato (IV:1, Paris, 1926, pp. XIII ff.).

2. Cf. below pp. 96 ff.

3. Perhaps on the pattern of the drama, see Henrik Zilliacus, "Boktiteln i antik litteratur" (*Eranos*, 36, 1938), p. 10, cf. Ernst Nachmanson, *Der griechische Buchtitel* (Göteborgs Universitets Årsskrift, 1941:19), pp. 10 ff.—The *Phaedo* is called after the relator of the Dialogue, who, however, was present at the discussions.

4. In the MSS, the Dialogues are usually provided with three titles, for to the first—the Platonic one—two subtitles are added, the former indicating the content, the latter to which of the following eight categories the Dialogue belong: Πειραστικός, ἠθικός, λογικός,

μαιευτικός, ἀνατρεπτικός, ἐνδεικτικός, πολιτικός, φυσικός. In many modern editions the subtitles are omitted. Both kinds of subtitles are mentioned by Diogenes Laertius, who says (III 57) that Thrasylus—or Thrasyllus († A.D. 36)—the editor of Plato, διπλαῖς τε χρῆται ταῖς ἐπιγραφαῖς καθ'ἕκάστου τῶν βιβλιῶν, τῇ μὲν ἀπὸ τοῦ ὀνόματος, τῇ ἀπὸ τοῦ πράγματος. The word χρῆται cannot be interpreted as meaning that Thrasylus "invented" the second titles (obviously not the third ones), as was rightly pointed out by Henri Alline, *Histoire du texte de Platon* (Bibliothèque de l'École des Hautes Études, 218, Paris, 1915), pp. 55 ff., and A. G. Hoerber, "Thrasylus' Platonic Canon and the Double Titles" (*Phoenix*, 2, 1957, pp. 10–20), who does not quote Alline. Both assert that the double titles were not only in use long before Thrasylus but that they go back to the Old Academy, judging from the fact that Aristotle refers to the *Symposium* as οἱ ἐρωτικοὶ λόγοι (*Politics* II 4, 1262 b 11) and to the *Menexenus* as ἐπιτάφιος (*Rhetoric* III 14, 1415 b 30). Perhaps they were invented by Plato himself, in favour of which hypothesis Hoerber adduces the certainly spurious *Ep.* XIII 363 A, cf. also Alline, *op.cit.*, p. 55 n. 4. Even apart from that, the argument is not conclusive, for it is only natural to designate the *Menexenus* as a funeral oration and the *Symposium* as a series of speeches on Love, as, indeed Plato himself indicates at the very beginning of the Dialogue (177). The Callimachean epigram (*AP* VII 471) where the *Phaedo* is referred to as τὸ περὶ ψυχῆς belongs to Hellenistic times. As Nachmanson—who is ignored by Hoerber—pointed out (*op. cit.*, pp. 11 ff.), most Neoplatonists—e.g. Proclus and Olympiodorus—distinguished between the old, Platonic titles and the new ones, see especially Proclus, *Commentarii in Platonis Rem publicam*, ed. W. Kroll, I (Leigzig, 1899), pp. 8 ff. Only two of the Neoplatonists, Elias and David, seem to have regarded the double titles as authentically Platonic. It seems extremely un-Platonic to use so obvious—and so misleading—labels as the subtitles are. In his recent study, "The Platonic Corpus" (*Phoenix*, 24, 1970, pp. 296–308), J. A. Philip, too, believes that second titles—indicating the subject—are very old but appears not to ascribe them to Plato himself.—As Nachmanson says (p. 10), the quotations of his own writings (*Politicus* 284 B and 286 B) prove that Plato had himself coined the title *Sophist*. Nachmanson's doubt, whether Plato provided all of his dialogues with titles seems unfounded, for by then the booktitle was in common use and the absence of a title would have been very awkward, the more so as the Dialogues do not begin with the author's name, cf. below, p. 93.

5. Aristotle proceeded in the same way, cf. Zeller, *op. cit.*, II: 1⁶, pp. 448 ff.

6. Stein, *Sieben Bücher zur Geschichte des Platonismus*, I, pp. 5 ff.

7. Thus the late Philip Merlan in his remarkable posthumous paper, "Bemerkungen zum neuen Platobild" (*AGPh*, 51, 1969, pp. 111–126), p. 125: "Es sieht nicht danach aus, als ob Plato je versucht habe, die Dialoge einandern nicht widersprechen zu lassen, noch danach, als ob ihm je daran gelegen gewesen sei."

8. Olof Gigon asserts that Plato was not conscious of his contradictions and changes but viewed his written works as a homogenous whole, see *Grundprobleme der antiken Philosophie* (Bern, 1959), pp. 145 ff. This view of Plato resembles alarmingly that entertained by Richard Robinson, see below, pp. 22 f.

9. See Wilamowitz's splendid eulogy in *Geschichte der Philologie* (Leipzig, 1959; reprint of the third ed., 1927), p. 67, and Hermann Diels's obituary in Zeller, *Kleine Schriften*, III (Berlin, 1911), pp. 465–511.

10. First edition in three volumes (Tübingen, 1844–52), subsequently expanded into six volumes. Shortly before, Zeller had expounded his conception of a history of Greek philosophy in the papers, "Die Geschichte der alten Philosophie in den letzt verflossenen 50

Jahren" and "Wie soll man Geschichte der Philosophie schreiben?" (*Kleine Schriften*, I, pp. 1–99).

11. Zeller, *Op. cit.*, II: 1⁶, p. 586.

12. *L.c.*

13. *Op. cit.*, II: 1⁶, pp. 570 ff.

14. See, e.g., *op. cit.*, II: 1⁶, pp. 626, 707, 758.

15. *Op. cit.*, II: 1⁶, pp. 581 f. Hegel, too, disapproved of the Platonic myths, see *Vorlesungen über die Geschichte der Philosophie* (Sämtliche Werke, Jubiläumsausgabe, 18, 3 ed., Stuttgart, 1959), II, pp. 188 ff.

16. I–III (London, 1865).

17. *Op. cit.*, I, pp. IX ff., cf. II, pp. 393 ff.

18. *Op. cit.*, I, pp. 214 f.

19. *Op. cit.*, I, p. XI.

20. *Op. cit.*, I, p. IX.

21. *Op. cit.*, II, p. 394.

22. Cf. Zeller's criticism (*op. cit.*, II: 1⁶, p. 472).

II. The Resort of the Scalpel

1. *Matthew* 18:8, cf. *Mark* 9:43–45.

2. Concerning the ancient atheteses of Plato's works, see Zeller, *op. cit.*, II: 1⁶, p. 441 n.1, Leisegang, "Platon", col. 2365, and Ulrich von Wilamowitz-Moellendorff, *Platon*, II (2d ed., Berlin, 1920), pp. 325 ff.

3. See Zeller, *op. cit.* II: 1⁶, pp. 475 ff., cf. Wilamowitz's indignant protest (*op. cit.*, II², p. 7). The first wholesale representative of the athetizing school was Friedrich Ast, *Platon's Leben und Schriften* (Leipzig, 1817), see the chapter on Plato's dubious and spurious works (pp. 376 ff).

4. *Op. cit.*, II², p. 9.

5. Ernst Hoffmann, *Platon* (Zürich, 1950), p. 126.

6. Especially Paul Shorey and Harold Cherniss, cf. the posthumous book by L. Edelstein, *Plato's Seventh Letter* (Leyden, 1966), which is very representative of the present reaction against Wilamowitz.

7. In *Platonische Studien* (1839), see Zeller, *op. cit.*, II: 1⁶, pp. 976 ff.

8. See, eg., Olof Gigon's declaration that the *Laws* should not be used unreservedly, because its doctrine is a Platonism "in decomposition" (*Entretiens sur l'Antiquité classique*, III, *Recherches sur la tradition platonicienne*, Verona, 1957, p. 20).

9. Walter Bröcker, *Platos Gespräche* (Frankfurt, 1964), p. 10.

10. If only as a matter of curiosity, I may mention Josef Zürcher's odd book, *Das Corpus Academicum* (Paderborn, 1954), which pretends that the extant *Corpus Platonicum* is in fact a *Corpus Academicum*, compiled by Polemo, the scholarch of the Academy from 315 to 270 B.C., and published by his successor Arcesilas. The *Corpus* contains some amount of real Platonic matter but mixed up with much later stuff. Zürcher seems to have convinced nobody of his fancies; they are nevertheless symptomatic of the present situation in Platonic scholarship.

11. Günther Jachmann's radical doubt about the reliability of our present Plato text (*Der Platontext*, Nachrichten von der Akademie der Wissenschaften in Göttingen, Philolog.hist. Klasse, N. F., Fachgruppe I: 4:7, 1940–41, pr 1942) has not convinced other scholars, cf. H. Langerbeck's review (*Gn*, 22, 1950, pp. 375–380), Ernst Bickel, "Das platonische Schriften-

korpus der 9 Tetralogien und die Interpolation in Platontext" and "Geschichte und Recensio des Platontextes" (*Rh M,* 92, 1943, pp. 94–96; 97–159), and Hartmut Erbse in *Geschichte der Textüberlieferung der antiken und mittelalterlichen Literatur,* I (Zürich, 1961), pp. 261 ff. In any case the scholars of whom I am speaking are not inspired by Jachmann.

12. Thus Gerhard Müller, "Die Philosophie im pseudo-platonischen 7. Brief" (*Archiv für Philosophie,* 3, 1949), p. 276.

13. See G. Müller, *Studien zu den platonischen Nomoi* (Zetemata, 3 München, 1951), cf. H. Cherniss's review (*Gn,* 25, 1953, pp. 367–379). In the "Nachwort zur zweiten Auflage" (*op. cit.,* 1968, pp. 191–210), Müller tries to refute Cherniss, at the same time as he tries to cast suspicion on the text of Aristotle's *Politics,* II, where the *Laws* are twice explicitly called Platonic (1264 b 27, 1271 c 2). According to Müller, these testimonies are not due to Aristotle himself but to some ignorant pupil of his or a later editor. Obviously without knowing it, Müller repeats an argument of Fr. Ast, *op. cit.,* p. 390 n.

14. Zeller, *op. cit.,* II: 1⁶, pp. 946 ff.

15. To the very end, Zeller stuck to his opinion about the un-Platonic nature of the *Laws,* and found in it many interpolations, see *op. cit.,* II: 1⁶, pp. 978 ff.

16. See Ast's revealing remarks (*op. cit.,* pp. 9 ff.) about "the true Platonic spirit", the presence or absence of which in a Dialogue settles its authenticity. Thanks to this principle, Ast could reject, e.g., the *Apology,* for the very intention to justify Socrates against his detractors is "un-Platonic" (*op. cit.,* pp. 10 ff.).—A good modern example of this method of arguing is the way in which G. Müller declares *Republic* VII 540 D ff. spurious, because its content—the establishment of the ideal city by exiling all grown-up people, so that the children can be freely educated by the ruling Philosophers—presupposes that the ideal city can be realized in this world, something which, according to Müller, is absolutely un-Platonic (*Studien,* pp. 149 ff.). It is only too obvious that the farfetched stylistic and linguistic arguments adduced as proofs against the authenticity of the passage in question are not the true reasons why Müller rejects it. He does so, because it is contrary to his conception of Plato as a purely unworldly scholar, inimical to politics (*op. cit.,* pp. 141 ff.).—In a similar way, Müller athetizes *Republic* 465 C—471 C, because in this passage Plato makes a fundamental distinction between Greeks and Barbarians, which Müller refuses to accept as Platonic (*Die Philosophie* etc., p. 274 n. 48). Thus he manages to widen the gap between the *Republic* and the *Laws*—where the distinction just mentioned is stressed—and confirm his suspicions about the authenticity of the latter work.

17. Cf. Heinz Kimmerle's Introduction to Schleiermacher's *Hermeneutik* (Abhandlungen der Heidelberger Akademie der Wissenschaften, philos.-hist. Klasse, 1959: 2), pp. 17 ff.

18. A pertinent characterization and criticism of the athetizing school is to be found in L. Stefanini, *Platone* (2d ed., Padua, 1949), pp. XVIII ff.

III. The Triumph of Progress

1. See *Plato's Earlier Dialectic* (2d ed., Oxford, 1953), cf. the reviews of the first edition (1941) by H. Cherniss (*AJPh,* 68, 1947, pp. 133–146) and Paul Friedländer (*CPh,* 40, 1945, pp. 253–259), which Robinson took into consideration in his second edition (*op. cit.,* p. VII), and the review of that edition by Philip Merlan (*The Journal of Philosophy,* 52, 1955, pp. 351–353). See further the detailed criticism in Manasse, *Bücher über Plato,* II, pp. 140 ff.

2. Though very reluctantly, see "Plato's Consciousness of Fallacy" (Mind, 1942; reprinted

in *Essays in Greek Philosophy,* Oxford, 1969, pp. 16–38). There Robinson argues that conscious fallacies occur only in the earliest Dialogues, in which "Plato's purpose is *almost entirely* (italics mine) to depict an unusual personality, and he has little or no interest in defending the logical validity of any argument which that person uses" (p. 21). This is, indeed, to beg the question!

3. See, e.g., Wilhelm Erkert, *Dialektischer Scherz in den früheren Gesprächen Platons* (Diss. Erlangen, 1911), the Chapter on "Sophismen" in G. J. de Vries's important book, *Spel bij Plato* (Amsterdam, 1949), pp. 116–152, more recently Maurice C. Cohen, "The Apories in Plato's Earlier Dialogues" (*JHI,* 23, 1962, pp. 163–174), and Rosamond Kent Sprague, *Plato's Use of Fallacy* (London, 1967).

4. *Essays in Greek Philosophy,* pp. 28 ff., see Sprague, *op. cit.,* p. 7 n. 5.

5. Thus for instance, we would be bound to conclude—as Gladstone did—that Homer could not discern Blue as a separate colour, because he has no special word for it, see, e.g., Rudolf Horchheim, *Die geschichtliche Entwickelung des Farbensinnes* (Innsbruck, 1884), and Hermann Schultz, "Das koloristische Empfinden der älteren griechischen Philosophie" (*Neue Jahrbücher für das klassische Altertum,* 14, 1911, pp. 11–22).

6. *Plato's Earlier Dialectic²,* p. VI, cf. Robinson's review of Miss Sprague's book, which reproaches her for not having reflected enough "on the nature of the progress of thought" (*The Philosophical Quarterly* 14, 1964, pp. 78–80).

7. *Plato's Earlier Dialectic²,* p. 6.

8. *Essays in Greek Philosophy,* p. 88.

9. *Plato's Earlier Dialectic²,* p. 83.

10. *Nicomachean Ethics* II 7 (1108 a 20 ff.) and IV 14 (1127 b 22 ff.).

11. See the Chapter on "Elenchus" (*Plato's Earlier Dialectic²,* pp. 7–19).

12. See my *Plato's Idea of Poetical Inspiration,* pp. 11 ff.

13. *A History of Formal Logic,* translated and edited by Ivo Thomas (Notre Dame, Indiana, 1961), p. 5.

14. *Op. cit.,* p. 12.

15. *Op. cit.,* pp. 15 f.

16. *Op. cit.,* p. 17.

17. *Op. cit.,* p. 33.

18. *Op. cit.,* pp. 34 ff.

19. It makes no difference that Robinson in the Preface to *Plato's Earlier Dialectic²* (p. VI) declares that Plato "was a very great logician" for his "evolutionism" deprives this praise of any real value. Judged by modern—i.e. Robinson's—standards, Plato could not reason logically. In his review of Robinson's book, Philip Merlan says sarcastically but pertinently: "All this adds to a picture of a Plato sadly confused, with Socrates as the villain of the piece, a bad logician himself, merely destructive (one imagines Robinson joining Cleitophon and changing from Socrates to Thrasymachus, who gives you something constructive) and hypocrite with his use of irony" (*op. cit.,* pp. 352 ff.).

IV. The Genetic Approach

1. Heidelberg, 1839.

2. *Op. cit.,* pp. 347 ff., 370 ff.

3. Schleiermacher, *Platons Werke,* I: 1 (3d ed, Berlin, 1855), pp. 32 ff., cf. Zeller's remarks (*op. cit.,* II: 1⁶, pp. 500 ff.).

4. See the survey in A. E. Taylor, *Plato: The Man and his Work* (London, 1926; I use a reprint, New York, 1956, of the sixth edition, 1952), pp. 18 ff.

5. See below, n. VI 201.

6. I–II:1–2 (Leipzig, 1855–60; there is a modern reprint, Osnabrück, 1967).

7. *Op. cit.,* I, pp. 1 ff.

8. See Hermann, *op. cit.,* pp. 384 ff.

9. See the table of contents in Susemihl, *op. cit.,* I.

10. *Op. cit.,* II: 2, p. 696.

11. *Op. cit.,* I, p. VIII.

12. *Op. cit.,* II: 2, p. 558; Susemihl points out that Aristotle's philosophy gives the solution of Plato's fundamental problem.

13. But Walter Bröcker seems to share it, when he finishes his account of the Platonic Dialogues with the words: "Die Wahrheit Platos ist Aristoteles" (*Platos Gespräche,* p. 560). Bröcker does not refer to Susemihl.

14. I–II (Leipzig, 1863–64).

15. See the attack on Susemihl in *Genetische Darstellung,* II. pp. 58 ff., 86 ff. Ribbing's copy of Susemihl's work, now in Uppsala University Library, is full of exclamation marks in the margins.

16. *Op. cit.,* II, pp. 47 ff., 96 ff. Like Schleiermacher, Ribbing regarded the *Phaedrus* as Plato's first dialogue (*op. cit.,* II, pp. 191 ff.).

17. *Op. cit.,* I, pp. 69 ff., 79 ff.; II, pp. 87 f., 109 f.

18. *Op. cit.,* II, p. 117.

19. *Op. cit.,* II. p. 118.

20. *Op. cit.,* I, pp. 57 ff., 88 ff.; II, p. 87.

21. *Op. cit.,* II, p. 122.

22. See above, pp. 19 ff.

23. *Op. cit.,* II, pp. 155 ff.

24. This was vehemently denied by Paul Shorey, who tried to demonstrate the essential agreement between the *Laws* and the other Dialogues, especially the *Republic,* see "Plato's *Laws* and the Unity of Plato's Thought" (*C Ph,* 9, 1914, pp. 345–369) and *What Plato Said* (Chicago, 1933), pp. 355 ff., in conformity with his general belief in the unity of Plato's thought, see below, pp. 52 ff. But the very fact that Shorey found himself compelled to make such a demonstration shows the existence of the problem. Concerning Zeller's difficulty in accepting *the Laws,* see above, p. 20.

25. On earlier wholesale or partial rejections, see Zeller, *op. cit.,* II: 1⁶, pp. 976 ff., on modern ones, Friedländer, *Platon,* III², pp. 360 ff., 502 ff., and Ada Babette Hentschke, *Politik und Philosophie bei Platon und Aristoteles* (Frankfurt, 1971), pp. 2 ff.

26. On Aristotle's account, see below, pp. 82 ff.

27. *Op. cit.,* II: 2, p. 560.

28. See below, pp. 92 ff.

29. Hermann, *op. cit.,* pp. 3 ff.

30. *Op. cit.,* pp. 4 ff., 137 ff.

31. *Op. cit.,* pp. 130 ff., 138.

32. *Op. cit.,* p. 5. Hermann even goes so far as to say that the Platonic philosophy resembles a tragedy, "wo die Grösse des Helden nur um den Preis seines Untergangs erkauft wird" (p. 8).

33. *Op. cit.,* p. 7, cf. p. 366.

34. *Op. cit.*, pp. 345 ff., 365 ff.

35. See the dedication to Creuzer (*op. cit.*, p. XVIII).

36. *Op. cit.*, pp. 351 ff.

37. *Op. cit.*, p. 9.

38. *Op. cit.*, p. 347.

39. *Op. cit.*, p. 345.

40. *Op. cit.*, p. 8.

41. Hermann speaks of Plato's partiality for Sparta, "Die auf die Gestaltung seiner ganzen philosophischen Lebensansicht so entscheidende Einflüsse geübt hat" (*op. cit.*, p. 25).

42. For to Hermann, Socrates is the Xenophontean one, as he maintains in polemic against, e.g., Schleiermacher, see *op. cit.*, pp. 249 and 331 (n. 333).

43. *Op. cit.*, pp. 45 ff., 384 ff., 570 ff.

44. *Op. cit.*, pp. 510 ff.

45. *Op. cit.*, pp. 129 ff., 512 ff.

46. *Op. cit.*, pp. 352 ff., where Hermann polemizes against Schleiermacher.

47. *Op. cit.*, p. 344. One understands, why the philosopher Ribbing sarcastically said that he had in Hermann's "weitläufigen Untersuchungen wenig mehr gefunden ... als dass er einer der Philologen ist, die in und mit ihren linguistischen Forschungen über die Werke der Alten noch dazu die Einsicht in die philosophischen Ansichten dieser zu bekommen glauben" (*op. cit.*, I, p. 42 n. 78).

48. As to the change in Hermann's view of Plato, see below, pp. 67 ff.

49. Hans Raeder, *Platons philosophische Entwickelung* (Leipzig, 1905), pp. 1 ff., gives a survey of earlier genetic interpretations.

50. Schleiermacher's Introduction to his translation of the *Republic* is characteristic of this attitude, see *op. cit.*, III: 1 (2d ed., Berlin, 1862), pp. 42 ff., though he was a liberal German patriot.

51. See the short survey of "the later history of Plato's political thought" in Sir Ernest Barker, *Greek Political Theory. Plato and his Predecessors* (4th ed., London, 1951), pp. 383 ff.

52. From Nietzsche's Lectures on Plato, printed in extracts in *Gesammelte Werke, Musarionausgabe*, IV (München, 1921), p. 369, cf. pp. 382 ff. The Lectures ought to be published *in extenso*.

53. On Nietzsche and Plato, see, besides E. Eberlein's superficial paper 'Nietzsche und Platon' (*Gymnasium*, 72, 1968, pp. 62–73), Ernst Müller's unprinted dissertation *Nietzsche und Platon* (Tübingen, 1924), a mere collection of *loca probantia*, which I have consulted thanks to the *bona officia* of the Tübingen University Library.

54. See *Geschichte des Altertums*, III (Halle, 1901), p. 287; V (Halle, 1902), pp. 350 ff., 502 ff. Well before Meyer, Jacob Burckhardt had declared the *Seventh Epistle* authentic, "weil ein Schüler diesen *Ton* kaum möchte getroffen haben" (*Gesamtausgabe*, VIII, *Griechische Kulturgeschichte*, I, Leipzig, 1930, p. 270 n. 4). But this remark was published only in 1898.

55. See the survey of the debate on the *Epistles* in Friedländer, *Platon*, I³, pp. 249 ff., 388 ff.

56. First published London, 1945; I use the fourth revised edition, I–II, London, 1962.

57. *Op. cit.*, I⁴, pp. 33 ff.

58. Popper's subsequent praise of such interpretations—see his approval of W. Fite and A. D. Winspear, *op. cit.*, I⁴, pp. 217 (n. 31), 267 (n. 14), 313 (n. 59), 315 (n. 64), added to the original text—seems scarcely compatible with his philosophic principles. In the same way he approves of H. Kelsen's psychoanalytical interpretation, see *op. cit.*, I⁴, pp. 217 (n. 31), 284 (n. 60), 313 (n. 59), though he is by no means favourable to psychoanalysis, see *op. cit.*, II⁴, pp.

215 ff. Obviously, Popper's hatred of Plato makes him accept virtually any argument which can be turned against Plato, cf. Ronald B. Levinson, *In Defence of Plato* (Cambridge, Mass., 1953), p. 21.

59. See, e.g., Kurt Singer, *Platon der Gründer* (Leipzig, 1927), and Kurt Hildebrand, *Platon. Der Kampf des Geistes um die Macht* (Leipzig, 1933; a second, slightly revised edition, with a Postscript, was published Berlin 1959).

60. See the accounts by Fr. J. Brecht, *Platon und der George-Kreis* (Das Erbe der Alten, 2d Ser., XVI, Leipzig, 1929)—sympathetic but not uncritical, cf. Richard Harder's review (*DLZ*, 5, 1930, cols. 972–982)—Leisegang, *Platondeutung der Gegenwart*, pp. 41 ff., 172 ff.—strongly critical. Friedländer's monograph is decisively influenced by the "George-Kreis", see below, pp. 49 f.

61. This combination of George and Hitler—much against the former's intention—is represented by, e.g., Joachim Bannes, *Platon. Die Philosophie des heroischen Vorbildes*, Berlin, 1935, who two years earlier had published *Platons Staat und Hitlers Kampf* (Berlin, 1933).—Such antidemocratic, totalitarian interpretations form the real, though unacknowledged, basis of Popper's attack on Plato, for he has simply and uncritically accepted them, only burning what they adore, cf. Levinson, *op. cit.,* pp. 441 ff., and Reinhart Maurer, *Platons 'Staat' und die Demokratie* (Berlin, 1970), pp. 302 ff.

62. See Kelsen's study 'Die platonische Gerechtigkeit (first printed in *Kant-Studien,* 35, 1933.; I quote from the reprint in *Aufsätze zur Ideologiekritik*, Darmstadt, 1964), p. 230.—Concerning this and the other Platonic studies by Kelsen, see Manasse's severe criticism, *op. cit.,* II, pp. 165 ff.

63. See the copiously annotated section on Plato in *The Legend of Sparta,* I, pp. 244–276, 532–560. As I said there, the modern attacks on Plato are more revealing with regard to the attackers' own frame of mind and their times than to Plato.

64. From the viewpoint of Platonic scholarship, the debate on Plato's politics has been singularly barren. It now shows signs of petering out, cf. Maurer, *op. cit.,* pp. 22 ff.

65. New York, 1934, cf. Levinson, *op. cit.,* pp. 9 ff., and passim.

66. New York, 1940, cf. Levinson, *op. cit.,* pp. 583 ff.

67. London, 1939, cf. F. M. Cornford's criticism, "The Marxist view of Ancient Society" (*The Unwritten Philosophy,* Cambridge, 1950, pp. 117–137).

68. I–II, London, 1949–55, cf. also *Aeschylus and Athens* (2d ed., London, 1946).

69. See Yvon Brès, *La Psychologie de Platon* (Paris, 1968), pp. 21 ff. Despite its title, this big book is very disappointing; it does not throw any new light on the relations between Plato the Man and Plato the Philosopher, cf. J. Moreau's review (*REA,* 91, 1969, pp. 146–150).—See further Reino Palas, *Die Bewertung der Sinnenwelt bei Platon* (Annales Academiae Scientiarum Fenniae, B XLVIII: 2, Helsinki, 1941), pp. 220 ff., which is influenced by Jaspers und Kretschmer.

70. "Die platonische Liebe". Originally published in the official organ of Freudian Psychoanalysis, *Imago,* 19, 1933, pp. 34–98, 225–255); I quote the reprint in *Aufsätze zur Ideologiekritik*, pp. 114–197. Cf. Levinson, *op. cit.,* pp. 100 ff., 466 ff., 586 ff. The reprint is only partial, the second part, "Kratos", being omitted, perhaps owing to its attack on Socrates.

71. *Aufsätze*, pp. 118 ff.

72. *Imago*, pp. 236 ff.

73. *Op. cit.,* pp. 238 ff.

74. This was rightly stressed by Levinson, *op. cit.,* pp. 107 ff., 586 ff. What Kelsen says about Plato's feelings of guilt and inferiority because of his homosexuality may be true of an

Austrian professor of philosophy in A.D. 1933, certainly not of an Athenian citizen of the fifth and fourth century B.C. Cf. also Palas's criticism (*op. cit.,* pp. 177 ff.).

75. *Aufsätze,* pp. 121 ff.

76. As Kelsen himself admits: "Was wir aus dem Leben Platons wissen, ist wenig, und das Wenige ungewiss" (*op. cit.,* p. 120). He even goes as far as to say: "Nicht einmal das Verhältnis zu seiner Mutter Periktione ... hat in seinen Werken eine Spur hinterlassen" (pp. 122 f.). That does not deter Kelsen from indulging in loose speculations about Plato's relations with his parents.

77. *Studies in Ancient Greek Society,* II, p. 322.

78. No less than four works of Stalin are listed in the bibliography (*op. cit.,* II, p. 354), and he is reverently quoted not only "on basis and superstructure", and "on bourgeois and proletarian revolutions", but also "on the discovery of iron" ("General Index", p. 366).

79. In an otherwise interesting and valuable book, R. Maurer makes the astonishing statement that two thirds of Plato's works belong to political philosophy (*op. cit.,* p. 27). Probably, Maurer considers both the *Republic* and the *Laws* as purely political works, unmindful of the fact that much of the content of these two works cannot be called "political", even in a wide sense of this word, cf. above, p. 14. A similar erronous argumentation can be found in Auguste Diès's Introduction to the Budé-edition of the *Republic,* I (Paris, 1932), pp. V ff.

80. Thus Thomson, *op. cit.,* II, p. 328: a dangerous concession which would hardly have won Stalin's approval. A still more orthodox Marxist, the East German Georg Mende assures us that Plato's so-called Objective Idealism was nothing but an ideological disguise of his one, dominating aim: "die gesellschaftliche Struktur der Sklavenhalteraristokratie vor jeglicher Erschütterung zu bewahren". See the discussion between Mende and Rudolf Schottlaender in *Das Altertum,* 10 (1964), pp. 142–154, 230–234.

81. Kelsen, *Aufsätze,* p. 117, speaks of "die schuldige Ehrfurcht vor einem ganz Grossen im Reiche des Geistes" which one should not infringe upon. Whereupon he proceeds to expatiate upon Plato's pathological psyche.

82. *Plato's Idea of Poetical Inspiration,* pp. 11 ff.

83. *Republic* IX 592 B, cf. 472 D–E. With these words and Glaucon's approval of them, the *Republic* ends, for Book X is an addition, as Plato stresses himself. I use the translation in Paul Shorey's edition of the *Republic* in the *LCL* (II, London, 1935, pp. 414 ff.).

84. See, e.g., *Republic* I 336 C, 341 C; IV 426 D–E; V 468 B–C; VII 529 A–B; 536 C; VIII 568 A–B, cf. G. J. de Vries, *Spel bij Plato,* pp. 176 ff., 184., 198, and Maurice Vanhoutte, "La réalisation d'un plan politique selon Platon" (*Proceedings of the XIth International Congress of Philosophy,* XII, Amsterdam, 1953, pp. 77–82). See further Maurer, *op. cit.,* pp. 293 ff., and Victor Goldschmidt, *Questions platoniciennes* (Paris, 1970), pp. 190 ff.

85. *Republic* III 414 B ff., see, e.g., Popper, *op. cit.,* I⁴, pp. 138 ff., cf. the rejoinder by Erich Unger, "Contemporary Anti-Platonism" (*The Cambridge Journal,* 1, 1947; reprinted in *Plato, Popper and Politics,* Cambridge, 1967, pp. 96 ff.). It is not a matter of chance that there is no entry "Irony" in the copious Index to Popper's book. See also Cornford, *The Unwritten Philosophy,* pp. 132 ff.

86. See *The Legend of Sparta,* I, pp. 261 ff., 549 ff.

87. Contrary to what Gerhard Müller asserts, *Studien zu den platonischen Nomoi²,* p. 117 n. 1: "Die Nomoi haben keine Ironie, weil sie nicht die Trennung von Sein und Schein kennen, und weil sie in ihrem starren Dogmatismus nicht die überlegene Sicherheit des Sokrates haben, die die Wahrheit unbesorgt um ihren Bestand in Frage stellen darf." In order to prove this astonishing statement, Müller has, whether consciously or unconsciously, passed over in

silence *all* the passages, quoted below, in which the Platonic irony appears so strongly. In his "Nachwort zur zweiten Auflage", Müller repeats his statement, explaining that he refers to "die sokratische Ironie, die im Platon aus dem Zusammentreffen der philosophischen Sehweise mit der unphilosophischen notwendig entsteht" (p. 205 n. 1). This explanation marks no progress, for it reveals that the religious foundation of the Socratic irony escapes Müller, cf. de Vries, *op. cit.*, pp. 22 ff., and *Plato's Idea of Poetical Inspiration*, p. 12. The same must be said of Kelsen's interpretation of those passages in the *Laws* as due only to old Plato's bitter resignation, see *Imago*, p. 241.

88. *Laws* III 685 A; IV 712 B; VI 769 A; VII 803 B–C, cf. *Plato's Idea of Poetical Inspiration*, p. 62.

89. *Ep.* VI 323 B.

90. As, e.g., Kelsen, *Imago*, pp. 231 ff., conceives Plato, cf. *Aufsätze*, pp. 118 ff.

91. In his lecture, "Plato in den Augen der Zeitgenossen", C. R. van Paassen has strongly rejected de Vries's conception of Platonic irony, wisely abstaining from discussing the texts adduced by the latter, see *Arbeitsgemeinschaft für Forschung des Landes Nordrhein-Westfalen*, 89 (Köln, 1960), pp. 16 ff.

92. See *Plato's Idea of Poetical Inspiration*, pp. 11 ff., and below, pp. 104 f.

93. See below, pp. 101 ff.

94. Very typical of this attitude to Plato is A.-H. Chroust, "A Second (and Closer) Look at Plato's Political Philosophy" (*Archiv für Rechts- und Sozialphilosophie*, 48, 1962, pp. 449–485), which is a passionate protest against "the most savage and uncompromising attack upon progressive (and humanitarian) ideas that have ever been recorded in Western history", viz. Plato's political and social theories. Chroust ends solemnly: "in a time such as the present, when the free democratic societies are once more under deadly attack, both from without and from within, Plato is the last person to whom we should turn for comfort and advice as to how we may survive as free men".

95. Surveys of the sources can be found in Ueberweg-Praechter, *op. cit.*, pp. 179 ff., Geffcken, *op. cit.*, II: 2, pp. 1 ff. (n. 3): Leisegang, "Platon", cols. 2342 ff. None of these surveys contains a real analysis. The old survey in Karl Steinhart, *Platon's Leben* (Platon's sämmtliche Werke, IX, Leipzig, 1873), pp. 4–31, is superficial and uncritical.

96. *Sieben Bücher zur Geschichte des Platonismus*, II, pp. 158–197 ("Der biographische Mythus und die literarische Tradition").

97. For what Steinhart says (*op. cit.*, p. 31) is no answer. When he accuses Stein of not having undertaken the hard task of analysing the biographical tradition in detail, it must be stressed that he is far from having himself even attempted such an analysis. His survey is simply a *bibliographie raisonnée*. Cf. Stein's reply (*op. cit.*, III, pp. 410 ff.).

98. Thus Taylor, *Plato*, p. 1 n. 1.

99. *Platon*, II², pp. 1–20.

100. *Op. cit.*, II², p. 6.

101. *Op. cit.*, I², p. 6.

102. On Wilamowitz's monograph, see below, pp. 40 ff.

103. *Op. cit.*, II, pp. 162 ff.

104. Diogenes Laertius III 2 = Speusippus fr. 27–28 Lang, cf. Paul Lang, *De Speusippi Academici Scriptis. Accedunt Fragmenta* (Diss. Bonn, 1911), pp. 32 ff., 60 ff. Besides Diogenes Laertius, this work—oration or pamphlet?—is mentioned in Apuleius, *De Platone* I 2.

105. Xenocrates fr. 53 a–c Heinze, cf. Richard Heinze, *Xenokrates* (Leipzig, 1892), pp. 158 and 179.

106. Diogenes Laertius II 106 and III 6 refers to Hermodorus, who is also quoted by Simplicius, *In Aristotelis Physica* I 9 (192 a 3); the last-mentioned text is printed in Kurt Gaiser, *Platons ungeschriebene Lehre* (2d ed., Stuttgart, 1968), p. 495. On Hermodorus, see *Philosophorum Academicorum Index Herculanensis,* ed. S. Mekler (Berlin, 1902), p. 34.

107. Erastus, Asclepiades, Philippus the Opuntian, cf. the surveys quoted above, n. IV 95, and Mekler's *Index,* p. 35. The ἐγκώμιον on Plato by Aristotle, mentioned in Olympiodorus' Commentary on the *Gorgias* (ed. W. Norvin, Leipzig, 1936, p. 197), was rejected as spurious by Zeller, *op. cit.,* II: 2⁵, p. 57 n. 2, because this work is never mentioned by any other writer, as should be expected, if it really was by Aristotle, but it is apparently accepted by Fritz Wehrli, see *Die Schule des Aristoteles,* III, *Klearchos* (2d ed. Basle, 1969), pp. 45 ff. Zeller's argument, however, seems irrefutable.

108. See Wilamowitz, *op. cit.,* II², p. 3: "wir müssen uns eingestehen, dass zwar eine reiche Überlieferung der ersten Generation nach Platons Tode vorhanden war, aber von den Späteren ganz ungenügend ausgenützt ist", and p. 4: "Es scheint dass die Primärquellen in der Kaiserzeit schon ganz verschüttet waren."

109. Cf. Leisegang, "Platon", col. 2343.

110. In fact, the introduction to Olympiodorus' commentary on the *Alcibiades Maior,* see above, Introd. n. 2.

111. Printed by K. Fr. Hermann in his *Platonis Dialogi secundum Thrasylli Tetralogias dispositi,* VI (Leipzig, 1853), pp. 196–222. The short and incomplete biography in Apuleius, *De Platone et eius dogmate* I 1–4, seems to have a source in common with the biographical account in the *Prolegomena,* see T. Sinko, "De Apulei et Albini doctrinae Platonicae adumbratio" (*Rozprawy Akademii Umiejętności, Wydzial filologiczny,* Ser. II, Tom. XXVI, 1906, pp. 175 ff.).

112. Geffcken disparagingly calls both Olympiodorus' *Vita* and the *Prologomena* "klägliche Leistungen neuplatonischer Unfruchtbarkeit" (*op. cit.,* II: 2, p. 30).

113. Fundamental is Johannes Geffcken, "Antiplatonika" (*H,* 64, 1929, pp. 87–109), see also Ingemar Düring, *Herodicus the Cratetean. A Study in Anti-Platonic Tradition* (K. Vitterhets Historie och Antikvitets Akademiens Handlingar, 51: 2, Stockholm, 1941), who does not refer to Geffcken. A painstaking collection of material can be found in Reinhold Feuk's dissertation, *Adversarii Platonis quomodo de indole ac moribus eius iudicaverint* (Jena, 1913), quoted by Düring but not by Geffcken. František Novotny, "Die antiken Platonlegenden" (*Opera Universitatis Purkepsianae Brunensis Facultas Philosophica,* 92, 1964, pp. 161–179), does not add anything new.—An ancient defender of Plato—and of Aristotle—against his detractors was the Peripatetic Aristocles of Messene (second half of the second century A.D.) in his big work, *On Philosophy,* see Hermann Heiland's good dissertation, *Aristoclis Messenii reliquiae* (Giessen, 1925), pp. 33, 34 ff., 104 ff. Cf. Werner Jaeger, *Aristotle* (2d ed. Oxford, 1948), p. 106.

114. Unfortunately, the title of C. R. van Paassen's paper, "Platon in den Augen der Zeitgenossen" (se above, n. IV 91), promises what the contents do not keep, for it is only a new sample of current Plato-reviling, whose main aim is to demonstrate the author's democratic *Gesinnungstüchtigkeit*—to use the appropriate German word, which has no Englich equivalent—see. e.g., the preposterous remark on the *Protagoras* (p. 10).

115. See the fragments of Demochares' speech, *Against Philo,* in *Oratores Attici,* ed., J. G. Baiter & Hermann Sauppe, II (Zürich, 1845–50), pp. 341–342. To these fragments should be added Athenaeus XI 509 B, see K. Swoboda, "Demochares" (*RE,* IV: 2, 1901), col. 2864. On Demochares' anti-Socratic and anti-Platonic polemics, see Düring, *op. cit.,* pp. 147 ff.

Wilamowitz's outburst against the "bad orator and historian" in his juvenile work, *Antigonos von Karystos* (Philologische Untersuchungen, IV, Berlin, 1881), pp. 189 ff., is more amusing than convincing. A less biassed appreciation can be found in Swoboda, *op. cit.,* cols. 2863–2867.

116. This is a subject on which only too much has been written. I confine myself to referring to Hans Gärtner's article, *KP,* II (1967), and the literature quoted there, e.g., K. Ries, *Isokrates und Platon im Ringen um die Philosophie* (Diss. München, 1959). See further Wilamowitz, *Platon,* II², pp. 106–125, and Gunnar Rudberg, "Isokrates und Platon" (*Symbolae Osloenses,* II, 1924, pp. 1–24).

117. The fragments of Theopompus' Καταδρομὴ τῆς Πλάτωνος διατριβῆς are to be read in *F Gr Hist,* II B, pp. 591, 595, 600; II D, pp. 390, 393.

118. Concerning the relations between Socrates, Plato, and Xenophon, see the latest survey in H. R. Breitenbach, "Xenophon", *RE,* XVIII A (1967), cols. 1769 ff.

119. This subject, too, has attracted scholars and inspired them to farfetched hypotheses, the more so as all of Antisthenes' writings are lost. I abstain from quoting any of the many works on this topic, see the latest account in W. K. C. Guthrie, *A History of Greek Philosophy,* III (Cambridge, 1969), pp. 310 ff., who is very cautious. Concerning Antisthenes' political ideas, see my *Legend of Sparta,* II, pp. 33 ff., where I have dealt in detail with Karl Popper's odd idea of turning the anti-democratic and pro-Spartan Antisthenes into a good Athenian democrat, the only true follower of Socrates.

120. Düring, *op. cit.,* p. 137. M. L. West entertains a far too positive view of these authors, when he calls them "researchers into the past", see *Early Greek Philosophy and the Orient* (Oxford 1971), pp. 197 ff. He offers no proofs.

121. Aristoxenus' remains, except for his writings on musical theory, are edited and commented upon by Fritz Wehrli, *Die Schule des Aristoteles,* II (2d ed., Basle, 1967), see especially fr. 51–60 (Σωκράτους βίος) and 61–68 (Πλάτωνος βίος) (pp. 24 ff., 27 ff., 65 ff.). See further Wehrli's article, *RES,* XI (1968) and K. Ziegler's article, *KP,* I (1964), and the literature quoted there. On Aristoxenus as a biographer, see Friedrich Leo, *Die griechisch-römische Biographie nach ihrer litterarischen Form* (Leipzig, 1901), pp. 102 ff., Wilamowitz, *Platon,* I², p. 94, D. R. Stuart, *Epochs of Greek and Roman Biography* (Sather Classical Lectures, IV, Berkeley, Calif., 1928), pp. 119 ff., cf. *The Legend of Sparta,* I, p. 233, and Wehrli, *op. cit.,* X (2d ed., Basle, 1969), pp. 117 ff. In his recent lectures on *The Development of Greek Biography* (Harvard, Mass., 1971), pp. 73 ff., Arnaldo Momigliano gives a rather favourable portrait of Aristoxenus.

122. Düring believes Aristoxenus' motives to have been: "Pythagorean fanatism, personal aversion, and the conceit of a musician" (*op. cit.,* p. 157). This seems a bit hard on the musicians. Wehrli declares: "Die Verunglimpfung Platons geschieht im Eifer für die Pythagoreer" (*op. cit.,* II², p. 67).

123. See, e.g., A.-H. Chroust's solemn denunciation of Plato, quoted above, n. IV 94, and C. R. van Paassen's passionate diatribe, quoted above, n. IV 114 and IV 91.

124. See, e.g., Winspear, *op. cit.,* pp. 80 ff., 85, 111, 233 f., who strongly asserts Aristoxenus' reliability against the criticism of A. E. Taylor and John Burnet, the former calling Aristoxenus "a singularly mendacious person" (*Plato⁶,* p. 1 n. 1), the latter speaking of "the scandalmonger Aristoxenus" (*Greek Philosophy,* I, London, 1914), p. 129 n. 2.

125. I do not find it necessary to give detailed references, as all the relevant texts are collected and commented upon by Feuk, Geffcken, and Düring. Zeller, *op. cit.,* II: 1⁶, pp. 427 ff., gives an excellent summing up. The accusations of plagiarism have been treated of by

Eduard Stemplinger, *Das Plagiat in der griechischen Literatur* (Leipzig, 1912), pp. 25 ff.

126. See the works of Leo, Stuart, and Momigliano, quoted above, n. IV 121. Cf. further the articles on Greek Biography by F. W. Walbank in *OCD²* and by M. Fuhrmann, *KP*, I.

127. The special edition of Book III, *Diogenis Laertii Vita Platonis* (Basle, 1907), by H. Breitenbach. Fr. Buddenhagen, A. Debrunner, and P. von der Mühl, does not quite deserve of Wilamowitz's scorn (*Platon*, II², pp. 6 ff.). At least, the copious testimonia are very useful. But there is still need of a new, commented edition of Diogenes' *Life of Plato*, on the pattern of Olof Gigon's excellent edition of the *Vita Aristotelis Marciana* (Kleine Texte, 181, Berlin, 1962). The new Oxford-edition of Diogenes Laërtius by H. S. Long (I–II, 1964) is unfortunately not satisfactory, cf. Gigon's review (*DLZ*, 86, 1965, cols. 101–105); I have preferred to use R. D. Hick's edition in *LCL* (I–II, London, 1925). See further Wilamowitz, *Antigonos von Karystos*, pp. 45 ff., *Platon*, II², pp. 1 ff., Leo, *op. cit.*, pp. 54 ff., Eduard Schwartz's fundamental article, *RE*, V: 1 (1903), and the recent articles on Diogenes by H. Dörrie, *KP*, II, and H. S. Long, *OCD²*.—The many attempts to discern Diogenes' immediate sources in which he found most of the authors he quotes but did not read have all proved unsuccessful. But see O. Gigon, "Das Proemium des Diogenes Laertios: Struktur und Probleme" (*Horizonte der Humanitas*, Bern, 1960, pp. 37–64).

128. The important anti-Platonic passages in Athenaeus are to be found in Books V 215 c ff. and XI 504 e ff., where the main source is the anti-Platonic pamphlet of Herodicus of Babylon, Πρὸς τὸν φιλοσωκράτην, see the monograph of Düring (above, n. IV 113), who has edited and annotated the fragments of this work.

129. This holds especially true of Plato's contemporaries among the writers of the Middle Comedy. For, to paraphrase Dr Johnson, when writing a comedy, an ancient Athenian was not upon his oath—a circumstance conveniently forgotten by van Paassen, who tries hard to prove Plato's bad character by quotations from the comic poets. Thus Amphis' harmless joke about Plato's frowning eyebrows, "lifted high up as a snail" (Diogenes Laertius III 28 = Amphis fr. 13 Kock) becomes to van Paassen a certain proof that Plato "ein unangenehmer Mensch war" (*op. cit.*, pp. 8 ff.). Van Paassen defends this conclusion with the naïve argument that his contemporaries would "Amphis sicher auf die Finger geklopft haben, wenn seine Beschreibung Platons mit der Wirklichkeit nicht übereingestimmt hätte" (p. 9). As if the good Athenians cared for such matters, provided the poet made them laugh—at the expense of Plato or somebody else! But then van Paassen believes in the historicity of the Aristophanean Socrates, too, arguing that the essence of a caricature is that it resembles the original. But Aristophanes' "caricatures" are often radical distortions. To what conclusions van Paassen's way of arguing leads, was well demonstrated in H. Müller-Strübing's amusing old book, *Aristophanes und die historische Kritik* (Leipzig, 1873), where we read the golden words that the primary condition of understanding the Attic comic poets is a sense of humour.—Actually, as Düring points out, "in the preserved fragments and the allusions to lost comedies there are however—and this is a remarkable fact—no derogatory or contemptuous insinuations about Plato's person, apart from the harmless mocking on the subject of his σεμνότης" (*op. cit.*, p. 138). If the comic poets' anodyne jokes about Plato entitle us to form a negative idea of his personality, what shall we think of other philosophers who are far worse treated in the Middle Comedy? For one of the favourite topics of this Comedy is philosopher-baiting, cf. Jacob Burckhardt's caustic remarks, *Griechische Kulturgeschichte*, III (Gesamtausgabe, V), p. 265. Rudolf Helm, *Lucian and Menipp* (Leipzig, 1906), pp. 376–386 ("Die Philosophen in der Komödie") has collected a rich material concerning the treatment of the philosophers in the Attic Comedy, see especially pp. 376 ff., on the Middle Comedy.

Another detailed treatment of this subject can be found in T. B. L. Webster, *Studies in Later Greek Comedy* (Manchester, 1953), pp. 50 ff., 110 ff., who stresses that "on the whole the comic poets are not unfriendly, if slightly contemptuous, of philosophers in general and the Academy in particular".—Frowning eyebrows were generally regarded as a sign of real or conceited severity, "superciliousness", see Helm, *op. cit.*, p. 377, Heinrich Jacoby, *Comicae Dictionis Index* (*Fragmenta Comicorum Graecorum*, ed. A. Meineke, V: 2, Berlin, 1857), s.v. ὀφρύς, and the many examples quoted in Henricus Stephanus, *Thesaurus Linguae Graecae*, V (Paris, 1842–46, col. 2463), s.v. ὀφρύς.

130. Stein, *op. cit.*, II, p. 178. Jacob Burckhardt was of the same opinion: "Ferner herrscht das Anekdotische in der ganzen Lebensgeschichte Platos, sowohl bei Diogenes von Laerte als bei den übrigen Biographen. Selbst die wahren Tatsachen werden mit Gesprächen, Umständen och Witzen referiert, welche das grösste Misstrauen rege machen, so dass schliesslich fast jeder Punkt im Leben des Philosophen bestritten ist" (*Griechische Kulturgeschichte*, III, pp. 400 f.).

131. See now the penetrating and interesting remarks by Margherita Isnardi Parenti, "Rileggendo *il Platone* di Ulrich von Wilamowitz-Moellendorff" (*Annali della Scuola Normale Superiore di Pisa*. Classe di Lettere e Filosofia, III, 1973, pp. 147–167).

132. See above, p. 37.

133. *Platon*, I², p. 6.

134. *Op. cit.*, I², p. 4.

135. *Op. cit.*, I², p. 6.

136. *Op. cit.*, II², p. 20.

137. *Op. cit.*, II², p. 7. In his review of Wilamowitz's book, his old friend, Eduard Schwartz, called Hermann's attempt "verfrüht", but added "aber er war von Notwendigkeit erzeugt und hinterliess durch sein Scheitern eine Lücke, die die Philologie früher oder später ausfüllen musste. Das ist jetzt geschehen" (*HZ*, 122, 1920, p. 292).

138. *Op. cit.*, II², p. 8.

139. See above, n. IV 47.

140. *Op. cit.*, I², pp. 3 ff.

141. *Op. cit.*, I², p. 3.

142. See Karl Reinhardt, *Vermächtnis der Antike* (Göttingen, 1960), p. 367.

143. *Platon*, I², p. 153.

144. *Op. cit.*, I², pp. 124 ff. The Chapter on these Dialogues is called "Jugendübermuth".

145. *Op. cit.*, I², p. 208.

146. *Op. cit.*, I², pp. 234 ff.

147. *Op. cit.*, I², pp. 254 ff.

148. *Op. cit.*, I², pp. 269, 279 ff.

149. *Op. cit.*, I², p. 394.

150. *Op. cit.*, I², pp. 250, 475 ff.

151. *Op. cit.*, I², pp. 489 ff.

152. *Op. cit.*, I², p. 711.

153. *Op. cit.*, I², p. 16.

154. *Op. cit.*, I², p. 711.

155. *Op. cit.*, I², pp. 508 ff.

156. *Op. cit.*, I², pp. 511 ff.; II², pp. 221 ff.

157. *Op. cit.*, I², p. 1.

158. *Op. cit.*, I², p. 711; Wilamowitz refers to *Republic* VII (520 A–E).

154. Concerning Wilamowitz's ambiguous relations with the "George school", see below, n. IV 188.

160. Albert Rivaud, "Platon" (*Revue de Synthèse*, VI: 3, 1933), p. 186, cf. *The Legend of Sparta*, I, pp. 244 ff., 534 ff. Even so cautious a scholar as Auguste Diès declared: "Platon n'est pas venu en fait à la philosophie que par la politique et pour la politique" (Introduction to The Budé-edition of the *Republic*, VI, p. V). See now Victor Goldsmidt's sharp protest, *Questions platoniciennes*, pp. 63 ff., 177 ff.

161. Friedländer, *op. cit.*, I³, p. 6.—Many years earlier, Paul Wendland had said much the same thing, see his interesting paper, "Entwicklung und Motive der platonischen Staatslehre" (*Preussische Jahrbücher*, 136, 1909, pp. 193–220), p. 219.

162. I use the translation of Glenn R. Morrow, *Plato's Epistles* (Revised ed., New York, 1962), though with some alterations.—Concerning *Ep*. VII, see further below, pp. 69 f., 73 f.

163. See above, pp. 31 f.

164. *Op. cit.*, I³, p. 3.

165. *Platons Selbstbiographie* is the title of Heinrich Gomperz's booklet (Berlin, 1928), see below, pp. 61 f.—This view of the Epistle as an autobiography is the point of departure for Georg Misch's rejection of its authenticity, see *Geschichte der Autobiographie*, I: 1 (Bern, 1949), pp. 114–158.

166. It is useless to recoil from this word as Geffcken did (*op. cit.*, II: 1, p. 160).

167. Thus Ernst Howald in his Introduction to *Ep*. VII (*Die echten Briefe Platons*, Zürich, 1951), p. 17, with whose interpretation I in the main agree, though not in regard to the so-called philosophic excurses, cf. below, pp. 73 f.

168. "Er schreibt in Abwehr nach vielen Richtungen" (Howald, *l.c.*).

169. Morrow rightly stresses that the passage on the Thirty is a selfdefense (*op. cit.*, pp. 52 ff.).

170. *Ep*. VII 330 D—331 D; the passage is an apology for his political inactivity at Athens, as Morrow points out (*op. cit.*, p. 224 n. 23). In the *Fifth Epistle*—whether Platonic or not—there is a similar apology (322 A–B), see Morrow, *op. cit.*, pp. 137 ff.

171. As Howald, *op. cit.*, pp. 23 ff., 27 ff., points out, Plato's heart was not in the matter. Thus also Wilamowitz, *op. cit.*, II², p. 290, and R. S. Bluck, *Plato's Seventh and Eight Letters* (Cambridge, 1947), pp. 20 ff., but see Morrow, *op. cit.*, pp. 59 ff.

172. Nietzsche declared: "Ich würde auch einer Lebensgeschichte Platon's von ihm selbst geschrieben, keinen Glauben schenken" (*Fröhliche Wissenschaft*, 91, Gesammelte Werke. Musarionausgabe, XII, München, 1924, p. 119). As his library at Weimar shows, Nietzsche was interested in the biographical section of *Ep*. VII, though at that time the Epistle was generally considered spurious, see H. J. Schmidt, *Nietzsche und Sokrates* (Monographien der philosophischen Forschungen, 59, Meisenheim am Glan, 1969), p. 370 n. 1164.—In his *Platons Leben* (Zürich, 1923), pp. 46 ff., Ernst Howald said: "Als Platon im höchsten Alter im sogenannten siebenten Briefe eine Art Rechenschaftsbericht über sein Leben ablegte, hatte er keine ganz genaue Vorstellung mehr von seiner früheren Entwicklung." He sincerely believed that he had been interested in politics from his early youth on. In reality, Plato was in his youth totally under the influence of Socrates, the asocial individualist and rationalist, whose evil genius led Plato astray and compelled him to do things incompatible with his true nature. Only in his mature age, Plato to a certain extent succeeded in freeing himself. This view of the relations between Socrates and Plato is inspired by Nietzsche, though the latter is not cited in Howald's book. Cf. above, n. IV 53.—A similar conception of Socrates as

influencing Plato in a way contrary to the latter's true inclinations, has been expressed by R. Palas (see above, n. IV 69).

173. Cf. Wilamowitz, *op. cit.,* II², p. 282.

174. Wilamowitz explained that the Epistle's silence about the Academy was due to the circumstance that in this way Plato avoided mentioning Dion's murderer Callippus, who was an Academic (*op. cit.,* I², p. 648; II², p. 299). But *Ep.* VII 333 E, Plato speaks obviously of Callippus—though without mentioning his name—and there he stresses that Callippus and his brother were Dion's friends οὐκ ἐκ φιλοσοφίας, which must mean that Dion and Callippus were not fellow-Academics. Athenaeus, of course, asserted (508 E–F) that Callippus was a member of the Academy, see Düring, *Herodicus,* pp. 38 and 83. Cf. also Kurt von Fritz, *Platon in Sizilien* (Berlin, 1968), p. 133, who finds it possible that Callippus had belonged to the Academy, "nur vorübergehend".

175. See the pertinent remarks of Jula Kerschensteiner in her and W. Neumann's edition, *Platon: Briefe. Griechisch-Deutsch* (München, 1967), pp. 187 ff.

176. Although Friedländer based his picture of Plato on the *Seventh Epistle,* he was not unaware of its omissions, see *op. cit.,* I³, pp. 136 ff.

177. See below, pp. 73 f.

178. Morrow, *op. cit.,* p. 67. The word omitted is "naturally". Morrow goes too far in trying to repudiate what he calls "the alleged irrelevance of a discussion of epistemology in a letter of political advice" (p. 61), for, as Wilamowitz pointed out (*op. cit.,* II², p. 293), if the Excursus is omitted, no gap results between 341 E and 344 A. The argumentation is clearly interrupted by the digression.

179. Representative of this reaction is Kurt Hildebrandt's severe review (*Preussische Jahrbücher,* 186, 1921, pp. 268–271). In *Platons Leben,* pp. 9 ff., 13 ff., Ernst Howald vindicated the scholar's right to interpret Plato contrary to his own words. To Howald, Wilamowitz's *Platon* is a mosaique, "das der inneren Einheit und der Folgerichtigkeit entbehrt", for the task of the biographer is to discover the inner unity of Plato's life which cannot be found in the texts but is "eine Deutung". In this way, the great individual becomes timeless. Here, the spirit of the George-school is speaking, see below, pp. 49 f.

180. *What Plato Said,* pp. 2 ff.—Even as staunch an admirer of Wilamowitz as Johannes Geffcken could not wholly conceal his doubts, see *op. cit.,* II: 1, p. 36; II: 2, pp. 29 (n. 2) and 41, cf. also Karl Praechter's objections (*op. cit.,* pp. 65ˣ ff.).

181. *Platon,* I², pp. 202 ff.

182. *Op. cit.,* I², p. 721.

183. "Resignation" is the heading of Wilamowitz's chapter on the *Laws* (*op. cit.,* I², pp. 654–704).

184. *Op. cit.,* I², p. 722; italics mine.

185. *Op. cit.,* I², p. 655.

186. *Op. cit.,* I², pp. 715 ff.

187. *Op. cit.,* I², pp. 723 ff.

188. On the George-school, see above, p. 32. The relations between it and Wilamowitz were curiously ambiguous. Outwardly, it was a relationship of sheer enmity, as appears from Kurt Hildebrandt's famous paper, "Hellas und Wilamowitz", in *Die Grenzboten,* 69 (1911), I, pp. 412–421. But Hildebrandt's own *Platon* (see above, n. IV 59) is strongly dependent on Wilamowitz, as he subsequently admitted, see the Postscript to the second edition (p. 372). The points in common—above all the exaltation of Plato's personality—are so many, that we again note that the fiercest opposition often arises between two kindred positions.

189. See, e.g., Hildebrandt, *Platon*², pp. 388 ff. A similar attitude in Howald, *Platons Leben,* pp. 10 ff., cf, above, n. IV 179.

190. *What Plato Said,* pp. 66 ff. In his criticism of Hermann, Ribbing argued in the same way, see *Genetische Darstellung der platonischen Ideenlehre,* II, pp. 54 ff. A similar criticism was voiced by Auguste Diès, *Autour de Platon,* II, (Paris, 1927), pp. 290 and 296 ff., and Jacob Klein, "Aristotle, An Introduction" (*Ancients and Moderns,* Essays in Honour of Leo Strauss, New York, 1964), p. 52.

191. *What Plato Said,* p. 67.

192. The first edition was published in two volumes (Berlin, 1928–30); the second, enlargened and revised, edition in three volumes (Berlin, 1954–60); the third edition—as yet only Vol. I–II (1964)—differs from the second only in details. There is an English translation of the second edition. All quotations are from Vol. I³, II³, and III² of the German edition.—Any discussion about Friedländer's work should take into account Julius Stenzel's remarkable review (*Gn,* 8, 1932, pp. 401–415). See also H. Kuhn's review of the second German edition (*Gn,* 27, 1955, pp. 545–551; 34, 1962, pp. 535–541)—quoted as Kuhn, I & II—and Manasse, *op. cit.,* II, pp. 11 ff.

193. See Kurt Hildebrandt's malicious remarks in "Das neue Platonbild" (*Blätter für deutsche Philosophie,* 4, 1930–31, pp. 190–202), p. 200.

194. In the first edition, the subtitle of Volume I was "Eros—Paideia—Dialogos". This solemn use of Greek words is characteristic of the "Georgean" style. In the second edition, the subtitle was changed to "Seinswahrheit und Lebenswirklichkeit". In the Preface to the third edition, Friedländer says: "'Idee und Existenz' könnte man auch dafür setzen." This change expresses Friedländer's dissociation from George und rapprochement to Jaspers and Heidegger, a phenomenon that appears in the second edition, cf. Stenzel, *op. cit.,* pp. 409 ff., Kuhn, I, pp. 548 ff.; II, pp. 540 ff., and Manasse, *op. cit.,* I, pp. 13 ff. Very "Georgean" is also the quotation from Nietzsche which Friedländer chose as a motto: "Was kann uns allein wiederherstellen? Der Anblick des Vollkommenen". This motto remains in the second and third editions.

195. As appears from Hildebrandt's criticism (above, n. IV 193); in his *Platon,* he is appreciative (*op. cit.*², p. 376).

196. See Stenzel's criticism with which I entirely agree.

197. Kuhn accuses Friedländer of attempting to combine biography with "Problemgeschichte", something that, according to Kuhn is impossible. But I fail to find any "Problemgeschichte" in Friedländer.

198. Cf. above, pp. 17 f., à propos of Grote.—As far as I see, Friedländer never squarely faces the problem.

199. First published in 1926. The subtitle reads "The Man and his Works". But the introductory Chapter on "The Life of Plato" is very short and matter of fact, Taylor regarding the ancient biographical tradition with great suspicion, cf. above, n. IV 98. Taylor's well-known theory about the relationship between Socrates and Plato does not essentially mar his account of the works, though he tends to "christianize" Plato, cf. Manasse, *op. cit.,* II, pp. 36 ff. Taylor denies that Plato had any system and hails Grote as his model (*Plato,* pp. VII ff.). Recently, G. J. de Vries has rightly stressed "Taylor's excellent contributions to Platonic scholarship", see "Miscellaneous Notes on Plato" (Medeelingen der K. Nederlandse Akademie van Wetenschappen, afd. Letterkunde, N. R., 38: 1, 1975) pp. 33 ff.

200. Concerning the Third Humanism, see, besides Jaeger's *Humanistische Reden und Vorträge* (Berlin, 1937; 2d ed., 1960), the collective work, *Das Problem des klassischen und der*

Antike, edited by Jaeger (Berlin, 1931), discussed in Karl Reinhardt's important study, "Die klassische Philologie und das Klassische" (*Vermächtnis der Antike,* pp. 334–360).

201. See, e.g., the introductory Chapter, "Kulturidee und Griechentum", in *Platos Stellung im Aufbau der griechischen Bildung* (Berlin, 1928), pp. 7–19.—The three lectures which constitute this book were also published in the organ of the Third Humanism, *Die Antike,* IV (1928).

202. Vol. I was published in German (Berlin, 1934); Vol. II–III first in Gilbert Highet's English translation (New York, 1943–44). I quote from the Oxford edition in English, I–III 01944–45). Cf. Manasse, *op. cit.,* I, pp. 6 ff.

203. See Jaeger's own comment in his late work, *Early Christianity and Greek Paideia* (Cambridge, Mass., 1961), pp. 190 ff.

204. See *Platos Stellung,* pp. 34–49 ("Die platonische Philosophie als Paideia").

205. *Paideia,* II, p. x.

206. *Op. cit.,* II, pp. 82 ff., 96 ff.

207. *Op. cit.,* II, p. 198.

208. *Op. cit.,* II, pp. 104 ff.; italics Jaeger's.

209. *Op. cit.,* II, pp. 105 and 385 (n. 52), cf. also pp. 92 ff. The repudiation of the genetic interpretation was expressed earlier, in *Platos Stellung,* pp. 27 ff., where Jaeger also very politely dissociates himself from Wilamowitz.

210. *Paideia,* II, p. 198. In a characteristically philological way Jaeger tries to prove his view that Plato was no system-builder by the argument that the very word σύστημα "is not used to describe a body of scientific or philosophical doctrine before the Hellenistic age, of which it is a characteristic product" (p. 400 n. 4). The argument is not conclusive, for a thing can exist long before there is a special word for it, cf. above, n. III 5. Actually, σύστημα in this sense occurs already *Epinomis* 991 E: ἀριθμοῦ σύστημα, cf. E. des Places in the Budé-Plato, XII: 2 (1956), p. 159.

211. *L.c.*

212. See J. Tate's review (*cr,* 59, 1945, pp. 54–56). But on the other hand, Tate accuses Jaeger of reducing philosophy to history.

213. See Léon Robin's long and very appreciative review (*Critique,* 1947, III, pp. 196–216, 334–336), p. 325, cf. below, pp. 59 ff.

V. *The Search for Unity*

1. *The Decennial Publications of the University of Chicago.* First Series. Vol. VI (Chicago, 1904). Jaeger refers to it *Paideia,* II, p. 385 (n. 52).

2. Shorey, *op. cit.,* p. 3. I quote according to the separate pagination.

3. *Op. cit.,* p. 88.

4. *Op. cit.,* p. 8.

5. *Op. cit.,* p. 5.

6. *Op. cit.,* p. 6.

7. *Op. cit.,* p. 6.

8. *Op. cit.,* p. 7.

9. See, e.g., *op. cit.,* pp. 26 ff. (à propos of *Republic* 580 D ff.) and pp. 38 ff. (à propos of *Sophist* 248 A ff.).

10. *Op. cit.,* pp. 40 ff.

11. *Op. cit.,* p. 41.

12. *Op. cit.,* p. 7.

13. See above, pp. 47 f.

14. *Op. cit.,* pp. 50 ff., 57 ff., 60 ff.

15. *Op. cit.,* p. 8.

16. *Op. cit.,* p. 8.

17. *Op. cit.,* p. 9.

18. Chicago, 1933.

19. *What Plato Said,* p. v.

20. *Op. cit.,* p. 73.

21. The *Meno* is dealt with in five pages!

22. Albert Rivaud in *Revue Critique,* 67 (1933), pp. 198–199; Ernst Hoffmann was equally negative (*Gn,* 15, 1939, pp. 481–482). Other critics were more positive, see especially Constantin Ritter's eulogy (*Ph W,* 55, 1935, cols. 1025–1039).

23. See, e.g., *What Plato Said,* pp. 233 ff., 290 ff., 294 ff., 298 ff.

24. *Sather Classical Lectures,* 14 (Berkeley, Calf., 1938).

25. *Platonism,* p.p. 44., cf. p. 16 and *What Plato Said,* p. 33.

26. *Platonism,* p. 233.

27. Cf. Manasse's criticism (*op. cit.,* II. pp. 52 ff.).

28. See C. G. Field's review (*CR,* 47, 1933, pp. 181–182). In his review of J. Stenzel's *Zahl und Gestalt bei Platon und Aristoteles,* Shorey went as far as to assert that "Plato is the clearest and most explicit of writers" (*C Ph,* 19, 1924, p. 382)— a truly astonishing remark. *What Plato Said,* p. 320, we are told that Plato's "method everywhere is to be almost painfully and minutely clear and explicit".

29. Cf. Hoffmann: "Von diesem primitiven Niveau aus ist ein Zugang zur Platonischen Geisteswelt nicht zu gewinnen" (*l.c.*).

30. Cf. A. E. Taylor's review of *What Plato Said* in *The Philosophical Review,* 42 (1933), p. 627–634; even Field complains of Shorey's "harsh dogmatism" (*l.c.*).

31. See *Unity,* p. 28, where the Platonic Ideas are compared to Kant's *Ding-an-sich* and Herbert Spencer's "Unknowable". Cf. also Shorey's paper, "The Question of the Socratic Element in Plato" (*Proceedings of the Sixth International Congress of Philosophy, Harvard September 13–17 1926,* New York, 1927, pp. 576–583), and the Introduction to his LCL-edition of the *Republic,* I (London, 1935), pp. xvi and xxiii ff.

32. See *Platonism,* pp. 12 ff., where Plato is praised as "the chief and best source of ethical and natural religion throughout European literature", and his ambiguous attitude to the popular religion compared to that of Matthew Arnold. But subsequently, Shorey admits "the fundamental difference between Christianity and Platonism between Socrates and Christ": "Platonism is intellectual and aristocratic ... Christianity is emotional and popular" (p. 87). Yet it seems that to Shorey "the moral idealism of Jesus" was not too dissimilar to that of Plato, see Ch. III, "Plato and Christianity" (pp. 62–87).

33. Typical is Shorey's treatment of the *Laws,* see *What Plato Said,* pp. 355 ff., where he does not shrink from suggesting that the proceedings against the atheists in Book X are "perhaps not entirely serious", cf. also his paper, "Plato's *Laws* and the Unity of Plato's Thought", quoted above, n. IV 24.

34. *What Plato Said,* p. 67.

35. Published in Zeller, *op. cit.,* II: 1 (5th ed., Leipzig, 1922; here, too, I use the reprint, Hildesheim, 1961).

36. *Op. cit.,* II: 1⁶, p. 1059.

37. See below, pp. 74 f.
38. *Op. cit.*, II: 1⁶, pp. 1064 ff.
39. Collected in *Platonismus und christliche Philosophie* (Zürich, 1960).
40. *Platon* (Zürich, 1950).
41. *Platon*, pp. 56 ff., 63 ff., 88 ff., cf. also the account of Platonism in "Platonismus and Mittelalter" (*Platonismus und christliche Philosophie*, pp. 230–295).
42. *Platon*, p. 57.
43. *Op. cit.*, pp. 62 ff. Hoffmann's use of these terms is not strictly Platonic, see J. L. Ackrill's criticism (*M*, 60, 1951, pp. 129–132). Cf. Édouard des Places, *Lexique de la langue philosophique et religieuse de Platon* (The Budé-edition of Plato, XIII–XIV, Paris, 1964) s.v.
44. *Platon*, pp. 112 ff.
45. *Op. cit.*, pp. 30 ff., and *Platonismus*, pp. 436 ff.
46. See, besides Ackrill's review, quoted above, n. V 43, the criticism by Harold Cherniss (*CPh*, 47, 1952, pp. 259–260) and by E. Manasse, *op. cit.*, I, pp. 16 ff.
47. This opinion inspires Hoffmann's long paper, "Platonismus und Mittelalter" (see especially *Platonismus*, pp. 297 ff.).
48. See the paper on "Platon and Kant" (*Platonismus*, pp. 428 ff.).
49. See *Platon*, pp. 128, 140, 195, and 209, cf. Manasse, *op. cit.*, I, p. 17.
50. *Platon*, pp. 17 ff., 22 ff.
51. *Op. cit.*, pp. 22 ff., 26 ff.
52. *Op. cit.*, pp. 22 and 129.
53. *Op. cit.*, p. 119.
54. *Op. cit.*, pp. 149 ff. The four phases do not wholly correspond to the three groups into which Hoffmann distributes the Dialogues (pp. 129 ff.).
55. Thus Ackrill, *l.c.*, cf. Manasse, *op. cit.*, I, p. 19.
56. *Platon*, p. 16, cf. Manasse, *op. cit.*, I, p. 18.
57. See the interesting paper on "Philosophiegeschichtliche Methode" (*Platonismus*, pp. 5–41).
58. See above, pp. 16 f.
59. *Platon* (Paris, 1935). See further the papers on Plato published in *La pensée hellénique des origines à Epicure* (Paris, 1942), and the lectures on *Les rapports de l'Être et de la Connaissance d'après Platon*, published posthumously (Paris, 1957). In the Budé-edition of Plato, Robin edited the *Phaedo*, the *Symposium*, and the *Phaedrus* (IV: 1–3, Paris, 1926–38).
60. *Platon*, p. VII.
61. *Op. cit.*, p. 254.
62. *Op. cit.*, pp. 275–316.
63. *Op. cit.*, p. VII, cf. pp. 12 ff.
64. Paris, 1908.
65. *Théorie platonicienne*, pp. 5 ff.
66. *Op. cit.*, pp. 442 ff., 585 ff.
67. See especially Albert Rivaud's review (*REG*, 1908, pp. 397–402), cf. further Cornelia de Vogel, *Een Keerpunkt in Plato's denken* (Diss. Utrecht, 1936), pp. 229 ff. her "Thesis" III, and "La dernière phase de la philosophie de Platon et l'interprétation de Léon Robin" (*Philosophia*, I, pp. 243–255), Harold Cherniss, *Aristotle's Criticism of Plato and the Academy*, I (Baltimore, 1944), pp. XIX ff., and *The Riddle of the Early Academy* (2d ed., New York, 1962), pp. 26 ff.
68. See, e.g., *Théorie platonicienne*, pp. 69 ff., 98 ff., 186 ff., 260 ff., 428 ff., 577.

69. See below, pp. 81 ff.

70. *Platon,* pp. 141 ff.

71. *Op. cit.,* p. 31.

72. *Op. cit.,* p. 141.

73. See, e.g., *op. cit.,* pp. 68, 99, 146 ff., 168 ff. Cf. Glenn R. Morrow's review (*The Philosophical Review,* 45, 1936, pp. 616–619), which gives a clearer account of Robin's complicated reconstruction of the Platonic system than the latter's own book, which presupposes a close study of his dissertation.

74. Robin, *Platon,* pp. 142 f., 169 ff., 246 ff., cf. *Théorie platonicienne,* pp. 585 ff.

75. Morrow, *op. cit.,* p. 617.

76. *Théorie platonicienne,* p. 598.

77. See Auguste Diès's review (*Bulletin de l'Association Guillaume Budé,* No. 51, april 1936), p. 30.

78. See Albert Rivaud's review (*REG,* 49, 1936, pp. 484–486). In his earlier review of *La Théorie platonicienne*—see above, n. V 67—Rivaud had pointed out that Robin's whole argumentation presupposes the existence of a Platonic system (pp. 401 ff.).

79. Thus A. E. Taylor in his otherwise appreciative review (*M,* 44, 1936, pp. 373–378), and Morrow (above, n. V 73).

80. *Platon,* p. 332. A reader familiar with the French literature of that time is reminded of Gide.

81. *Op. cit.,* pp. 332 ff.

82. *Op. cit.,* p. 330.

83. This was rightly stressed by Rivaud: "Le livre donne le sentiment d'une lutte perpetuelle contre une pensée qui se dérobe, et l'on est sûr, en le fermant, que l'auteur lui-même, au terme d'un si loyal effort, en a reconnu les limites" (*l.c.*).

84. Perhaps for this reason, Robin's monograph—in contrast to his thesis—has been overlooked by the modern Esoterists, as Ph. Merlan pointed out, see his "'ΑΠΟΡΗΣΑΙ 'ΑΡΧΑΙΚΩΣ" (*RhM,* 111, 1968), p. 121 n. 1.

85. *Platons Selbstbiographie* (Berlin, 1928).

86. See below, pp. 73 f.

87. *Op. cit.,* pp. 44 ff.

88. See the "Vorbemerkung".

89. "Platons philosophisches System" (*Proceedings of the Seventh International Congress of Philosophy Oxford September 1–6 1930,* Oxford, 1931, pp. 420–431).

90. See above, p. 58.

91. Partly perhaps because the lecture was not listed in the *Année philologique.*

92. However, the modern Esoterists have not forgotten Gomperz's attempt, see, e.g., H. J. Krämer, *Arete,* p. 479 n. 193–194, and "Fragen" p. 120 n. 52 (see below, n. VI 6 and VI 54). The lecture was reprinted in an English translation in Gomperz's *Philosophical Studies* (Boston, 1953).

VI. The Hidden System

1. See below, pp. 74 f.

2. See in the first place *From Platonism to Neoplatonism* (3d ed., The Hague, 1968; the first edition was published in 1953), where Merlan's other works on this topic are listed.

3. The several studies of Miss de Vogel are now collected in *Philosophia*, I (Assen, 1970), see especially the hitherto unprinted paper, "Some Controversial Points of Plato Interpretation Considered" (pp. 183–209).

4. *Tübinger Beiträge zur Altertumswissenschaft*, 40 (Stuttgart, 1959).

5. Stuttgart, 1963; 2d ed., Stuttgart, 1968, with a postscript.—Further works by Gaiser will be noted below.

6. *Abhandlungen der Heidelberger Akademie der Wissenschaften. Philosophisch-historische Klasse*, 1959: 2; subsequently quoted as *Arete*.

7. Amsterdam, 1964; quoted as *Geistmetaphysik*.—Further works by Krämer will be noted below, but it may be pointed out here that *Idee and Zahl* (Abhandlungen der Heidelberger Akademie der Wissenschaften, Philosophisch-historische Klasse, 1968: 2) contains a series of interesting papers on the problem of esoteric Platonism by Gaiser, Krämer, and others.

8. No less a scholar than Albin Lesky has—though with some reservations—accepted Gaiser's and Krämer's theories, see his *Geschichte der griechischen Literatur* (3d ed., Bern, 1971), pp. 606 ff. This book has become the authoritative textbook on the history of Greek literature and has been translated, e.g., into English. Jürgen Wippert has edited a collection of papers concerning *Das Problem der ungeschriebenen Lehre Platons. Beiträge zum Verständnis der Platonischen Prinzipienphilosophie* (Wege der Forschung, Band CLXXXVI, Darmstadt, 1972). Unfortunately, this anthology gives a very misleading view of the state of the problem in present Platonic scholarship. Being an ardent believer in an Unwritten Doctrine, as appears from his lengthy Introduction, the Editor has, with one exception, only printed studies in support of his own belief. The exception is a chapter from Harold Cherniss's book on the Early Academy, which is, indeed, an important book, but which by now is forty years old and—so Wippert confidently tells us—"refuted" by later scholars (p. XV n. 9). *None* of the many recent serious criticisms of and objections to a belief in an Unwritten Doctrine has been found worthy to appear in the anthology, though they are mentioned in the bibliography. One can only hope that the Redactors of the Series *Wege der Forschung* will find it possible to add a new volume on the question, containing proofs of the adversary criticism. *Audiatur et altera pars!*

9. See Krämer, *Arete*, p. 381. However, the list given p. 381 n. 2 is neither complete nor reliable, as will be proved subsequently. Many of the texts adduced by Krämer do not refer to any secret doctrine. Nevertheless, Krämer's assertion has been uncritically accepted by Stanley Rosen, *Plato's Symposium* (New Haven, 1968), p. XVI.

10. *Physics* 209 b 13–16, cf. Cherniss, *The Riddle of the Early Academy* (see above, V 67), pp. 14 ff., but see Merlan, "Zwei Bemerkungen zum aristotelischen Plato" (*RhM*, 111, 1968, pp. 1–15) p. 5 n. 15.

11. Schleiermacher, *Platons Werke*, I: 1³, p. 13. Rosen's criticism reveals that he has missed the point of Schleiermacher's argumentation (*op. cit.*, p. XXVI).

12. See below, pp. 82 ff.

13. Even H. J. Krämer has been unable to find any earlier texts—apart from those statements of Plato which he misinterprets, see subsequently in the text.

14. Albinus, *Didascalicus* XXVII: πάνυ γοῦν ὀλίγοις τῶν γνορίμων καὶ τοῖς γε προκριθεῖσι τῆς περὶ τοῦ ἀγαθοῦ ἀκροάσεως μετέδωκε (Albinos, *Epitomé*, ed. P. Louis, Paris, 1945, pp. 128–129). Louis's translation is misleading, like many other passages in his translation, cf. H. Cherniss's review (*AJPh*, 70, 1949), pp. 77 ff.—Incidentally, Albinus' statement is contrary to Aristoxenus' well-known story about the reception of this lecture,

quoted below, p. 71. Curiously enough, the passage in Albinus is missing in the "Testimonia" in Gaiser, *Platons ungeschriebene Lehre,* though it is mentioned in Krämer, *Arete,* p. 440 n. 123. The denial of R. E. Witt, *Albinus and the History of Middle Platonism* (Cambridge, 1937), p. 87, that Albinus asserted the existence of an esoteric doctrine is incompatible with Albinus' own words. On Albinus, see further Heinrich Dörries's article, *RES,* XII (1970), cols 14–22, and J. H. Loenen, "Albinus' Metaphysics. An attempt at Rehabilitation" (*Mn,* 1956, pp. 296–319; 195–197, pp. 33–56).

15. See below, pp. 70ff.

16. Krämer, "Die platonische Akademie und das Problem einer systematischen Interpretation der Philosophie Platons" (*Kant-Studien,* 55, 1964; quoted subsequently as "Akademie"), p. 75 n. 6, interprets the Albinus-passage as showing conscioussness of Platonic esoterism, "was um so bedeutsamer ist, als sich im mittleren Platonismus selbst keine gleichartige Esoterik feststellen lässt".

17. On Numenius, see the monograph by E. A. Leemans, *Studie over den wijsgeer Numenius van Apamea med uitgave der fragmenten* (Académie R. de Belgique. Classe des Lettres et des Sciences Morales et Politiques. Mémoires. Collection in in –8°. Deuxième Serie, t. XXXVII: 2, 1935), R. Beutler's comprehensive article, *RES,* VII (1940), cols. 664–678, Krämer, *Geistmetaphysik,* pp. 63 ff., the Chapter on Numenius in Ph. Merlan, "Greek Philosophy from Plato to Plotinus" (*The Cambridge History of Later Greek and Early Medieval Philosophy,* ed. A. H. Armstrong, Cambridge, 1967; quoted below as *Cambridge History*), and Dörrie's article, *KP,* IV (1970).—I have made use of the English translation in K. S. Guthrie's otherwise worthless book, *Numenius of Apamea* (Diss, Columbia, 1917). Guiseppe Martano's small Italian monograph (Naples, 1950)—not listed in *L'Année Philologique*—is of little value, as is also the case with J. M. van der Ven, "Leven, leer en beteckenis van Numenius van Apamea" (*Bijdragen van de philosophische en theologische fakulteiten der Nederland-Jezuieten,* I, 1938, pp. 236–272). Numenius should now be studied in Édouard des Places's Budé-edition, *Numenius, Fragments* (Paris, 1973), with a French translation, a long introduction and copious notes.

18. Ἀπόρρητος (ἄρρητος) is a word belonging to the language of mysteries, see the numerous relevant texts in Odo Casel, *De philosophorum Graecorum silentio mystico* (Religionsgeschichtliche Versuche und Vorarbeiten, XVI: 2, Giessen, 1919). On Numenius, *ibid.* pp. 111 ff.

19. Numenius fr. 30 (Leemans, *op. cit.,* p. 143)=fr. 23 Des Places (*op. cit.,* pp. 61 ff.)

20. Numenius fr. 1 (Leemans, *op. cit.,* p. 115)=fr. 24 Des Places (*op. cit.,* pp. 62 ff.).

21. More exactly, the doctrine that there are three gods, which Numenius ascribes to Plato, who got it from Socrates, according to Numenius' interpretation of the pseudo-Platonic *Ep.* II 312 E, cf. Merlan, "Drei Anmerkungen zu Numenius" (*Ph,* 106, 1962), pp. 137 ff., and *Cambridge History,* p. 97.

22. Thus, e.g., Krämer, *Geistmetaphysik,* p. 64.

23. See the critical Budé-edition of the *Theologia Platonica* by H. D. Saffrey & L. G. Westerink, I– (Paris, 1968–), which, when complete, will entirely supersede the old, unsatisfactory edition by Aemilius Portus (Hamburg, 1618). The modern Italian translation by Enrico Turolla (Bari, 1957) is helpful, though it must be used with circumspection, being full of gross errors, as was pointed out by R. Gnolli in a detailed and severe criticism of it (*Parola del Passato,* 16, 1961, pp. 136–159).—On Proclus' opinion—*Theologia Platonica,* I, pp. 5 ff.—cf. Olof Gigon, "Zur Geschichte der sogenannten neuen Akademie" (*MH,* 1, 1944), pp. 97 ff.

24. This has recently been stressed by Willy Theiler, "Diotima neuplatonisch" (*Untersuchungen zur antiken Literatur,* Berlin, 1970), p. 503.

25. *Theologia Platonica,* I 5 (I, pp. 23 ff. ed. Staffrey & Westerink).—In his Chapter on "The Later Neoplatonists" in *Cambridge History,* A. C. Lloyd says: "Proclus claims in the introduction that alongside the philosophy of the Ideas there is to be found in Plato a secret philosophy which Plotinus and his successors have helped to expound" (p. 306). Lloyd gives no references, and I fail to discover any such statements in Proclus; on the contrary, as stated in the text, he stresses the mystic, esoteric, divine character of *all* Platonism. Probably, Lloyd is thinking of the passage I 1 (I, pp. 6 ff.). But the distinction made there is between true Platonism which is a mystery religion and a superficial philosophy which is no Platonism at all and certainly not to be found in Plato's Dialogues; of the Ideas there is no mention. (I, pp. 5 ff., cf. p. 131 n. 2).

26. *Theologia Platonica* I 7 (I pp. 30 ff.).

27. See Karl Praechter, "Richtungen und Schulen im Neuplatonismus" (*Genethliakon Carl Robert,* Berlin, 1910), pp. 126 ff., and his papers (*Byzantinische Zeitschrift,* 18, 1909, pp. 511–518, and *GGA,* 1905, pp. 505–535). Cf. further the old work by E. Vacherot, *Histoire critique de l'école d'Alexandrie,* II (Paris, 1846), pp. 432 ff.; III, pp. 467 ff., Thomas Wittaker, *The Neoplatonists* (Cambridge, 1961; a reprint of the 3d ed., 1928), pp. 221–341, and A.-J. Festugière, "L'ordre de lecture des dialogues de Platon au Ve–VIe siécle" (*MH,* 26, 1964, pp. 281–296).

28. See Vacherot's pertinent discription of the Neoplatonic interpretation of earlier thinkers: "Il (Neoplatonism) admet tout dans sa synthèse, mais en tout transformant: loin de se plier aux doctrines qu'il adopte c'est lui qui les asservit à sa propre pensée. C'est en modifiant, en corrigeant, en épurant, parfois en dénaturant la pensée d'autrui, sous prétexte de l'interpréter qu'il fait rentrer toutes les Écoles dans son système. Quand il croit simplement commenter Platon, Pythagore, Aristote, Zenon, c'est sa propre pensée qu'il développe le plus souvent. Partout et toujours il se met à la place des doctrines qu'il interprète; par une sorte d'illusion facile à expliquer, dans toutes les pensées d'autrui il ne voit que la sienne" (*op. cit.,* III, pp. 467 ff.).

29. See Armstrong, "Plotinus" (*Cambridge History*), pp. 213 ff.

30. The Neoplatonic dogmatization and systematization of Plato is analysed in R. F. Hathaway, "The Neoplatonic interpretation of Plato" (*Journal of the History of Philosophy,* 7, 1969, pp. 19–26).

31. It is interesting to note that, to my knowledge, none of the modern Esoterists has seriously discussed the Neoplatonic interpretation. Krämer says only that until the eighteenth century Plato's work were "im Sinne der neuplatonischen Tradition systematiziert und konstruktiv umgedeutet" ("Akademie", p. 69).

32. *The Decline and Fall of the Neoplatonic Interpretation of Plato* (Societas Scientiarum Fennica. Commentationes Humanarum Litterarum, 52, 1974).

33. See *Decline and Fall,* pp. 57 ff.

34. See *Decline and Fall,* pp. 64 ff.

35. See the general introduction to Schleiermacher's translation (1804), *Platons Werke,* I³, pp. 10 ff. The Introduction has been reprinted in *Das Platonbild. Zehn Beiträge zum Platonverständnis* (Hildesheim, 1969).—Concerning Schleiermacher's refutation of the Esoterists, see *Decline and Fall,* pp. 5 ff.

36. See below, pp. 84 and 87 f.

37. See above, p. 26.

38. *Geschichte und System*, pp. 552 ff., 709 ff. Hermann referred also to the *Epistles*, especially the *Seventh*, which he considered written by a well-informed disciple of Plato's and therefore a good source.

39. *Op. cit.*, p. 554, cf. pp. 711 ff. (n. 750), where, adducing Schleiermacher, Hermann even seems willing to retract what he had said about the special character of Plato's oral teaching.

40. *Abhandlungen und Beiträge zur classischen Literatur und Altertumskunde* (Göttingen, 1849), pp. 281–305. The lecture has been reprinted in *Das Platonbild.*—An outline was printed in *Verhandlungen der zweiten Versammlung deutscher Philologen und Schulmänner in Mannhein 1839* (1840), pp. 21–26.

41. See, e.g., Gaiser, *Platons ungeschriebene Lehre²*, p. 335 n. 1. Cf., to the contrary, Zeller's criticism (*op. cit.*, II: 1⁶, p. 484 n. 3).

42. *Abhandlungen*, p. 291.

43. *Op. cit.*, pp. 289 ff.

44. Hermann adduces not only *Ep.* VII but also *Ep.* II, though he calls it "späteres Machwerk" (*op. cit.*, p. 284).

45. *Op. cit.*, p. 289. Hermann explicitly denies that Plato distinguished between a discussion and a lecture, pp. 287 ff., cf. below, pp. 97 f. This is in accordance with Hermann's assertion—against Schleiermacher—that the dialogue was not essential to Plato's philosophic thought but a mere external form, borrowed from earlier writers (pp. 285 ff.), cf. above, p. 30.

46. *Op. cit.*, pp. 298 ff.

47. *Op. cit.*, p. 293.

48. *Op. cit.*, p. 305.

49. The words "wer Augen hat zu sehen" are curiously ambiguous.

50. Which did not escape Zeller's attention (*l.c.*, see above, n. VI 41).

51. *Phaedrus* 276 A; I follow R. Hackforth's translation, *Plato's Phaedrus* (Cambridge, 1927), pp. 158 ff., cf. *Protagoras* 329 A.

52. *Ep.* VII 341 B; as to the translation, see *Plato's Idea of Poetical Inspiration*, p. 9 n. 13.

53. *Ep.* II 314 B; I follow the translation by Glean R. Morrow, *Plato's Epistles*, pp. 197 ff.

54. See Krämer, *Arete*, pp. 22 ff., 393 ff., 405 ff., 443 ff., 461 ff.; p. 395 Krämer exclaims: *"Die Behauptung, die Dialoge enthalten die platonische Philosophie schlechthin, setzt sich folglich mit Platon selbst, und zwar mit dem Platon eben der Dialoge, direkt im Widerspruch"* (italics Krämer's). See further his papers "Akademie", passim, "Retraktationen zum Problem des esoterischen Platons" (*MH*, 21, 1964, pp. 136–167; quoted subsequently as "Retraktationen"), pp. 148 ff., and "Die grundsätzlichen Fragen der indirekten Platonüberlieferung" (*Idee und Zahl*, pp. 106–150; quoted subsequently as "Fragen"), and Gaiser, *Platons ungeschriebene Lehre²*, p. 452 n. 7.

55. *Plato's Idea of Poetical Inspiration*, pp. 8 ff. To the literature indicated there, I wish to add Giorgio Pasquali, *Le lettere di Platone* (Florence, 1938), pp. 89 ff., and Stefanini, *Platone*, I², pp. XXVIII ff. I regret that I omitted to mention Gunnar Rudberg's discussion of the relations between the *Phaedrus* and the *Seventh Epistle* in his *Kring Platons Phaidros* (Göteborg, 1924), pp. 47 ff.

56. In an attempt to combine a belief in the Dialogues as the main evidence of Plato's philosophy with the belief in an esoteric teaching, Stanley Rosen has tried to interpret the statements in *Ep.* II and VII as ironical (*Plato's Symposium*, New Haven, 1968, pp. XIII ff.). He offers no real proofs, except a general assertion that irony dominates all Plato's teaching, whether written or oral. This "pan-ironical" interpretation of Plato will be dealt with in a later

context, see below, pp. 95 f. Here it suffices to say that it does not seem possible to discover any irony in the relevant passages in *Ep. VII*, whether written by Plato or not. As to the interpretation of *Ep.* II, see below, n. VI 63.

57. Recently, Robert Muth asserted: "Der grundliegende Unterschied des Erlebnisart, ob ein Literaturwerk durch Hören aus dem Munde eines andern oder durch Lesen aufgenommen wird, bleibt bestehen, auch wenn man laut liest" ("Randbemerkungen zur griechischen Literaturgeschichte", *WS,* 79, 1966, p. 248 n. 8). This simply proves, how difficult it is for a modern man—even for a professor of Greek—to understand the ancient Greeks. Muth's assertion is refuted by the statements of the Greeks themselves, see especially Polybius XII 27, 1–4—written, *nota bene,* in Hellenistic times, by a writer who certainly was a big book-reader. In his paper, "Über Plato's schriftstellerische Motive", discussed above, K. Fr. Hermann had maintained the same opinion as Muth (*op. cit.,* pp. 287 ff.). Cf. further Richard Harder, "Bemerkungen zur griechischen Schriftlichkeit" (*Kleine Schriften,* Munich, 1960, pp. 57–80).

58. To the literature quoted in my earlier study, p. 10 n. 19 and 20, should be added A. E. Taylor's pertinent observation: "It was one of Plato's foremost convictions that nothing really worth knowing can be learned by merely listening to 'instruction'; the only true method of 'learning' science is that of being actually engaged, in company with a more advanced mind, in the discovery of scientific truth" (*Plato*[6], p. 6). In a paper published posthumously, Philip Merlan expressed a similar opinion, see "Bemerkungen zum neuen Platobild" (*AGPh,* 51, 1969), pp. 115 ff. But the right thing had already been said by Schleiermacher, *op. cit.,*I[3], pp. 14 ff.

59. Krämer believes that when Plato speaks of πολλὴ συνουσία γενομένη περὶ τὸ πρᾶγμα αὐτὸ (*Ep.* VII 341 C), he is thinking of his lectures περὶ τἀγαθοῦ, because these lectures—(or this lecture) are by later writers called συνουσίαι (*Arete,* p. 404). It should, however, be obvious that συνουσία here means "being together", "discussion", cf. E. des Places, *Lexique,* s.v. R. S. Bluck comments: "Personal contact between pupil and teacher is necessary" (*Plato's Seventh & Eight Letters,* p. 120); Kerschensteiner translates "aus häufigem gemeinsamen Bemühen um die Sache selbst" (*Platons Briefe* p. 89); Ernst Howald: "aus dem Zusammensein in ständiger Bemühung um das Problem" (*Die echten Briefe Platons,* p. 107). In his big commentary upon the *Epistles,* Frank Novotny refers to the use of συνουσία *Gorgias* 461 B and *Laws* XII 968 C, where the sense is clearly "discussing together", and to *Ep.* VII 344 B: μετὰ τριβῆς πάσης καί χρόνου πολλοῦ (*Platonis Epistulae,* Brunn, 1930, p. 217). Krämer tries to neutralize these facts by declaring in another passage (p. 14 n. 4) that the περὶ τἀγαθοῦ was not, properly speaking, a lecture but a "Lehrgespräch"—a term coined by Krämer in order to escape from the difficulties of his own making, see below, pp. 88 f.—To the passages quoted by Novotny may be added *Apology* 19 E. See s.v. συζῆν and συνουσία Des Places, *Lexique,* II, pp. 470 and 486.

60. The "illumination" of which Plato speaks, *Ep.* VII 344 B, is not any mystical revelation, as has rightly been pointed out by Morrow, *op. cit.,* Kerschensteiner, *op. cit.,* p. 206 n. 65, J. Stenzel, *Platon der Erzieher* (2d ed., Hamburg, 1961), pp. 317 ff., and especially in the chapter on "Arrheton" in Friedländer, *Platon,* I[3], pp. 63–89. Plato was no mystic like Plotinus. Cf. also Joseph Souilhé in the Budé-edition of Plato, XIII: 1 (Paris, 1926), pp. LIV ff. F. M. Cornford, "Mathematics and Dialectic in the 'Republic' VI–VII" (*M,* 1932; reprinted in *Studies in Plato's Metaphysics,* ed. R. E. Allen, London, 1965, pp. 61–95, from which I quote), pp. 93 ff., calls the experience described in *Ep.* VII "a vision" and finds that Plato in describing it "adopts the language of the Eleusinian mysteries". But in the mysteries there were no exchange of

thought, like that which leads to the Platonic illumination. In fact, Cornford adds that "the experience Plato means is ... rather an act of metaphysical insight or recognition—certainly nothing of the nature of trance or ecstasy". It may further be added that the Platonic 'vision' is not only shared by two or several persons but presumes their collaboration. Nothing can be more unlike the Plotinian φυγὴ τοῦ μόνου πρὸς τὸν μόνον.

61. See *Plato's Idea of Poetical Inspiration*, pp. 9 n. 14, 10 n. 12. Krämer seems to agree with the interpretation of the two works given here, when he says: "Gemeinsam (to them) aber ist der normative Richtpunkt dialektischer Mündlichkeit, hinter der der innere Dialog der Seele mit sich selbst steht" ("Fragen", p. 124). This view is hardly compatible with Krämer's usual conception of Plato's teaching in the Academy, see below, pp. 73 f.

62. See, e.g., Howald, *op. cit.*, pp. 156 ff., Souilhé, *op. cit.*, pp. LXXIX ff., Pasquali, *op. cit.*, pp. 177 ff., Morrow, *op. cit.*, pp. 11c ff., Kerschensteiner, *op. cit.*, pp. 116 ff.

63. That is the conclusion of Howald, Pasquali, Morrow, and Kerschensteiner—and, as far as I know, of most modern scholars. Cf. also Josef Pavlu, "Der zweite und dritte sogenannte Platonbrief" (*Mitteilungen des Vereines klassischer Philologen in Wien*, VII, 1930, pp. 1–35). Burnet, *Greek Philosophy*, I, p. 212. and Taylor, *Plato*[6], p. 15, did, indeed, accept *Ep.* II as authentic but they accepted almost all the letters. Paul Friedländer, *Platon*, I[3], pp. 254 ff., tried to defend the authenticity of *Ep.* II by explaining it as being fiercely ironical, and succeeded in impressing Lesky, see *Geschichte der Griechischen Literatur*[3], p. 575. A similar interpretation has recently been given by Eugen Dönt, "Platons Spätphilosophie und die Akademie" (*Österreichische Akademie der Wissenschaften, Philosophisch-historische Klasse, Sitzungsberichte*, 251:3, 1967), pp. 28 ff. These attempts to discover irony behind the pomposity of the Epistle do not carry conviction. The right thing about *Ep.* II was said as early as by Fr. Ast, *Platons Leben und Schriften*, pp. 511 ff. See also the discussion between J. Stannard and R. S. Bluck (*Phronesis*, 5, 1960, pp. 53–55 and 140–157), the former accepting, the latter rejecting the authenticity.

64. Gaiser regards *Ep.* II as Platonic, see *Platons ungeschriebene Lehre*[2], pp. 3, 480 (22 B), 533 (52), but in "Platons *Menon* und die Akademie" (*AGPh*, 46, 1964), p. 292 n. 17, he declares that the authenticity of the Epistle is as yet uncertain. On the other hand, Krämer rejects it as an "intolerable" imitation of *Ep.* VII, see *Arete*, p. 462 n. 164, and *Geistmetaphysik*, p. 221 n. 76, but tends to regard it as a product of the Early Academy (*l.c.*). For linguistic reasons, the Epistle must have been written in pre-Hellenistic times.

65. Thus Souilhé, *op. cit.*, p. LXXXI. It is precisely the esoterism of *Ep.* II which impressed him as Pythagorean. Cf. John M. Rist, "Neopythagoreanism and 'Plato's Second Letter'" (*Phronesis*, 10, 1965, pp. 78–81).

66. But see Ph. Merlan, "War Platons Vorlesung 'Das Gute' einmalig?" (*H*, 96, 1968), p. 706 ff., who finds it possible that both Themistius and Proclus also used other sources, independent of Aristoxenus.

67. Aristoxenus, *Harmonics* II (30, 10 Meib.), see Paul Marquard, *Die harmonischen Fragmenten des Aristoxenus* (Berlin, 1868), pp. 44–45, Henry S. Macran, *The Harmonics of Aristoxenus* (Oxford, 1902), pp. 122 and 187, Rosetta da Rios, *Aristoxeni Elementa Harmonica* (Rome, 1954), pp. 39 and 45. I have in the main used Macran's translation but with some alterations, especially those made by Sir David Ross, *Plato's Theory of Ideas* (Oxford, 1951), pp. 147 ff.

68. I assume that τὸ πέρας is used adverbially, cf. Macran, *op. cit.*, p. 256, Cherniss, *The Riddle of the Early Academy*, p. 87 (n. 2), Ross, *l.c.*, Düring, "Aristoteles" (*RES*, XI, 1968), col. 307, Krämer, *Arete*, p. 424, Gaiser, *Platons ungeschriebene Lehre*[2], p. 453. Ross's translation

of ὅτι ἀγαθόν ἐστιν ἕν "that there is one Good" (*l.c.*) seems improbable, for that would be intolerably banal, as Krämer rightly says (*op. cit.*, pp. 433 ff.). Subsequently (p. 244), Ross concedes that the phrase could be understood as meaning "the One is good", but finds it impossible to decide what Plato really said. Cherniss, *l.c.*, finds the phrase unintelligible. Nor is Miss da Rios's translation, "il Bene-che è uno solo", acceptable. Düring, *l.c.*, translates, 'Das Gute ist Eins'. G. J. de Vries, "Marginalia bij een esoterisch Plato" (*Tijdschrift voor Filosofie*, 28, 1964), p. 706 translates: "en als bekroning dat het Goede éin is (of het Ene is)".

69. See above, pp. 38 ff.

70. The bias of the Aristoxenian account has not entirely escaped Gaiser: "Schon in dem Bericht des Aristoxenus ist freilich eine Tendenz spürbar ... das Vorgehen Platons als 'weltfremd' und ehrgeizig hinzustellen" (*op. cit.*, p. 452). ("Weltfremd", yes, but "ehrgeizig"?) Unfortunately, Gaiser feels compelled to introduce, here too, his 'King Charles's head', viz., Plato's "regelmässige Lehrtätigkeit in der Akademie", for he asserts that just this bias proves that Aristotle's criticism of Plato's procedure "eigentlich nicht auf ein einmaliges Hervortreten Platons zu beziehen sind, sondern eher auf die regelmässige Lehrtätigkeit in der Akademie". This is a typical sample of the way in which the Esoterists interpret the texts. Cf. further de Vries, "Marginalia", p. 709.

71. See, e.g., Wilamowitz, *Platon*, I², p. 715, Friedländer, *Platon*, I³, p. 369 (n. 3), Hermann, *Geschichte und System der platonischen Philosophie*, I, pp. 79 and 123 (n. 178), who, however, refers to Themistius, not to Aristoxenus. On the contrary, Zeller, *op. cit.*, II: I⁶, p. 417 n. 3, asserts that the lecture was attended only by Plato's students. A. E. Taylor, who believed that Plato lectured "habitually in the Academy" (*Plato*, p. 10), speaks of "a particularly famous lecture" (*l.c.*) and of "the famous lecture on 'the Good'" (p. 503), cf. also Burnet, *Greek Philosophy*, I, p. 221. See further Cherniss, *op. cit.*, p. 12, and the literature quoted there.

72. See Krämer, *Arete*, pp. 404 ff., "Akademie", pp. 72 ff., and "Retraktationen", pp. 139 ff. Krämer's lengthy, strongly polemical papers for the most part simply repeat the argumentation in his main work, *Arete*. See further Gaiser, *op. cit.*, pp. 452 ff. Krämer and Gaiser seem, however, not to agree about the character of Plato's audience, for while Krämer declares that "die Teilnehmer nicht beliebige waren" (*Arete*, p. 406, and "Retraktationen", p. 141), and that in this way Plato tried his disciples, as he had tried Dionysius II (*Ep.* VII 340 B–341 A), Gaiser says that Aristoxenus' story "zeigt dass die Lehrvorträge Platons—jedenfalls gelegentlich und zu Beginn—allgemein zugänglich waren" (*op. cit.*, p. 452 n. 7).

73. See Merlan, "War Platons Vorlesung 'das Gute' einmalig?" (*H*, 96, 1968, pp. 705–709), G. J. de Vries, "Aristoxenus über περὶ τἀγαθοῦ (*ibid.*, pp. 124–126)—against Krämer, "Aristoxenus über Platons περὶ τἀγαθοῦ (*ibid.*, pp. 111–112)—Gregory Vlastos's review of Krämer's *Arete* (*Gn*, 35, 1963), pp. 650 ff., Düring, "Aristoteles", col. 307, and Dönt, "Platons Spätphilosophie", p. 9.

74. Gaiser, "Quellenkritische Probleme der indirekten Platon-überlieferung" (*Idee und Zahl*, pp. 31–84; quoted subsequently as "Probleme"), p. 36. Thus also Krämer, "Retraktationen", p. 139, and "Fragen", p. 112.

75. Krämer, "Fragen", pp. 112 ff.

76. Thus Simplicius, *In Aristotelis Physica*, pp. 151 and 453 ff. Diels, reproduced by Gaiser, *op. cit.*, pp. 453 and 481 ff. Cf. Cherniss, *Riddle*, p. 90 (n. 57) and Aristotle's *Criticism of Plato and the Academy*. I (Baltimore, 1944), pp. 169 ff. (n. 96), who points out that Simplicius' source was Porphyry who in his turn used Dercyllides' book on Platonic philosophy. See

further Gaiser's hypothetical attempt to reconstruct the transmission of the lecture ("Probleme", pp. 35 ff.), and Krämer, *Geistmetaphysik,* p. 55 (n. 121).

77. Cherniss, *op. cit.,* p. 12.

78. Krämer, *Arete,* p. 408.

79. See Paul Moraux, *Les listes anciennes des ouvrages d'Aristote* (Louvain, 1951), pp. 39 ff., 195 ff., 202, 295. The catalogue in the so-called *Vita Menagiana*—believed to be based on the *Onomatologus* of Hesychius Illustris—ascribes only *one* Book to the περὶ τἀγαθοῦ, whereas Ptolemaeus Chennus seems to have ascribed *five* Books to it, but we do not have his catalogue at first hand. Since Alexander of Aphrodisias, who used Aristotle's work, quotes from its *Second* Book, the statement in the *Vita Menagiana* cannot be right, see Moraux, *op. cit.,* p. 202. It seems therefore hypercritical to say, as H. Cherniss does, "Some War-Time Publications Concerning Plato" (*AJPh,* 68, 1947), p. 236 n. 7, that "the discrepancy of the three lists deprives all of them of authority in this matter".

80. Gaiser, "Probleme", pp. 35 ff., cf. Krämer, *Arete,* p. 376 n. 250. Walter Burkert, *Weisheit und Wissenschaft* (Erlanger Beiträge zur Sprach- und Kunstwissenschaft, X, Nürnberg, 1962), p. 31 n. 31, says about Aristotle's account of Plato's lecture: "er verband auch die Aufzeichnung von π.τἀγ. mit Kritik".

81. Thus Krämer, *Arete,* pp. 404 ff., 407 n. 50. As his quotation from Simplicius and Philoponus unintentionally reveals, the singular and the plural are used indiscriminately, so that no certain conclusion can be drawn from their use. Modern translators render Aristoxenus' ἀκρόασις sometimes by "lecture" (so Marquard, *op. cit.,* p. 46), sometimes by "lectures" (so Macran, *op. cit.,* p. 187, and da Rios, *op. cit.,* p. 451). Purely linguistically, both translations are possible, but the context proves decisively that the singular is intended. As Cherniss, *l.c.,* pointed out, in the *Poetics* (1459 C 21 f.), Aristotle speaks of tragedies, performed "at one sitting" (εἰς μίαν ἀκρόασιν).

82. As Krämer seems to believe, "Retraktationen", p. 140.

83. See Krämer, *Arete,* pp. 400 ff., "Retraktationen", pp. 140 ff., "Fragen", pp. 115 ff. As usual with Krämer, the later papers repeat the thesis of his main work, without adding anything substantially new. See further Gaiser, *Platons ungeschriebene Lehre²,* p. 452.

84. *Ep.* VII (340 B).

85. As Gundert does, "Zum philosophischen Exkurs im 7. Brief" (*Idee und Zahl,* pp. 85–105), pp. 88 ff., finding it probable that in other cases, too, Plato used this method. Thus also Egidius Schmalzriedt, *Platon, Der Schriftsteller und die Wahrheit* (München, 1969), pp. 13 ff., 353 ff., though he admits that Plato says, "indeed" (zwar), "diese Prüfung sei auf einen ganz bestimmten Personenkreis zugeschnitten" (p. 14). Nevertheless, Schmalzriedt insists that the subsequent description of the test has general validity, though he polemizes against Krämer's conclusion (p. 359 n. 31).

86. As Krämer believes (*Arete,* pp. 405 ff.), cf. Burkert, *op. cit.,* p. 17 n. 21.

87. Simplicius, *In Aristotelis Physica,* pp. 453 ff. Diels (reproduced in Gaiser, *op. cit.,* pp. 481 ff.) says, indeed, that Plato's disciples ἀνεγράψαντο τὰ ῥηθέντα αἰνιγματωδῶς, ὡς ἐῤῥήθη and speaks of τὰ ἐν τῇ περὶ τἀγαθοῦ συνουσίᾳ αἰνιγματωδῶς ῥηθέντα, Cherniss interprets this as meaning that, in the opinion of his disciples, Plato had spoken "in riddles" (*Riddle,* p. 12); thus also Merlan, "Bemerkungen zum neuen Platobild", pp. 114 ff. But, as Krämer points out, Simplicius *can* have meant no more than to say that his immediate sources—Porphyry or Dercyllides—did not understand the disciples' accounts of the lecture (*Arete,* p. 408 n. 5)—which Simplicius himself had not read. But, with one of his usual contradictions, Krämer subsequently conceded that Plato "insofern in 'Rätseln' sprach, als er

die letzten Schlussfolgerungen zuweilen den Hörern selbst überliess, um die Spontaneität des Verstehens anzustacheln" ("Fragen", p. 147 n. 134). It is not easy to make out what Krämer really means. Sir David Ross translates the passage in Simplicius: "Aristotle, Heraclides, Hestiaeus, and other associates of Plato attended these /lectures/ and wrote them down in the enigmatic style in which they were delivered" (*The Works of Aristotle*, XII, *Selected Fragments*, Oxford, 1952, p. 120).

88. *Ep.* VII 341 A.

89. See Plutarch, *Dion* 13, cf. Wilamowitz, *Platon*, I², pp. 549 ff.

90. See above, pp. 69 f.

91. "Bemerkungen zum neuen Platobild", pp. 115 ff.

92. *Ep.* VII 341 D, cf. Merlan, *op. cit.*, p. 117, and Dönt, "Platons Spätphilosophie", p. 22 ff.

93. *Ep.* VII 341 C–D and 344 B. Morrow translates καί τοι τόσον δέγε οἶδα, ὅτι γραφέντα ἢ λεχθέντα ὑπ' ἐμοῦ βέλτιστ' ἂν λεχθείη (341 B) by "And this I know: if these matters are to be expounded at all in book or lectures, they should best come from me" (*Plato's Epistles*, p. 237).

94. Krämer, *Arete*, pp. 27 n. 27 and 401, cf. also p. 22: "dem Suchenden nur in dialektischen Gespräch ... zugänglich".

95. See below, pp. 88 f.

96. See *Arete*, pp. 393, "Retraktationen", pp. 143 ff., and "Fragen", p. 122 n. 54—against H. D. Voigtländer's review of *Arete* (*AGPh*, 45, 1968, pp. 194–211), pp. 205 ff. Stating that there is not nor will ever be a book by him on the highest principles (*Ep.* VII 341 C, see above, p. 80), Plato uses the word σύγγραμμα. Schmalzriedt, *op. cit.*, pp. 16 ff. and 358 (n. 14), tries hard to prove that σύγγραμμα means "Lehrbuch", "Kompendium", "Lehrschrift", but that the Dialogues were not by Plato considered σύγγράμματα and therefore escaped condemnation—thus also Jacques Sulliger, "Platon et le problème de la communication de la philosophie" (*Studia Philosophica*, XI, 1951), p. 164, not quoted by Schmalzriedt. As the context shows, Plato is thinking primarily about Dionysius' τέχνη (341 B) and it is such a work which he finds impossible to write. The Dialogues are simply not discussed. But in the *Phaedrus* the condemnation of the written word is wholesale. That it occurs in one of Plato's greatest Dialogues is a paradox which we have to accept and, if possible, explain, not suppress.

97. For Plato says of Dionysius' τέχνη: οὔτε γὰρ ὑπομνημάτων χάριν αὐτὰ ἐγραψεν—οὐδὲν γὰρ δεινὸν μή τις αὐτὸ ἐπιλάθηται, ἐὰν ἅπαξ τῇ ψυχῇ περιλάβῃ (344 D); pointed out by Burkert, *Weisheit und Wissenschaft*, p. 18 n. 25, see also Hentschke, *Politik und Philosophie bei Platon und Aristoteles* p. 55 n. 18, who refers to *Ep.* VII 341 C, 342 A, where Plato seems to expect other similar publications. The passage *Ep.* VII 344 D is not discussed in Krämer's *Arete*. To say, as Krämer subsequently does—"Fragen", p. 117, and in his review of Dönt (*Anzeiger für die Altertumswissenschaft*, 21, 1968), col. 221—that Plato's anger with Dionysius and other unnamed persons for having written about matters about which Plato himself found it impossible to write or speak proves that it *is* possible to write about such matters, seems little more than a bad joke.

98. See *Arete*, pp. 14 and 462 n. 162, cf. also Gaiser, *Platons ungeschriebene Lehre²*, p. 454, and "Probleme", p. 81 n. 121. As Krämer points out, the originator of this interpretation was Werner Jaeger, see his *Studien zur Entstehungsgeschichte der Metaphysik des Aristoteles* (Berlin, 1912), p. 146 n. 3.

99. See *Arete*, pp. 25 ff., and 411 ff. Krämer gives no proof of his assertion, for the

circumstance that, when referring to the περὶ τἀγαθοῦ, Simplicius does not mention that the accounts of the disciples were "published" constitutes no proof. As Krämer well knows, Simplicius did not himself directly use any of those accounts, see e.g. *Arete*, p. 248. Gaiser, too, speaks of a "für den Gebrauch und die Weiterüberlieferung in der *Schule* bestimmte Niederschrift" (*Platons ungeschriebene Lehre*², p. 454; italics Gaiser's) but accuses Aristotle of having "profaned" Plato's teaching by publicly discussing its esoteric principles in his dialogue *On Philosophy* (pp. 313 and 400 n. 208). Erich Franck, too, thought that *Ep.* VII 341 D "may refer also to such a report as the Aristotelian concerning the doctrine of the ideal numbers" (*Knowledge, Will, and Belief*, Zürich, 1955, pp. 478 ff., cf. p. 113), but his reason was that such a report deprives these thoughts "of their relation to the very self of the philosopher and represents them as a purely theoretical doctrine".—In his study "Merkwürdige Zitate in der Eudemischen Ethik des Aristoteles" (*Sitzungsberichte der Heidelberger Akademie der Wissenschaften, Philosophisch-historische Klasse*, 1962: 2), pp. 5 ff., Franz Dirlmeier asserts that Plato's Dialogues were published twice: "Nachdem sie durch Rezitation im Kreise der Akademie eine Erstpublikation, ihre Uraufführung gehabt hatten, verblieben sie nicht nur in einem Exemplar etwa als Archivstücke in der Obhut der Akademie, sondern sie wurden ein zweites mal, in dem uns geläufigen Sinne publik gemacht." Dirlmeier adduces no proofs of his assertion, for the excellent reason that no such proofs exist. We simply do not know whether Plato ever recited his Dialogues to the Academy or not. Nor do we know whether the Academy possessed 'deposit copies' of the Dialogues or not. (This applies also to the statements in B. A. van Groningen, "Ἔκδοσις", *Mn*, 1963, pp. 1–17). Nevertheless, K.-H. Ilting speaks about Dirlmeier's "Feststellung" that the Platonic Dialogues were published in this way. Furthermore, Ilting asserts that the *On the Good* was an unfinished outline of a philosophic system, made in ca. 366–355 B.C., published before 352 B.C., without Plato's authorization, by at least five of his disciples ("Platons 'Ungeschriebene Lehre': der Vortrag über das Gute", *Phronesis*, 13, 1968, pp. 1–31). Ilting even knows that this work was about the same size as an average Dialogue and that Plato's recitation of it lasted a whole day!

100. On Albinus, see above, pp. 64 f., cf. above, n. VI 14.

101. To my knowledge, in his energetic fight for the esoteric character of the περὶ τἀγαθοῦ Krämer adduces Albinus only twice, "Akademie", p. 75 n. 6, and *Geistmetaphysik*, p. 110, where he rightly says that Albinus' source cannot have been Aristoxenus, "weil das Motiv der Esoterik fehlt"—a remarkable admission.

102. *Geschichte und System der Platonischen Philosophie*, I, pp. 78 ff. As we have seen, Hermann subsequently changed his mind, se above, pp. 67 ff.

103. *Op. cit.*, II, p. 139 n. 2.

104. *Op. cit.*, II: I⁶, pp. 416 ff.

105. *Platon*, I², pp. 494.

106. *Platon*, I³, pp. 96 and 369 (n. 3).

107. *Studien zur Entstehungsgeschichte der Metaphysik des Aristoteles*, pp. 140 ff., Jaeger's declaration has naturally been quoted with high approval by the Esoterists, see Krämer, *Arete*, pp. 14, 19, 22, and passim, and Gaiser, *Platons ungeschriebene Lehre*², p. 16. Subsequently, however, Jaeger seems to have abandoned this view, for it does not appear in his later writings on Plato, where, on the contrary, he comes nearer to the position of Schleiermacher, see above, pp. 50 ff.

108. *Plato*⁶, p. 10.

109. *Op. cit.*, p. 503.

110. *Greek Philosophy*, I, pp. 220 ff.—Of course, Taylor's and Burnet's main reason for

such a view was their belief that Plato became an independent thinker only in his old age, after having written most of the Dialogues.

111. See Krämer, *Arete*, pp. 19 ff. and passim—with characteristical reservations against Stenzel's interest in the Dialogues—and Gaiser's Introduction to a reprint of Stenzel's *Platon als Erzieher* (2d ed., Hamburg, 1961; the original edition was published in 1928).

112. Stenzel, *op. cit.*, pp. 96 ff., 309 ff., and his assertion, supporting Jaeger, that there was a Platonic philosophy "besides" the Dialogues, see "Literarische Form und philosophischer Gehalt des platonischen Dialoges" (*Studien zur Entwicklung der platonischen Dialektik*, 3d ed., Stuttgart, 1961), p. 123.

113. Pp. 56 ff.

114. See, e.g., Krämer, *Arete*, pp. 17 ff., 33 ff., 381 ff.; "Akademie", p. 80; "Retraktationen", p. 162, Gaiser, *Protreptik und Paränese*, passim., and *Platons ungeschriebene Lehre*[2], pp. 1 ff., 8 ff., 15 ff., 335 ff. Gaiser is generally less negative towards the Dialogues than Krämer, but see the latter's admission, quoted below, p. 89.

115. Pp. 69 f.

116. See *Plato's Idea of Poetical Inspiration*, pp. 12 and 62, and the literature quoted there, especially de Vries, *Spel bij Plato*. Cf. also the observations in R. Maurer, *Platons 'Staat' und die Demokratie*, pp. 226 ff.

117. *Arete*, pp. 461 ff.

118. *Laws* III 685 A, cf. IV 712 B, VI 769 A.

119. *Laws* VII 803 C, cf. de Vries, *op. cit.*, pp. 22 ff. Characteristically, this passage is not quoted by Krämer.

120. Krämer, *Arete*, pp. 389 ff., cf. "Fragen", pp. 136 ff. The passages in question are: *Protagoras* 357 B; *Republic* 506 D ff.; *Phaedrus* 246 A and 274 A; *Sophist* 254 C ff.; *Statesman* 262 C, 263 B, 284 C, *Timaeus* 28 C, 48 C, 53 D. Cf. K. von Fritz, "Die philosophische Stelle im Siebenten Brief und die Frage der 'esoterischen' Philosophie" (*Phronesis*, 11, 1966), pp. 139 ff.

121. Thus the passages in the *Phaedrus* can hardly be called "refusals" nor the passages in the *Sophist* and the *Statesman*.

122. *Republic* VI 506 E–507 A; I follow Paul Shorey's translation in the LCL-edition of the *Republic*, II (London, 1935), pp. 95 ff.

123. See, e.g., Shorey, *op. cit.*, II, p. 95 n.f., *What Plato Said*, pp. 76 and 454, and especially "The Idea of God in Plato's *Republic*" (*University of Chicago Studies in Classical Philology*, I, 1895, pp. 188–239), Friedländer, *Platon*, I[3], pp. 156 ff. and Merlan, "Form and Content in Plato's Philosophy" (*JHI*, 8, 1947, pp. 407–430), p. 421.

124. *Ep.* VII 344 B, see above, pp. 69 f.

125. As, à propos of the passage in the *Republic*, Friedländer excellently says: "Da ist es die Unsagbarkeit der höchsten platonischen Sicht, die durch die Ironie des sokratischen Nichtwissens symbolisiert wird" (*op. cit.*, I[3], p. 157). See also Paul Plass, "Philosophic Anonymity and Irony in the Platonic Dialogue" (*AJPh*, 85, 1964, pp. 254–278). Krämer reveals himself as deaf to this irony, when, in a subsequent paper, he asserts that Socrates' refusal to speak about the Good "now", shows that the refusal is "nicht schlecht hin 'unsagbar', sondern dass Platon Sokrates absichtlich zurückhalten lässt" ("Fragen", p. 131 n. 87). Such an interpretation convinces only him that already believes in Krämer's thesis. This way of interpreting is a logical circle, *pace* Krämer, "Retraktationen", pp. 165 ff.

126. See H.-D. Voigtländer's review of Krämer's *Arete*, *AGPh*, 45 (1963), pp. 205 ff. Cf. also von Fritz, "Die philosophische Stelle", pp. 139 ff.

127. See "Retraktationen", pp. 143 ff.; most of Krämer's retort is simply a repetition of the argumentation in *Arete.*

128. Krämer calls these hints "hypomnematische Winke für die Teilnehmer des akademischen Unterrichts" ("Fragen", p. 131 n. 87).

129. In his paper, "Über den Zusammenhang von Prinzipienlehre und Dialektik bei Platon" (*Ph*, 110, 1966, pp. 35–70), Krämer tries to prove that the passage *Republic* VII 534 B–C about dialectics is intelligible only in the light of the Secret Doctrine.—Krämer much resents that Plato's unwritten doctrine is called "secret" ("Fragen", p. 121 n. 52 and p. 124). But "secret" it must have been to anyone who did not belong to the Academy.

130. *Arete,* p. 20 n. 15 a.

131. On Krämer's subsequent "retractatio", see below, pp. 88 f.

132. Gaiser declares that "*in den Dialogen jeweits nur einzelne Aspekte* in den Blick gerückt werden" (*Platons ungeschriebene Lehre*², p. 338 n. 8; italics Gaiser's).

133. The collection of Testimonia Platonica in Gaiser's *Platons ungeschriebene Lehre* is useful but neither complete nor correct, as he himself later admitted, see "Probleme", p. 31 n. 2, and the "Nachwort" to the second edition of the book (1968), pp. 578 ff., cf. the review of the first edition by de Strycker (*Revue belge de philologie et d'histoire*, 45 1967, pp. 116–123), p. 121, and K.-H. Ilting (*Gn*, 37, 1965), p. 144.

134. This is the case with the passage Sextus Empiricus, *Adversus Mathematicos* X 248–283, which P. Wilpert believed to be dependent on the περὶ τἀγαθοῦ, see his "Neue Fragmente aus περὶ τἀγαθοῦ" (*H*, 76, 1941, pp. 225–253) and *Zwei aristotelische Frühschriften über die Ideenlehre* (Regensburg, 1949). Wilpert's thesis was embraced by the Esoterists, and Gaiser printed the whole section in his Testimonia (*op. cit.*, pp. 496–502). Cf. also Ross, *Plato's Theory of Ideas*, pp. 185 ff. But other scholars have strongly rejected Wilpert's interpretation, see J. L. Ackrill's review of the former's book (*M*, 61, 1952, pp. 102–113), pp. 110 ff., Merlan, *From Platonism to Neoplatonism*³, pp. 203 ff., and Gregory Vlastos's review of Krämer's *Arete* (*Gn*, 35, 1963), pp. 644 ff. Although Gaiser preserved his belief in the Platonic origin of the Sextus passage, he changed his mind about its source. In the first edition of his book, he declared that it could be traced back to Aristotle's περὶ φιλοσοφίας cf. p. 497, but in the second edition (p. 578 n. 3) and in "Probleme", pp. 63 ff., he stated that the source of the passage was "eine Nachschrift von Platons περὶ τἀγαθοῦ aus der Alten Akademie", although in a Neopythagorean revision. *Adhuc sub iudice lis est.* The same must be said about Klaus Oehler's attempt to find "Neue Fragmente bei Porphyrios zum esoterischen Platon" (*H*, 93, 1965; reprinted in *Antike Philosophie und Byzantinisches Mittelalter*, Munich, 1969, pp. 222–233), for it was decisively rejected by Ilting, "Platons ungeschriebene Lehre" (*Phronesis*, 13, 1968), p. 15. n. 30, cf. now also I. Tarán's criticism (*Gn*, 46, 1974, pp. 545 ff.).

135. See Gaiser, "Probleme", p. 84, and Krämer, *Arete*, pp. 380 ff.

136. Taylor, *Plato*⁶, p. 503, cf. Burnet, *Greek Philosophy*, I, p. 222. Actually, as we have seen (above p. 64), Aristotle speaks only once of Plato's ἄγραφα δόγματα, cf. Cherniss, *Riddle*, p. 2.

137. Stenzel, *Platon als Erzieher*, p. 309. Earlier scholars had made similar suggestions, see Hermann, *op. cit.*, I, pp. 711 (n. 750). In *A history of Greek Philosophy*, III (Cambridge, 1969), p. 359 n. 1, W. K. C. Guthrie states that "from Aristotle's description (of the ἄγραφα δογματα) it does not sound as if they (Plato's later doctrines) were actually never committed to writing but rather that they were unpublished notes for use within the school". It is strange that the words "*unwritten* doctrines" should mean that the doctrines *were* written. But Guthrie

is not the inventor of this argumentation, for it occurs long before him in Tennemann, see *Decline and Fall,* p. 104 n. 521.

138. *Arete,* p. 14 n. 4, 376 n. 248, 409 n. 55.

139. Merlan, "Greek Philosophy from Plato to Plotinus" (*Cambridge History*), p. 15, cf. *From Platonism to Neoplatonism*[3], passim, especially pp. 195 ff., cf. further his paper "Zwei Bemerkungen zum aristotelischen Plato" (cf. above, n. VI 10). I have purposely quoted Merlan's summary, because he was favourably disposed towards the Esoterist. Other summaries can be found in Wilpert, *Zwei aristotelische Frühschriften* and in Cherniss, *Riddle,* pp. 7 ff. A very detailed survey of Aristotle's statements about Plato is given in Robin, *Theorie platonicienne,* see above, p. 60. But the most lucid exposition remains that in Zeller, *op. cit.,* II: 1[6], pp. 497 ff.—Shorey, *Unity,* pp. 82 ff., found the statements about Plato in the Aristotelian *Metaphysics* muddled and unintelligible, cf. also his review of Stenzel's *Zahl und Gestalt* (*CPh,* 19, 1924, pp. 381–383).

140. Gaiser's *Testimonia* is a convenient collection of texts but must be used with caution, cf. above, n. VI 133, 134. A more restricted and therefore more reliable selection of texts can be read in C. J. de Vogel, *Greek Philosophy,* I (2d ed., Leiden, 1957), pp. 277 ff. A translation of the relevant Aristotelian fragments by Sir David Ross is included in the Oxford translation of *The Works of Aristotle,* XII.

141. See the excellent survey of earlier scholarship in the Foreword to Cherniss, *Aristotle's Criticism of Plato and the Academy,* I, which relieves me of going into details.

142. Heinrich von Stein was one of them, see *op. cit.,* II, pp. 76 ff. However, he admitted the possibility that Aristotle was aided by Plato's oral utterances which "die dunklen Andeutungen der Dialoge in der von Platon beabsichtigten Richtung auffassen liessen" (p. 114). But to Stein, these oral utterances did not contain any "Geheimlehre" (p. 139).

143. Cf. Krämer, *Arete,* pp. 383 ff.

144. In his book, *Plato's Symposium,* cf. below, pp. 81, 97 f.

145. *Op. cit.,* p. XVII.

146. Actually, H. von Stein regarded Plotinus as a true Platonist; "in ihm kommt der ganze und wahrhafte Platon noch einmal zu Worte" (*op. cit.,* II, p. 317).

147. Although Krämer has made some valiant attempts, see above, n. VI 125 and VI 129. See also Gaiser, "Platons *Menon*" (above, n. VI 64). Miss de Vogel has defended the Neoplatonic interpretation of the *Parmenides*—on which see E. R. Dodds, "The *Parmenides* of Plato and the Neoplatonic 'One'" (*cR,* 22, 1928, pp. 129–143)—see her paper, "On the Neoplatonic character of Platonism and the Platonic character of Neoplatonism" (*M,* 62, 1953; reprinted in *Philosophia,* I, pp. 355–377), pp. 370 ff., but with formulations which reveal how different her viewpoint is from the Neoplatonic one. Concerning other modern attempts to renew the Neoplatonic interpretation of the *Parmenides,* see F. M. Cornford, *Plato and Parmenides* (London, 1939), pp. V ff. *Curiositatis causa,* we may mention Egil A. Wyller, *Platons Parmenides in seinem Zusammenhang mit Symposium und Politeia. Studien zur platonischen Henologie* (Skrifter utgitt af Det Norske Videnskaps-Akademie, II. Hist.-Filos. Klasse, 1959: 1)—a strange mixture of Proclus and Heidegger, cf. the reviews by W. Perpeet (*Philosophische Rundschau,* 10, 1962, pp. 254–262) and D. M. Balme (*Gn,* 34, 1962, pp. 308–310). As appears also from a little book in Norwegian (*Plato,* Oslo, 1960) and a bigger book in German (*Der späte Platon,* Hamburg, 1970), the mystical theology or metaphysics which to Wyller constitutes the essence of Platonism cannot be analysed or criticized according to the usual rules of interpretation, see *Plato,* pp. 22, 28 ff., for at least the philosophy of Plato's later years is based on a vision which the interpreter must elucidate intuitively, see *Der*

späte Platon, pp. 9 ff. Evidently, such an interpretation lies on a level different from that of mere philological interpretation.

148. Rosen, *op. cit.*, p. XVII.

149. *Op. cit.,* p. XXVI.

150. Rosen refers to Leo Strauss's interesting work, *Persecution and the Art of Writing* (Glencoe, Ill., 1952). But as a general method of interpreting pre-Enlightenment philosophic works, this viewpoint invites abuse.—On Numenius, see above, p. 65, on Tennemann, see *Decline and Fall,* pp. 9 ff., 66 ff., and 104 (n. 546).

151. It is a pity that both books lack Indices.

152. Baltimore, 1935. Werner Jaeger's critical but appreciative review (reprinted in his *Scripta Minora,* II, Rome, 1960, pp. 161–168) is of interest, not least because at first sight Jaeger would hardly appear to be the man to appreciate Cherniss's achievement.

153. Cherniss's general thesis has been strongly criticized by W. K. C. Guthrie, "Aristotle as a Historian of Philosophy" (*JHS,* 77, 1957, pp. 35–41). In his great work, *A History of Greek Philosophy,* of which hitherto four Volumes have appeared (I–IV, Cambridge, 1962–75)—the 'Zeller' of our times—Guthrie has had ample opportunity to voice his opposition to Cherniss. The latter's treatment of Aristotle's attitude to Plato has further been criticized in Friedrich Solmsen's important review of Cherniss's *Riddle* (*CW,* 40, 1946/47, pp. 164–168), in C. J. de Vogel's "Problems concerning Later Platonism, I–II" (*Mn,* 1949, pp. 197–216, 299–318; reprinted in a revised form, as "Problems concerning Plato's Later Doctrines" in *Philosophia* I., pp. 256–292), in Sir David Ross, *Plato's Theory of Ideas,* and in Merlan, *From Platonism to Neoplatonism*[3].

154. This applies especially to Krämer, whom Willy Theiler has jokingly called "the Anti-Cherniss" (*Untersuchungen zur antiken Literatur,* pp. 462 f.). See, e.g., *Arete,* pp. 380 ff., and "Fragen", passim; in *Geistmetaphysik,* too, Krämer, often polemizes against Cherniss.

155. *Plato's Idea of Poetical Inspiration,* p. 10 n. 21.

156. Epicrates fr. 11 Kock, see Cherniss, *Riddle,* pp. 62 ff.—The scanty and often elusive statements about Plato and the Academy in the Attic Comedy are well discussed by G. J. de Vries, "De filosof in de komedie" (*Hermeneus,* 27, 1955, pp. 2–9). See further above, n. IV 129.

157. See below, pp. 88 ff.

158. Cherniss, *op. cit.,* p. 55, cf. Solmsen's comments (*op. cit.,* p. 168).

159. This was also Erich Frank's view, see his paper "The Fundamental Opposition of Plato and Aristotle" (*op. cit.*), p. 94.

160. See the pertinent remarks in Gregory Vlastos's excellent review of Krämer's *Arete,* (*Gn,* 35, 1963, pp. 641–655), with which I in the main agree.

161. Pointed out by a believer in the Esoteric Plato, Philip Merlan, "Bemerkungen zum neuen Platonbild", p. 125. See above, p. 15.

162. Cf. Vlastos, *op. cit.,* p. 654 ff.

163. Cherniss, *Aristotle's Criticism,* I, p. IX. Cherniss does not quote the important passage in Cicero, *Tusculanae Disputationes* III 69, whose authenticity has recently been defended against Düring by Dirlmeier, "Merkwürdige Zitate", pp. 42 ff., cf. above, n. VI 99.

164. Stein, *op. cit.,* II, pp. 76 ff.

165. Taylor, *Plato*[6], p. 503.

166. *Platonism* (Sather Classical Lectures, V, 1928, Berkeley, Cal.), p. 56, cf. p. 121.

167. Thus Taylor, *l.c.,* and Burnet, *Greek Philosophy,* I, pp. 312 ff.

168. Cf. Cherniss, *Riddle*, p. 9, and von Fritz, "Zur Frage der 'esoterischen' Philosophie Platons" (*AGPh*, 49, 1967), pp. 258 ff.

169. "Fragen", p. 106.

170. *Platons ungeschriebene Lehre²*, p. 522. In another passage (p. 431 n. 291), Gaiser makes the astonishing statement (from his point of view) that Aristotle was never really a Platonist. For Plato said in the *Seventh Epistle* (344 E) that the knowledge of the highest principles, once grasped, can never be forgotten: "Da nun aber Aristoteles die platonische Prinzipienlehre im wesentlichen verwirft, ist anzunehmen, dass er die Ideenschau im Sinne Platons nie wirklich mitvollgezogen hat." Nevertheless, Gaiser is willing to rely on Aristotle's account of Plato's Secret Doctrine!

171. "On the Neoplatonic Character of Platonism" (*Philosophia*, I), p. 367 (cf. above, n. VI 147); that "perhaps" is curious.

172. *Plato's Theory of Ideas*, p. 143.

173. Cf. Cherniss, *Riddle*, p. 20.

174. See Ackrill's remarks in his review of Wilpert, quoted above, n. VI 134.

175. Gaiser says: "Jedenfalls muss bei der Rekonstruktion der mündlichen Lehre Platons damit gerechnet werden, dass schon die Berichte der unmittelbaren Schüler in verschiedener Weise durch Umdeutungen entstellt sind; und schon allein deshalb ist jede Untersuchung der von Schülern stammenden Zeugnisse über das esoterische System Platons methodisch genötigt, die Dialoge als Grundlage der Kritik anzuerkennen" (*op. cit.*, pp. 339 ff. n. 13)—an admission which in reality ruins the Esoterists' reconstruction, cf. below, pp. 88 f.—See further Merlan, "Greek Philosophy from Plato to Plotinus", pp. 16 ff., and Theiler, "Einheit und unbegrenzte Zweiheit von Plato bis Plotin" (*Untersuchungen zur antiken Literatur*, p. 40 n. 18): "wo Plato seinen famuli nicht alles zu enthüllen schien, mussten sich diese (in gewisser Weise auch Aristoteles) von sich aus die Sache zurechtlegen".

176. Burkert, *Weisheit und Wissenschaft*, p. 26.

177. Kurt von Fritz deplores the tendency of modern Platonic scholars, "gerade das am wenigstens zuverlässig Überlieferte als des Wertvollste, das wir haben, zu betrachten" ("Zur Frage der 'esoterischen Philosophie Platos'", p. 256). See also H.-G. Gadamer, "Platons ungeschriebene Lehre" (*Idee und Zahl*), p. 12.

178. Helmut Kuhn, "Platon und die Grenze philosophischer Mitteilung" (*Idee und Zahl*), pp. 157 ff.

179. See above, pp. 73 ff., and 77 ff., and below, pp. 90 f.

180. *Riddle*, pp. 3 and 9.

181. *From Platonism to Neoplatonism³*, p. 195, cf. p. 228.

182. *Op. cit.*, p. 231. Merlan maintained the same *epoché* in his survey of "Greek Philosophy from Plato to Plotinus" in *The Cambridge History*.

183. As was pointed out by H. Dörrie in his important review of the first edition of Merlan's *From Platonism to Neoplatonism* in *Philosophische Rundschau*, 3 (1955), pp. 14–25.

184. Although believing in a final phase of Plato's thought, "seine letzten Lehren", Wilamowitz issued a strong warning against the reports of the disciples: "Solche Berichte sind immer mit grosser Vorsicht aufzunehmen, und niemals darf, was ein Denker nicht selbst als Fertiges gegeben hat, auf gleiche Linie mit seinen Werken gestellt, noch viel weniger aus dem ergänzt werden, was die Schüler aus seinen letzten Andeutungen machen" (*Platon*, I², p. 715).

185. This is the position of, e.g., Paul Wilpert, *Zwei aristotelische Frühschriften*, passim, who speaks of Plato's "Altersphilosophie", and of Sir David Ross, *Plato's Theory of Ideas*, pp.

143 ff. Merlan, too, was inclined to think so, see his review of Gaiser's *Platons ungeschriebene Lehre* in *Gymnasium*, 72 (1963), pp. 543–546.

186. See Cherniss, *Riddle*, pp. 4 ff., and F. P. Hager, "Zur philosophischen Problematik der sogenannten ungeschriebenen Lehre Platos" (*Studia Philosophica*, 24, 1964, pp. 90–117).

187. As Taylor pointed out (*Plato*[6], p. 504).

188. As the Esoterists have not failed to observe, see Krämer, *Arete*, p. 21 n. 18, and "Fragen", p. 113. Gaiser, however, admits that in the disciples' report of the *On the Good* "wahrscheinlich die späteste Fassung der Lehre Platons festgehalten war" (*Platons ungeschriebene Lehre*[2], p. 15).

189. See the characteristic paper of Klaus Oehler, "Der Entwicklungsgedanke als heuristisches Prinzip der Philosophiegeschichte" (*Antike Philosophie und byzantinisches Mittelalter*, pp. 38–47).

190. See above, p. 67.

191. Krämer, *Arete*, pp. 33 ff.

192. *Op. cit.*, passim, see. e.g., pp. 298 ff., 319 ff., 443. See further "Fragen", p. 129, "Retraktationen", p. 166 n. 100, and "Akademie", p. 92. See also Oehler, *op. cit.*, pp. 75 and 90 ff.

193. *Arete*, pp. 487 ff.

194. *Op. cit.*, p. 485.

195. See Gaiser, *Protreptik und Paränese bei Platon*, cf. Oehler, *op. cit.*, pp. 78 and 90, and Krämer, "Akademie", p. 81.

196. Gaiser, *op. cit.*, p. 19.

197. Gaiser, *op. cit.*, p. 20: "Vorspiel und exoterisch-protreptische Hinführung zum wesentlichen sind die Schriften Platons."

198. Krämer, *Arete*, p. 471.

199. *Op. cit.*, p. 471 n. 181.

200. *Op. cit.*, p. 479 n. 195; Krämer adduces Merlan's more cautiously worded statement in his "Beiträge zur Geschichte des antiken Platonismus" (*Ph*, 89, 1934, pp. 35–53, 197–214), p. 213. But as we have seen, Merlan always hesitated to attribute the systematic tradition to Plato himself, cf. above, p. 84.

201. Although rejecting the genetic interpretation of Plato, the Esoterists accept without further discussion the current chronology of the Dialogues, cf., e.g., Gaiser, *Platons ungeschriebene Lehre*[2], pp. 15 ff.

202. See the hesitation of Gaiser, *l.c.*, who believes that in these Dialogues Plato "purposedly" suppressed the Esoteric Doctrine, and Krämer, "Fragen", p. 134 ff., who even says that we must take into account the possibility of an evolution of the Unwritten Doctrine itself—a dangerous concession, cf. below, p. 90. Krämer tries to bolster up his belief in an early fixation with the argument that most great philosophers—Kant being an exception—arrive at their final philosophy pretty early, between thirty and forty ("Akademie", pp. 93 f., and "Fragen", p. 134, a circumstance also proved by the Greeks dating a man's ἀκμή to the age of forty.) It is difficult to take so frivolous an argument seriously. Schelling and Nietzsche—to mention only these two—changed their philosophy several times, and, if Werner Jaeger and other scholars are to be believed, that is true of Aristotle, too. In such cases, the golden rule is that there is no golden rule.—On the motives of Apollodorus' use for the acme-conception in his *Chronica*—*inter alia* Pythagorean numerology—see Felix Jacoby, *Apollodors Chronik* (Philologische Untersuchungen, 16, Berlin 1902), pp. 41 ff., who gives a survey of popular Greek belief in the age of forty as being the climax of Man's life.

203. See Krämer, *Arete*, pp. 507 ff., 534 ff., cf., Gaiser, *Platons ungeschriebene Lehre*[2], pp. 395 ff. n. 190.

204. See Pierre Boyancé's eulogy *Latomus*, 29, 1970, pp. 543–547 and Merlan's sympathetic but critical review (*Philosophische Rundschau*, 15, 1968, pp. 97–100), cf. "Bemerkungen zum neuen Platobild", pp. 122 ff. On the contrary, the fellow-Esoterist Klaus Oehler declares brutally: "Krämers Unternehmen ist gescheitert" (*Gn*, 40, 1969; reprinted *op. cit.*, p. 161), cf. further Maurer, *Platons 'Staat' und die Demokratie*, pp. 226 ff., 251 ff.

205. *Arete*, pp. 520 ff. Krämer stresses: "*Die grosse Umwälzung, die sich von Sokrates zu Platon hin vollzieht beruht demnach ... auf dem dialektischen Durchbruch Platons zur letzten unbedingten Begränzung, dem Seinsgrund selbst, und damit zur Ontologie letzter Instanz* (pp. 528 f.; italics Krämer's).

206. "Plato ist nicht Sokrates", Krämer says irritatedly ("Fragen", p. 140 n. 118). On the Neoplatonic neglect of Socrates, see *Decline and Fall*, pp. 7 ff., 32 ff.

207. If we can trust the Indices, Socrates is not so much as mentioned in Gaiser's *Platons ungeschriebene Lehre*.

208. Even an admirer of Krämer, Karl Voretska, has felt compelled to protest against this neglect of Socrates, see his review of *Arete* in *Anzeiger für die Altertumswissenschaft*, 18 (1965), cols. 33–37.

209. See above, pp. 64, 75 ff.

210. "Fragen", p. 137.

211. See above, p. 63.

212. See the paper "Bemerkungen zum neuen Platobild", often quoted above.

213. Cf. the characteristically cautious statement: "Das es ein mündliches System Platos gegeben hat, sollte *doch wohl* (italics mine) zugegeben werden" (*op. cit.*, p. 123).

214. More than thirty years earlier, Merlan finished his "Beiträge zur Geschichte des antiken Platonismus" (*Ph*, 89, 1934, pp. 33–53, 197–214) with the revealing words: "Der 'unsystematische' Platon ist ein undankbares Studium; in gewisser Hinsicht ist Aristoteles viel leichter." He is, indeed.

215. "Der entmythologisierte Platon" (*Antike Philosophie und byzantinisches Mittelalter*), p. 89, see Merlan's remarks (*op. cit.*, pp. 118 ff.). Cf. Heinrich von Stein's description of an unexperienced reader's reaction at his first confrontation with Plato (*op. cit.*, I, 5 ff.), see above, p. 15. But Stein did not draw Oehler's conclusion.

216. Cf. what a modern philosopher who was also an expert on Greek philosophy said about this prejudice:

"Die Platonischen Dialoge, deren untersuchende Grundhaltung vorbildlich geworden ist, stellen den Urtypus echter philosophischer Einstellung auf die Probleme als solche dar. Die philosophische Ahnungslosigkeit der Philologen hat von jeher die scheinbare Resultatlosigkeit vieler dieser Dialoge missverstanden, ja sie deshalb für blosse Einführungs- und Populärschriften erklären zu müssen gemeint. Man glaubte zu wissen, dass der Kern der Platonischen Philosophie ganz wo anders liege, in einer „Ideenlehre", deren Systembild man nur sehr unvollkommen und in immer neuen Fassungen schillernd in diesen Schriften fand. Man ging stillschweigend davon aus, Platon sei ein Systembildner im Sinne seiner späten Nachfahren; man überlegte gar nicht erst, ob er nicht vielmehr die konstruktiven Konsequenzen gescheut habe. Und doch musste dem Sokratiker nichts näher liegen als das." (Nikolai Hartmann, *Kleinere Schriften*, Berlin, I, 1956, p. 4.)

A similar but cruder expression of the same attitude towards the Dialogues occurs in J. N.

Findlay, *Plato. The Written and Unwritten Doctrines* (London, 1974), pp. IX ff. The whole book is a very uncritical attempt to construct a Platonic system. Findlay accepts the Aristotelian account of the Platonic Number-Ideas, as also the Neoplatonic systematization of Platonism, and naturally adduces the modern Esoterists. Strange to say, Findlay asserts that the Unwritten Doctrine remained unwritten, "because it never became more than a programme, one that inspired all Plato's efforts, but that he was never able to implement fully. What he was unable to communicate to others was also what he was unable to say clearly to himself, the predicament of many great thinkers" (p. XI). After these disquieting words, Findlay adds confidently: "But, despite this, it is a thoroughly intelligible programme." That is to say: Plato did not understand himself, but Findlay does understand him—in contrast to Aristotle, who "never understood Plato's programme". A reconstruction of Plato's thought which is animated by such a naïve presumptuousness cannot be taken seriously. We are reminded of Tennemann, see *Decline and Fall*, p. 67.

217. In contrast to the Norwegian scholar Egil A. Wyller—see above, n. VI 147—who has renewed the Neoplatonic interpretation by amalgamating it with Heidegger's 'Existentialism'. Wyller finds it possible to extract a system from the Dialogues, though he seems to accept the Esoteric reconstruction of Plato's oral teaching (*Der späte Platon*, pp. 3 ff.). But his own interpretation keeps to the Dialogues, though interpreted philosophically, not philologically (*op. cit.*, pp. 5 ff.). To Wyller, Plato's philosophy—at least in the later Dialogues—is a metaphysical system, based on a "vision", experienced in his youth or early manhood (*op. cit.*, pp. 9 ff.). The Dialogues are not expressions of a quest for truth, for Plato knew in advance what he would find, but attempts to make the truth ever more present and clear to his readers (*op. cit.*, pp. 76 ff.). This conception of Platonism as a system consequently differs from that of Hegel or Zeller, as Wyller points out (*op. cit.*, p. 10). As has been stated above (n. VI 147), this systematization of Plato is based on an intuition which cannot be subjected to a rational criticism.

218. "Problem", p. 71.

219. *Arete*, pp. 14 n. 4, 318 n. 151, 376 n. 248, cf. "Fragen", p. 138 n. 109. It is strange that these statements are tucked away in notes, while in the text, the author continues to talk of lectures. But in another passage (*Arete*, p. 377), Krämer calmly states that these "Gespräche" were, "methodisch vielleicht auch literarisch", "weitgehend" counterparts to the Aristotelian lectures. But the Aristotelian πραγματεῖαι are no discussions.

220. *Arete*, p. 14 n. 4.

221. "Fragen", p. 147 n. 134. As if aware of the dangerous character of this statement, Krämer hastens to add: "freilich nicht, um Verstehen zu verhindern (as according to Krämer, the Socrates of the Dialogues does), sondern um es wirklich zu erzeugen".

222. See above, pp. 72 ff.—As pointed out above, n. VI 99, Gaiser seems to believe in the existence of a semi-official Academic record of Plato's lectures.

223. Krämer, "Fragen", p. 129, cf. Gaiser, *Platons ungeschriebene Lehre*, p. 337 (n. 3).

224. *Op. cit.*, pp. 198 ff.

225. *Platons ungeschriebene Lehre*, p. 5.

226. "Fragen", p. 136.

227. *Ibid.*, p. 137, but cf. *Arete*, p. 20 n. 15a, quoted above, p. 76.

228. *Op. cit.*, p. 336 n. 1, but see the statement, pp. 8 ff.

229. "Fragen", p. 140.

230. Oehler, *op. cit.*, p. 79.

231. *Op. cit.,* p. 87, cf. Merlan's commentary ("Bemerkungen zum neuen Platobild", pp. 118 ff.).

232. Krämer tries to parry this argument by asserting that Plato *could* have written down his last wisdom ("Fragen", p. 148). But this assertion does not tally with what, in the passages just quoted, both Krämer himself and Oehler say, still less with what the former says in the passage quoted below.

233. Krämer, *Arete,* pp. 464 n. 17, 480, 544 n. 107, and "Akademie", pp. 96 ff.

234. "Fragen", p. 140 n. 119. This comes dangerously close to Merlan's conception of a 'third' Plato, inaccessible to all, like the One of the Neoplatonists. (One wonders whether Merlan's three Platos were not unconsciously inspired by the three Neoplatonic Hyposthases).

VII. *The Fair Risk*

1. See above, p. 15.

2. Cf. Friedländer, *Platon, I*³, p. 134.

3. See above, p. 58. Cf. Lesky, *Geschichte der griechischen Literatur*³, p. 478.

4. This has been pertinently pointed out by Gerhard Krüger, *Einsicht und Leidenschaft* (Francfort, 1939), pp. 71 ff., though some of his conclusions may be doubted.

5. Cf. Lesky: "Zum Wesen dieser sublimen Spiele gehört die Kunst der Einleitungen" (*op. cit.,* p. 579). See further Fritz Muthmann's dissertation, *Untersuchungen zur "Einkleidung" einiger platonischen Dialoge* (Bonn, 1961), which, however, does not treat of the *Parmenides*.

6. *Parmenides* 126 A–127 A. I have used H. N. Fowler's translation in the LCL-Plato (VI, London, 1926).

7. *Parmenides* 137 B: ἐπειδή περ δοκεῖ πραγματειώδη παιδιὰν παίζειν. Of course, this ironical self-depreciation is as ambiguous as its numerous Socratic counterparts, cf. Karsten Friis Johansen, *Studier over Platons Parmenides i dess forhold til tidligere platonske dialoger* (Diss. Copenhagen, 1964), p. 242, who, however, does not discuss Antiphon's role.

8. Robert S. Brumbaugh, *Plato on the One* (New Haven, 1961), pp. 26 ff.

9. Edward G. Ballard, *Socratic Ignorance* (The Hague, 1965), p. 81.

10. See *Procli Philosophi Opera Inedita. Pars Tertia, continens Procli Commentarii in Platonis Parmenidem,* ed. Victor Cousin (Paris, 1864; I quote the reprint, Hildesheim, 1961), cols. 625 ff. Cf. the notes in A.-Ed. Chaignet's French translation, *Proclus le Philosophe, Commentaire sur le Parmenide,* I (Paris, 1900; I quote the reprint, Francfort, 1962), pp. 54 ff. Brumbaugh's belief that the nameless Clazomenians who had followed Aphalus to Athens were supporters of Anaxagoras, is already in Proclus (Cousin, col., 625, 10–14, cf. Chaignet, I, p. 54).

11. Cf. René Schaerer's commentary; "Et c'est distraitement, sans doute, en revant à ses pur sang et regrettant le temps qu'on lui fait perdre qu'il /Antiphon/ devidera son chapelet d'arguments" (*La question platonicienne,* p. 196). But when Schaerer adds: "Le prologue n'explique donc rien", we may wonder whether this very circumstance does not ask for an explanation. Wilamowitz says crossly about the Prologue: "Die wunderliche Erfindung hat nur den Zweck, das Gespräch irgendwie scheinbar zu beglaubigen und erfüllt ihn schlecht genug" (*Platon,* II², p. 21). On the contrary, Lesky, *op. cit.,* p. 579, speaks of "Die wohl überlegte Dissonanz zwischen Rahmen und Gehalt" in the *Parmenides*. Unfortunately, he does not further explain his statement. A. E. Taylor, who regarded the *Parmenides* as "an elaborate *jeu d'esprit*" (*op. cit.,* p. 351), thought that Plato "by insisting on the early date of the

conversation, and the fact that no one is living who could check the third-hand report of what passed ... frees himself from responsibility for the strict accuracy of his narrative" (p. 352).—Outdoing Proclus, Egil A. Wyller, finds a deep and sinister sense in Antiphon's desertion of philosophy, for unlike his brothers, he had penetrated the awful secret of the Dialogue: "Der platonische Logos pendelt *zwischen* der oberen Freiheit zum nihil mysteriosum und der unteren Freiheit zum Gar-nichts" (*Platons Parmenides,* pp. 178 ff.), cf. the critical remarks in Friis Johansen, *op. cit.,* pp. 266 ff. A different but equally fanciful over-pretation, this time of the Prologue to the *Symposium,* can be read in Rosen, *Plato's Symposium,* pp. 1–38, where we are told, e.g., that at the banquet in Agathon's house, "Socrates and Aristodemus are fundamentally Hellenes among Trojans" (p. 30). The whole book is interesting as an example of what an inventive and uninhibited reader may discover in Plato.

12. See *Plato's Idea of Poetical Inspiration,* passim, and especially pp. 11 ff., where the literature on this topic is indicated (p. 25).

13. In his *Plato* (II², p. 30), Wilamowitz spoke of "the unhappy exaggerations to which unfortunately good ideas irreparably fall a victim".

14. Rosen, *Plato's Symposium,* p. XIV (italics Rosen's).

15. *Op. cit.,* p. XXVII.—In the same passage Kierkegaard is also mentioned, see further, pp. 278 ff. It is not quite fair to adduce his famous doctoral dissertation, *On the Concept of Irony with Constant Reference to Socrates* (1841), for it was written from a Hegelian viewpoint which subsequently Kierkegaard sharply repudiated, radically altering his opinion on Socrates, see J. Himmelstrup, *Søren Kierkegaards Opfattelse af Sokrates* (Diss. Copenhagen, 1924), pp. 97 ff., 101 ff., 104 ff.

16. *Plato's Idea of Poetical Inspiration,* p. 12.

17. Cf. Schaerer, *op. cit.,* pp. 19–23 ("Le jeu sérieux").

18. *Ibid.,* pp. 43 ff.

19. Of the many treatments of this theme I will only refer to the excellent one in Friedländer, *Platon,* I³, pp. 134 ff. Nor shall I speak about the many attempts to eliminate Socrates more or less radically from the history of Greek and Platonic philosophy of which Olof Gigon, *Sokrates* (Bern, 1947), is easily the most intelligent, cf. *The Legend of Sparta in Classical Antiquity,* I, pp. 242 ff. The modern Esoteric interpretation of Plato amounts to a similar elimination, see above, pp. 86 ff.

20. *Ep.* VII 324 E.

21. On the character and purpose of the *Seventh Epistle,* see above, pp. 44 ff.—To me, the words about Socrates have always seemed a decisive argument in favour of the authenticity of the Epistle.

22. *The Legend of Sparta,* I, p. 242, cf. Friedländer, *op. cit.,* I³, p. 137.

23. Concerning the pre-history of the Socratic and Platonic Dialogue, see the survey in Lesky, *op. cit³.,* pp. 576 ff., and E. G. Schmidt, "Dialogos" in *KP,* II (1967). Rudolf Hirzel's old, solid work, *Der Dialog,* I–II (Leipzig, 1895), is still well worth reading.

24. *Poetics* 1447 b 11.

25. As Schaerer, *op. cit.,* pp. 78 ff., rightly stresses.

26. The unfinished character of the *Laws* appears not least from the circumstance that in long sections of the book the dialogue disappears.

27. As has been done, e.g., by F. M. Cornford in his translation of the *Republic* (Oxford, 1941).

28. See above, pp. 69 ff., 81 ff., and *Plato's Idea of Poetical Inspiration,* pp. 10 ff. To the

literature indicated there may now be added Hermann Gundert, *Dialog und Dialektik. Zur Struktur des platonischen Dialogs* (Amsterdam, 1971).

29. See above, p. 30.

30. See *Plato's Idea of Poetical Inspiration*, p. 6.

31. Thus Richard Robinson, see above, p. 23.—A curious instance of this attitude can be found in most of the contributions to *Studies in Plato's Metaphysics*, ed. R. E. Allen (London, 1965). The learned authors treat of the Platonic Dialogues, as if they were papers written to be read at the meetings of philosophic societies.

32. Zeller, *op. cit.*, II: 1^6, p. 578.

33. *L.c.*

34. Cf. Gundert, *Dialog und Dialektik*, pp. 7 ff.

35. This was no doubt due to Hegel's influence. For the latter—not least owing to his antipathy to the German Romantics, who cultivated the Dialogue, and to Schleiermacher, who stressed its importance to Plato—regarded the Dialogue as simply an impediment to our comprehension of Plato and regretted that his dogmatic works—in whose existence Hegel believed—were not extant, adding that we should not consider the Dialogue as the best form of philosophic exposition, see *Sämtliche Werke, Jubiläumsausgabe*, XVIII (3d ed. Stuttgart, 1959), pp. 179, 182 ff.

36. See above, pp. 16 f.

37. The difference between the two dialogues was pointed out by Stein, *Sieben Bücher zur Geschichte des Platonismus*, I, p. 28.

38. Cf. Schaerer, *op. cit.*, p. 45.

39. *Sophist* 284 B and 286 B, cf. Nachmanson, *Der griechische Buchtitel*, pp. 10 ff.

40. *Critias* 106 A–B.

41. *Theaetetus* 150 D; I use the translation of H. N. Fowler in the LCL-edition of Plato (II, London, 1921).

42. *Meno* 80 A–C; I use the translation of R. M. Lamb in the LCL-edition of Plato (IV, London, 1924).

43. *Theaetetus* 149 A.

44. Leo Strauss, "On a New Interpretation of Plato's Political Philosophy" (*Social Research*, 13, 1946, pp. 326–367), p. 351. The whole paper is well worth reading.

45. Cf. the warning of Ballard, *Socratic Ignorance*, pp. 32 ff., and of Gundert, *op. cit.*, p. 6. Friedländer has devoted two chapters of his monograph to Heidegger's and Jaspers's treatment of Plato (I^3, pp. 233–248).—Jaspers's last word on Plato—the substantial chapter in *Die Grossen Philosophen* I (Munich, 1957), pp. 234–318—is remarkable and testifies to his high admiration for Plato, but the interpretation is expressed in the categories of Jaspers's own thought. On Heidegger's attitude to Plato, see Manasse, *op. cit.*, I, pp. 21 ff.

46. See *Plato's Idea of Poetical Inspiration*, pp. 52 ff. Gerhard Krüger says rightly: "Plato kann Mythen nie ohne Ironie erzählen" (*Einsicht und Leidenschaft*, p. 57).

47. Rosen, *Plato's Symposium*, p. XXIV.

48. Ironically enough, this has happened precisely to a propounder of the 'pan-ironical' interpretation of Plato—a just fate, cf. above, pp. 95 f.

49. Rosen, *l.c.*

50. On the role of the *Logos*, see Schaerer, *op. cit.*, pp. 37 ff.

51. Cf. the similar exhortation *Philebus* 59 B.

52. *Republic* II 349 D and 365 D.

53. *Republic* X 607 B; *Crito* 48 C.

54. *Phaedo* 90 E; I use Fowler's translation of the LCL-edition of Plato (I, London, 1926).

55. *Meno* 86 B–C, cf. n. VII 42.

56. Jaspers, *op. cit.*, I, p. 310.

57. "In die Situation des totalen Unheils", as Jaspers has it (*op. cit.*, I, p. 309).

58. Strauss, *op. cit.*, p. 351.

59. Jaspers, *op. cit.*, I, p. 310.

60. R. E. Allen in his Introduction to *Studies in Plato's Metaphysics*, p. XII.

61. As Socrates says *Theaetetus* 151 B, speaking of Prodicus and other Sophists.

62. *Plato's Idea of Poetical Inspiration*, p. 26.

63. From his point of view, Jaspers found fault with Plato for trying to have any doctrines at all (*op. cit.*, I, pp. 307 ff.).

64. See above, pp. 35 f.

65. See above, pp. 102 f.

66. The New Academy has been rather neglected by scholars. Except for the recent, very unsatisfactory, edition by Bohdan Wiśniecki, *Karneades. Fragmente, Text und Kommentar* (Warsaw, 1970), there is no collection of the fragments and the testimonia, nor is there any comprehensive modern monograph. The most detailed treatment is still the old but solid book by L. Credaro, *Lo scetticismo degli Academici*, I–II (Rome-Milan, 1889–93); as this book is not easily accessible outside Italy, I am grateful to the Biblioteca Nazionale Braidense, Milan, for having put a copy at my disposal. More or less substantial chapters on the New Academy are to be found in general works about Greek scepticism, see, e.g., Rudolf Hirzel, *Untersuchungen zu Cicero's philosophischen Schriften*, III (Berlin, 1883), Victor Brochard, *Les sceptiques grecques* (Paris, 1887); Léon Robin, *Pyrrhon et le scepticisme grecque* (Paris, 1950); the two lastmentioned books have good bibliographies. See further Zeller, *op. cit.*, III: 1[6], (Hildesheim, 1963; reprint of the 4th ed. procured by Ed. Wellmann, 1909), pp. 507 ff., 609 ff., Überweg-Prächter, *op. cit.*, pp. 464–475, 141[x]–143[x], Hans von Arnim's articles, "Arkesilaos" (*RE*, II: 1, 1895), and "Karneades" (*RE*, X: 2, 1919), to which A. Weische has given a supplement (*RES*, XI, 1968), and Olof Gigon, "Zur Geschichte der sogenannten Neuen Akademie" (*MH*, 1, 1944, pp. 47–64). There are now some good remarks on the New Academy in H. J. Krämer, *Platonismus und hellenistische Philosophie* (Berlin, 1971).

67. Cicero's relations with the New Academy is treated in detail by Hirzel, Credaro, and especially by A. Weische, *Cicero und die Neue Akademie* (Münster, 1961), see further the important paper by W. Burkert, "Cicero der Platoniker und Skeptiker. Zum Platonverständnis der 'Neuen Akademie'" (*Gymnasium*, 72, 1965, pp. 175–200), and Pierre Boyancé's survey, "Le Platonisme à Rome. Platon et Cicéron" (1953), reprinted in his *Études sur l'humanisme cicéronien* (Bruxelles, 1970), pp. 222–247; p. 13 n 1. Boyancé announces the publication of a study on the "Academism" of Cicero in the near future.

68. See Cicero, *Academica* I 12, 46, cf. Gigon, *op. cit.*, pp. 62 ff., and Dal Pra, *op. cit.*, pp. 232 ff.

69. Concerning Numenius' accusation, see above, p. 65.

70. On this point, modern scholars have been of widely different opinions, see, e.g., Hirzel, *op. cit.*, III, pp. 22 ff., Zeller, *op. cit.*, III: 1[6], pp. 507 ff., Credaro, *op. cit.*, I, pp. 73 ff., 133 ff.; II, pp. 5 ff., 35 ff., 213–247, Brochard, *op. cit.*, pp. 94 ff., Robin *op. cit.*, pp. 45 ff., Dal Pra, *op. cit.*, pp. 78 ff. The attempt of Weische, *op. cit.*, pp. 51 ff., to derive the scepticism of the New Academy from the Peripatus of Theophrastus and Strato has been criticized by other scholars, see the review by A. Grilli (*Revista di filologia e di istruzione classica*, 92, 1964, pp.

206–209), and especially that by P. Boyancé (*Latomus,* 20, 1961, pp. 583–586), cf. also Karl Büchner, *Cicero* (Heidelberg, 1964), pp. 517 ff.

71. It may be questioned whether we should regard this return to Socrates and Plato as an expression of a general contemporary 'classisistic' attitude to philosophy, which teaches the return to the great masters of the past, as O. Gigon believes, see his paper, "Die Erneuerung der Philosophie in der Zeit Ciceros" (*Entretiens sur l'Antiquité Classique,* III, *Recherches sur la tradition platonicienne,* Verona, 1957), pp. 37 ff., cf. Boyancé's criticism (*Latomus,* 20, 1961, p. 685).—In agreement with Gigon's view would be the hypothesis, voiced by some modern scholars, that it was the New Academy which procured the collected edition of Plato's work that we now possess, see Wilamowitz, *Platon,* II², p. 326, who says of this edition, which contains so many spurious works: "Zur Zeit des Arkesilaos oder Lakydes ist das wohl glaublich, gerade weil der Platon der alten Akademie aufgegeben war"; thus also Giorgio Pasquali, *Storia della tradizione e critica del testo* (2d ed. Florence, 1952), pp. 261 ff. The existence of such an "Academic" edition of Plato was denied by Günther Jachmann but accepted by other scholars, cf. above, n. II 11. See further Antonio Carlini, "Alcuni dialoghi pseudo-platonici e l'Accademia di Arcesilao" (*Annali della Scuola Normale Superiore di Pisa,* Ser, II, Vol. XXI, 1962, pp. 33–63). In a recent paper, "The Platonic Corpus" (*Phoenix,* 24, 1970, pp. 296–308), J. A. Philip asserts that the Academy procured an edition of Plato in ca. 300 B.C., "when the dogmatism of the Early Academy and Xenocrates had begun to wane". But, A.-H. Chroust, "The Organization of the Corpus Platonicum in Antiquity" (*H,* 93, 1965, pp. 34–96, still believes in an Alexandrian edition of Plato, procured by Aristophanes of Byzantium.

72. The Platonism of the New Academy is a most controversial matter. Zeller, *op. cit.,* III: 1⁶, pp. 540 ff., recognized the Platonic element in it but found it far from Plato's true thought, thus also Brochard, *op. cit.,* pp. 30 ff. ("une parenté fort illégitime"). Robin, *op. cit.,* pp. 42 ff., stresses the Socratic rather than the Platonic aspect of the New Academy but ascribes a great importance to the influence of Pyrrhon; this is also the opinion of Dal Pra, *op. cit.,* pp. 77 ff. The Pyrrhonian influence was doubted by Pierre Couissin, "L'origine et l'évolution de l'ΕΠΟΧΗ" (*REG,* 42, 1929, pp. 373–397). In the same way, Gigon, *op. cit.,* pp. 44 ff., emphasized Arcesilas' independence of Pyrrhon and his attachment to Socrates, his aim being an aporetic not a dogmatic agnosticism; thus also Arnim, "Arkesilaos", cols. 1165 ff.—Cicero voices the New Academy's view of itself, when, in the Preface to the *De Natura Deorum,* I 5, 11, he speaks of the "ratio contra omnia disserendi nullamque rem aperte iudicandi profecta a Socrate, repetita ab Arcesila, confirmata a Carneade"; a statement Credaro, *op. cit.,* II, p. 182, curiously enough adduces in proof of the existence of a secret teaching, cf. n. VII 73. See now the interesting remarks by Krämer, *op. cit.,* pp. 54 ff., 65 ff., 106 ff., which are, however, marred by his persistent belief in an esoteric Platonic system.

73. The relevant texts—Cicero, *Academica* I fr. 21 Müller; *Academica* II 60; Numenius, fr. 2 and 7 Leemans (fr. 25 and 27 Des Places)= Eusebius, *Praeparatio Evangelica,* XIV 6, 5 and 8; Sextus Empiricus, *Pyrrhonicae Hypotyposes* I 234; Augustine, *Contra Academicas* III 17–18, 37–41; 20, 43; *Confessiones* V 10, 19 and 14,25—are all quoted and discussed in detail by Credaro, *op. cit.,* II, pp. 177–213, who believes in the secret doctrine, though he does not attempt to fix it. This is also the conclusion of Gigon, "Zur Geschichte der sogenannten Neuen Akademie" (above, n. VII 66), and of Claudio Moreschini, "Atteggiamenti scettici ed atteggiamenti dogmatici nella filosofia accademica" (*Parola del Passato,* 24, 1969, pp. 426–436), who, however, regards only Sextus' statement as reliable and believes that only Arcesilas had a secret doctrine, Carneades not. But most scholars have considered the

statement about a secret teaching of the New Academy legendary, thus Brochard, *op. cit.,* pp. 115 ff., Robin, *op. cit.,* pp. 67 ff., Dal Pra, *op. cit.,* pp. 111 ff. See further the equally negative opinion of Zeller, *op. cit.,* III: 1⁶, pp. 510 and 535 n. 1, Ueberweg-Prächter, *op. cit.,* pp. 467 ff., Hirzel, *op. cit.,* III, pp. 216 ff., Arnim, "Arkesilaos", col. 1167, Kurt von Fritz, "Philon", *RE,* XIX: 2 (1938), col. 2538, Weische, *op. cit.,* C. J. de Vogel, *Greek Philosophy,* III (Leiden, 1959), p. 200 (1117 a–d), and Krämer, *op. cit.,* p. 55 n. 212.—Of the testimonia adduced by Credaro, Numenius is late, inimical, and unreliable, as Credaro himself points out (I, pp. 67–74). Sextus again provides his statement about the secret dogmatism of Arcesilas with the reservation: "if one ought to credit also what is told about him". Nor should we forget that it is Sextus' endeavour to prove that the Academics were no true sceptics at all, see Hirzel, *op. cit.,* III, p. 220 n. 2. The only seemingly reliable testimony is that by Cicero, *Academica* I fr. 21 = Augustine, *Contra Academicos* III 20, 43. However, as I have showed in detail in my study, *The Decline and Fall of the Neoplatonic Interpretation of Plato,* pp. 8 ff., this statement does not in fact prove the existence of such a doctrine.

74. As Couissin *op. cit.,* proved in detail, the term ἐποχή is of Stoic origin and testifies to the deep negative influence of Stoicism upon the New Academy.

75. See W. Burkert's pertinent remarks ("Cicero der Platoniker und Skeptiker", pp. 189 ff.).

76. *Academica* I 12, 45–46, where Plato's position is identified with that of Arcesilas, cf. *Academica* II 5, 15 and 23–74.

77. The passage is pointed out by Burkert, *op. cit.,* p. 191.

78. This topic is dealt with in detail in my study, quoted above, n. VII 73.

79. *Platone,* I–II (2d ed., Padua, 1949; the first ed. was published in 1932–35).

80. *Op. cit.,* I, p. XXXIII.

81. *Op. cit.,* I, pp. XXXII, cf. II. p. 545.

82. *Op. cit.,* I, pp. XLI ff., cf. the criticism of the New Academy, I, p. LXXXII; ii, pp. 455 ff.

83. *Op. cit.,* I, pp. XLVI ff.

84. *Op. cit.,* I, pp. VV ff.

85. *Op. cit.,* I, pp. LVI ff., LXXXV ff.

86. *Op. cit.,* I, p. 55; cf. II, pp. 453 ff.

87. *Op. cit.,* II, p. 45 f.

88. *Op. cit.,* I, pp. XLVI ff.

89. See, e.g., *op. cit.,* II, pp. 16 ff., 160 ff., 266 ff., 327, 380 ff.

90. *Op. cit.,* II, p. 267.

91. *Op. cit.,* II, p. 352.

92. *Op. cit.,* II, p. 454.

93. See above, pp. 26 ff. As Stefanini often refers to Susemihl, the latter's view may have influenced him.

94. For that reason, perhaps, Stefanini's work seems to have been but little studied outside Italy, though Friedländer quotes it often.

95. As a modern Swedish philosopher, Anders Wedberg, has excellently put it: Much of Plato's "thinking is, essentially and merely in its literary expression, the mental dialogue of a sceptic with a faith" (Plato's Philosophy of Mathematics, Stockholm, 1955; I quote the reprint in *Plato. A Collection of Critical Essays,* ed. Gregory Vlastos, I, New York, 1971, p. 44 n. 20).

96. Strauss, "On a New Interpretation of Plato's Political Thought", pp. 351 f.

Index Nominum

The Index contains only the personal names mentioned in the text. The names "Plato" and "Socrates" are not included. Main passages are in italics.